EDUCATING HISPANIC STUDENTS

EDUCATING HISPANIC STUDENTS

Cultural Implications for Instruction, Classroom Management, Counseling and Assessment

By

HERBERT GROSSMAN, Ph.D.

Director, Bilingual/Cross Cultural
Special Education Programs
San Jose State University
San Jose, California

CHARLES C THOMAS • PUBLISHER
Springfield • Illinois • U.S.A.

Published and Distributed Throughout the World by

CHARLES C THOMAS ● PUBLISHER

2600 South First Street

Springfield, Illinois 62717

© *1984 by* CHARLES C THOMAS ● PUBLISHER

ISBN 0-398-05057-0

Library of Congress Catalog Card Number: 84-16950

Library of Congress Cataloging in Publication Data

Grossman, Herbert
  Educating Hispanic students.

  Bibliography: p.
  1. Hispanic Americans—Education—United States. 2. Hispanic Americans—Psychology.
3. National characteristics, Latin American. I. Title.
LC2670.G76   1984   371.97'6872'073   84-16950
ISBN 0-398-05057-0

Printed in the United States of America

PS-R-3

To Suzanne—
My extraordinarily wonderful
and fabulous wife. With all
my love.

PREFACE

This book presents the results of a study entitled "What Counselors, Educators, Psychologists and Others Should Know About the Hispanic Culture in Order to Work More Effectively with Hispanic Students and Their Parents" which was funded by the California Department of Education in 1982 and 1983. Approximately five hundred people from nineteen states, the District of Columbia, Puerto Rico, Costa Rica and Ecuador answered a four hundred item questionnaire which included descriptions of cultural traits supposedly characteristic of Hispanics living in the United States and suggestions for how professionals should take these cultural traits into account when working with Hispanic students and their parents.

The book is divided into three parts. Part One consists of an introductory chapter and a chapter which describes the study. The introductory chapter includes:

1. a discussion of the low success rate and the high failure rate Hispanic students experience in comparison to non-Hispanic students;
2. the proposition that the basic cause of this problem is that, with few exceptions, the schools provide Hispanics with a culturally inappropriate education;
3. a discussion of the purpose of the book, which is to provide an educationally relevant description of the Hispanic culture in the United States and specific suggestions for taking these cultural characteristics into account when working with Hispanic students and their parents;
4. a discussion of the seven objections raised by individuals who are not in favor of this approach to solving the problems encountered by Hispanic students.

The second chapter describes the theoretical basis of the study, the methodology it employed and the participants.

Part Two presents the results of the study. Chapters Three through Six deal with these results as they affect the instruction and classroom management of Hispanic students, the assessment (testing) of Hispanic students who are experiencing difficulty in school and the counseling of their parents. Chapter Seven presents the opinions of the participants regarding certain controversial issues. Chapter Eight includes comparisons of the responses of the Hispanic participants with those of the non-Hispanic participants and comparisons of the responses of non-Hispanic participants with considerable experience working with Hispanic students with those of non-Hispanics without such experience.

The results are presented in terms of whether the participants agreed or disagreed that certain traits attributed to the Hispanic culture actually tend to characterize Hispanics currently living in the United States and whether they agreed or disagreed with the specific suggestions offered for taking these cultural traits into consideration when working with Hispanic students and their parents. These results also contain examples of the written comments which the participants provided to explain why they responded to the items as they did. These comments are included in quotation marks as received except for minor editing. They are included so that the reader may obtain a better understanding of the reasons behind the participants' opinions about the various items.

Part Three contains the author's conclusions and his recommendations. A selected bibliography of articles and books about the Hispanic culture and its educational implications is also included for those who may wish to do additional reading.

This book has been written in the belief that while schools play an important role in the preservation of the American culture and its transmission to each new generation that lives within its boundaries, there is ample opportunity to accommodate methods and techniques to the individual needs of students. Counselors, educators, psychologists are already trained to accommodate their approaches to individual differences among students' motivation, learning style, attention span, handicapping conditions, etc., in order to help students learn more, lead more productive lives and feel better about themselves. Accommodating their approaches to cultural differences among students will lead to similar benefits for the many culturally different students currently living in the United States and for those who will be living among us in the future.

The author recognizes that this book deals with an extremely controversial topic. This is evident in the differences of opinion observed among the participants. In a number of instances their opinions and those of the author do not coincide. Nevertheless the author hopes he has presented both the results of the study and his conclusions and recommendations in a scholarly and professional manner. The results of the study reflect the opinions of the participants. The conclusions and recommendations are the author's personal interpretations of these results.

The author would like to express his sincere appreciation to the more than five hundred individuals who spent the five to ten hours necessary to complete the survey instrument. He hopes that their ideas and opinions will be as helpful to the reader as they have been to him.

ACKNOWLEDGEMENTS

The study described in this book was initiated with a small grant from San Jose State University. The major portion of the funding was contributed by the California State Department of Education. The author wishes to express his appreciation to Lalit Roy, a staff member of the California State Department of Education, who made many helpful suggestions regarding the format and contents of this report, and to Steve Aquino of San Jose State University, who assisted in the statistical analysis of the results.

CONTENTS

EDUCATING HISPANIC STUDENTS

PART I
THE STUDY

Chapter 1

INTRODUCTION

I t is an unfortunate fact of life in the United States that Hispanic students achieve less in school, drop out more often and earlier and are more often incorrectly placed in special education programs for the mentally retarded, learning disabled and behavior disordered than students from most other ethnic groups. The following quotations from four participants in the study offer personal opinions about the cause of this problem.

"When I began my 'educational career' I spoke almost no English. By the time I was able to understand my teachers I must have been two years behind grade level. Although my parents were uneducated they preached the value of education. They expected me to complete high school and hoped that I would go on to college. My teachers did not. Looking back at those years in retrospect I now can see that they treated me as if I were incapable of learning. It did not make a difference that well over half of us were Mexican-American —you would not have thought so to look at the curriculum. They never mentioned our foods, our holidays, our culture, or our contributions. It was always the Anglo culture. It was always hurry up and become Americanized which was idiotic since we were Americans. At the time I realized none of this. I had introjected their image of me as a loser. By the time I was 12 I was a psychological dropout. When I turned seventeen I made it official. It was not until the second year of my tour of duty in the Army that I became aware that I had the potential to learn. I returned to school, graduated and went on to college and graduate school determined to prevent as many Mexican-American students as possible from suffering the same fate that I almost suffered.

"While it is true that as a rule Hispanics have not done well in school, the reason is not because we are lazy or stupid as many Anglos have claimed. The true cause lies in the fact that our teachers were not prepared to teach us. They were concerned with making sure that we didn't speak Spanish anywhere on the school grounds, that we didn't act like Hispanics and that we learned to act like they did, and not concerned with learning who we were, what we were like and what they could do to adapt their Anglo teaching styles to us.

"Initially I had no interest in becoming a special educator. I believed that regular education used special education as a dumping ground for Hispanic students who were mislabeled retarded or learning disabled because the schools failed them. Now we have the assessment instruments to correctly identify Hispanic students who are retarded or learning disabled but there are too few special educators who speak Spanish and know the Hispanic culture to use these instruments. As a result my school district continues to misdiagnose Hispanic students.

"I have taught Hispanic graduate students in four Latin American countries and in the United States. My clear impression is that Hispanic university students in Latin America learned more of what they are taught than Hispanic students in the United States. This I attribute to the fact that the university system in the United States is not culturally appropriate to Hispanic students who have not completely acculturated to the American system. They learn less, drop out more often and have many more problems both personally and professionally with their professors who they often feel are either insensitive to their needs or outright prejudiced."

The central idea contained in these four quotations is that the major cause of the educational problems of Hispanic-American students is the culturally inappropriate education they receive. The study reported in this book was initiated because the author agrees with this explanation of the problem. This is not meant to imply that Hispanics are singled out as a group and purposely miseducated by prejudiced professionals. While far too many incidents of prejudicial treatment of Hispanic students have occurred in the past and continue to occur in the present, the author does not believe that the majority of the counselors, educators, psychologists and other school personnel who deal with Hispanic students are prejudiced people. They did not choose to work with children or adolescents in order to miseducate them and certainly not to abuse them. No, it is not prejudice toward Hispanic students but lack of information about their students' cultural background which causes so many professionals to fail in their duty toward them. The assumptions underlying this line of reasoning are:

1. Every culture prepares students to learn in specific ways.
2. The American educational system was not developed for Hispanic students and, with few exceptions, it is not staffed either by Hispanic professionals or by non-Hispanic professionals who have been prepared to work with Hispanic students.
3. As a result, Hispanic students are not educated in culturally appropriate ways.

If these assumptions are correct, then well-meaning educators, counselors, psychologists and others who work with Hispanic students should want to adapt their methods of instruction, classroom management, counseling and assessment to the cultural needs of their students in order to help them learn more and feel better about themselves. Also, special educators, speech and language therapists, psychologists, school administrators and others who are responsible for identifying, assessing, and placing Hispanic exceptional students in special education should want to improve their procedures so that they place only those Hispanic students who truly need these services.

The purpose of this book is to provide both an educationally relevant description of the cultural characteristics of Hispanics and specific suggestions for how professionals can accommodate their techniques to these cultural characteristics when they work with Hispanic students and their parents.

As stated above, the author assumes that well-meaning professionals will welcome the kinds of information provided in this book. This assumption was borne out by the fact that the vast majority of the participants agreed that such information would

be helpful. The few participants who did not agree with the goals
of the book cited seven reasons why they disagreed with the basic
purpose of the study. These reasons and the author's response to
them follow.

1. *The Hispanic culture is an inferior culture.* "Hispanics
are lazy." "Hispanics are unreliable." "Latin America will never
become industrialized and modernized because it is their culture
not their lack of resources, which they have plenty of, which holds
them back." "The Latino has no ambition to better himself."

Participants who expressed these opinions about the Hispanic
culture also believe that schools should not accommodate to the
cultural needs of Hispanics. They argued that Hispanic students
and their parents should give up those cultural characteristics
which have held them back and acculturate as completely and as
rapidly as possible to the American culture which they believe is
superior.

There are two obvious fallacies involved in this line of
reasoning. First of all, these negative stereotypes do not accurately
describe Hispanics. Secondly, there is no evidence that there are
superior and inferior cultures except in the eyes of individual
beholders who use their own subjective criteria for making such
comparisons. Cultures are different and because of these differences the members have different life-styles. However, there are no
universally acceptable criteria for evaluating these different life-
styles. For example, some people are brought up to believe that it
is better to start work promptly, to work rapidly and efficiently, to
make your mark, to climb up the ladder of success, to make a lot of
money in order to buy a lot of material things. But this may
require them to spend little time with their families, develop
ulcers or a heart condition and lose sight of the "simple pleasures
in life." Others may be equally convinced that it is better to work
at a more relaxed pace, accomplish less, not get ahead and not
have many of the things money can buy. While such a life-style
may enable them to lead a relaxed family centered life, it may also
be one of the major reasons why these groups of people remain
poor.

Which of these life-styles is better? Neither. Each one has its
advantages and disadvantages. However, people will probably
continue to talk about superior and inferior cultures and attribute
negative stereotypes to groups whom they know little about or
whom they perceive as different. Hopefully, fewer and fewer

professionals involved in the education of Hispanic students will base their educational policies or methodology on such misinformation. One of the purposes of this book is to correct these prejudicial stereotypes by providing a more accurate picture of the Hispanic culture as it currently exists in the United States.

2. *There is no Hispanic culture in the United States.*

Some participants argued that there is no single Hispanic culture in the United States, so it is not possible to accommodate educational techniques to the cultural needs of Hispanic students. As one participant put it,

"People are always telling us to become relevant to Hispanic students, to adapt our Anglo culture to the Hispanic culture. Well, I say that there exists no such 'Anglo culture.' Anglos are as diverse a group as can be imagined. There are people from many different European and Asian countries that might reasonably be considered as 'Anglos' if we are thinking of their contributions to American (United States) culture. The idea that there exists a monolothic 'Anglo culture' ignores a number of factors. For example, regional differences such as urban, rural, Northern, Southern, have more to do with the perceived differences than any factor. Religion is also important. A Mexican in Mexico and an American Catholic may be more alike in many respects than a Mexican and a Mexican Jehovah's Witness. It is true also for what are called 'Hispanic,' which is a diverse group ranging from the upper crust Spaniard from Castile to the barely acculturated into the Latin culture Indian; from right wing dictator to Central American revolutionary. I have lived in Mexico, South America and Spain with families from the very rich to the very poor. I've taught 'Hispanic' children for ten years. The beliefs and values of these people are as varied as that of the 'Anglo' population."

In a similar vein, another participant stated,

"Latin America is composed of developed industrialized countries such as Argentina and Chile and basically underdeveloped countries such as Bolivia, Honduras, Belize and Panama. Some countries have a strong European cosmopolitan influence, others have an American influence and others are still predominantly Indian. Some have high rates of illiteracy while others have well-developed educational systems which are as fine or better than those found in some states in the U.S. How then can we talk about a Hispanic culture in the U.S. when Hispanics come here from such diverse countries?"

A different point of view is presented in the following quotation from two other participants:

"Speaking from the point of view of a Chicano, Mexican (I respond to both), I can tell you that although we are all classified under one visually identifiable cultural group, there are individual differences. The degree of acculturation to the dominant group determines maintenance of cultural traditions and customs. Self-identification is determined by the origin of the group. Some Mexicans are descendants of original settlers such as those from New Mexico (1598). Then there are the Mexican people who are members and descendants of the three largest migrations into the United States from Mexico, 1910, 1920's and World War Two. And of course, we can't omit the most recent arrivals. Second- and third-generation Chicanos will certainly have cultural differences from first-generation Mexicans. The geographic areas of Mexico are so different that this also plays a part in the differences between Mexican Americans. Therefore, stereotyping should be avoided. Still the values and attitudes of the Mexicans are different enough from those of the dominant culture that not understanding these differences often creates cultural conflicts and misunderstandings.

"When I am with a group of fellow Latinos I'm conscious of our differences. Cubanos, Mexicanos, Puerto Riqueños, Colombianos, we are all different. Yet when I find myself among non-Latinos I realize how much alike we Latinos are."

The author has noticed many of the differences referred to above among the Hispanics he has known and worked with in Latin America and the United States. However, as important as these differences were, he too still observed many commonalities among Hispanics where he compared them to non-Hispanics living in the United States.

The participants in the study were also given an opportunity to express their opinion about whether there is a Hispanic culture in the United States. As will be seen from the information presented in Chapter 2, the majority agreed that there is.

Finally, the author suggests that the existence of federal and state laws and court decisions which require that culturally different students, especially Hispanics and Blacks, must be assessed and instructed in culturally appropriate ways and the existence of statewide examinations which are used to certify that individuals are culturally literate about Hispanics also attests to the widespread belief that there is a Hispanic culture in the United States.

3. *It would not be a good idea to provide professionals involved in educating Hispanic students with a prejudicial description of the Hispanic culture.*

Not everyone agreed that it would be a good idea to attempt to identify the cultural traits which characterize Hispanics in the United States. As the statements below indicate, some persons who were afraid that such an attempt would merely add one more voice to the existing chorus of prejudicial stereotyping of Hispanics opposed the study.

> "I believe enough good research has been done to dismiss bigoted stereotypes so as to warrant their exclusion from further pedantic endeavors. I, personally, get very tired of having to defend my culture against the mythical themes of the 'hot blooded, lazy, Latin.'"

> "Although I try to be objective about generalizations about Hispanics, it is difficult not to feel insulted by some statements. And I frankly resent the patronizing tone of some of those statements, particularly in those of them that attempt to deal with Hispanics as with a group of infantile persons. 'Let's-come-down-to-their-level-since-they-obviously cannot-rise-to-our-own' sort of thing."

On the other hand, the vast majority of the participants agreed that it would be helpful to provide professionals with information about the Hispanic culture. Only a few of them expressed reservations. The opinion of one participant who had such reservation was:

> "At first I was very reluctant to complete this survey because I felt that however well intentioned, it would perpetuate the stereotyped image of Hispanics, but then these stereotypes already exist. I have always felt that people have more in

common than they have differences even when faced with the reality of prejudice and discrimination. Still, there are many Hispanics that have special needs because they live differently than mainstream Americans. It is for this reason that I feel that the results of this survey may be useful in helping professionals become more sensitive to their needs."

One of the purposes of this study is to correct the inaccurate and prejudicial stereotypes of Hispanics which are all too prevalent in our society.

4. *Cultural descriptions can lead to misleading over-generalizations.*

A few people were not in favor of attempting to describe the Hispanic culture in the United States because they were concerned that such information could provide professionals with over-generalizations which could mislead them into believing that knowledge about Hispanics as a group is sufficient to understand an individual Hispanic student or his parents. This concern is expressed in the following statements.

"There are many common stereotypes of the Hispanic person such as never being on time, being deeply religious, etc. Those who work with Hispanics should be aware of this and guard against a generalized, stereotyped view of those they work with. This is not to say that a specific stereotype (like being deeply religious) may not apply to an individual. Rather, the individual should always be dealt with as a unique human being who may or may not exhibit certain attitudes, habits, and beliefs.

"A list of over-general attributes which describe certain socio-economic sub-groups of Hispanics such as the poor who may be more apt to have certain problems in school or the Indian who may be more apt to believe in *La Llorona* will not make educators more sensitive. Educators must recognize that children come to us from an infinitely varied array of backgrounds and not assume that all Hispanic students come from poor or Indian backgrounds."

While these comments reflect valid concerns, many other people shared these concerns and nevertheless believed that it is worthwhile to develop these cultural descriptions. The following statements are examples of this other point of view.

"While the teacher/counselor should keep in mind that culture influences the attitudes and values of many of the Hispanic people, Hispanics have been stereotyped and maligned so much that it is hard to know where reality really lies. For instance, Hispanics have been assigned the following social and attitudinal characteristics: subjugation to nature and God, present time orientation, low level of aspiration, work for present needs, sharing, non-scientific explanation for natural phenomena, humility and obedience to will of God. Not all of these are true and not all of them would be applicable to any given person. Despite this, as I note above, it is important to know how culture influences the attitudes and values of many of the Hispanic people.

"It is important for educators to be aware of our culture just so long as they refrain from thinking that we are all exactly alike. Just as knowing one Anglo would not enable a Hispanic to know all Anglos, so too knowing a few Hispanic students does not enable an Anglo educator to 'know' all Hispanic students either as a group or individually."

The author is also concerned that educators and others might overgeneralize from knowledge of Hispanic cultural tendencies to knowledge about an individual Hispanic student. That is why this study provides statements about cultural factors which Hispanics and others believe *may be* or *tend to be* characteristics of Hispanics *but not necessarily so*. In other words the study identified cultural characteristics which Hispanics and others agree persons who work with Hispanic students and their parents should be aware of as only *possibly* contributing to or influencing the behavior, attitude, etc., of an individual Hispanic student or parent.

5. *Culturally different students and their families should adapt to the mainstream culture in the schools, and not vice versa, because people living in the same country should all speak the same language, follow the same laws and share the same morality.*

This idea is embodied in the following five statements.

"We cannot survive as a culture with different laws for different people. Everyone must pay taxes, serve in the army, respect private property and the rights of others regardless of where they were born or what religion they profess."

"People who want to live in the United States should adapt to the American culture and not expect the American system to adapt to them. If they want to continue to live their life-styles they should stay where their life-styles are acceptable."

"Canada is on the verge of being torn apart by the French Canadian separatist movement. Their mistake was to allow a minority of their citizens to speak French and live French. We should learn from history not to repeat the mistakes of our neighbors to the North."

"The role of schooling traditionally has been one of acculturation. To change the role of schooling now would be to court disaster."

The quotations included above are based on two assumptions:

1. A multicultural educational approach in the classroom necessarily leads to having two or more national languages and different laws for different cultural groups;

2. There is a monolithic culture in the United States which must be preserved in order for the United States to continue to prosper.

The first assumption is not correct. Instructing students in their native languages while they learn English, permitting them to work at their own pace, developing the kinds of interpersonal relationships with them which make them feel comfortable, allowing them to choose whether to compete or not, etc., does not necessarily lead to adopting two or more national languages or sets of laws.

The second assumption is also false. While there is a dominant culture in the United States, there are so many sub-cultural differences among "Anglos" that the United States can truly be considered a pluralistic society. A few examples of differences in child-rearing practices are included to illustrate this point.

Some parents take La Maze classes and are active participants in their child's birth. Other mothers do not. Unprepared to partici-pate, they are put to sleep while the doctor delivers their children and later shows them to the proud parents. Some children are breast fed; others are given formula. When infants begin to crawl, some are allowed to roam the house. Their parents have placed any dangerous or breakable things out of reach so that they can explore their environments without restrictions. Other infants have no such freedom. Believing that children have to learn self-control from the beginning, their parents are teaching them what they are allowed and not allowed to do or touch. When some children are naughty, they are spanked, sent to their rooms or deprived of one or another privilege. Other children are made to feel guilty, ashamed, or disapproved of but are not spanked and seldom deprived of privileges.

During their elementary school years, some children have paper routes and are paid money for doing various jobs around the house. Other children are given allowances regardless of how they behave. When they are a little older, some are closely supervised to make sure they have completed all homework assignments before watching television or going out to play, while others are reminded as they are leaving to come back early if they have homework to do. As teenagers, some are allowed to have a little wine, beer, hard liquor and maybe even marijuana once in a while, but others are protected as much as possible from developing what their parents consider to be bad habits. Finally, some are encouraged to study hard because a good education can lead to a good job, while others are encouraged to study in order to become well-educated, well-rounded people.

These are just a few of many possible examples which could illustrate the fact that many different life-styles exist side by side in the United States, and while each individual may feel that his or her particular way of life is the best, there are many more who would disagree. The important thing to note is that Americans do not share a monolithic culture, a single way of life. Many different yet acceptable subcultures exist simultaneously outside the classroom. Therefore, it is entirely feasible and appropriate that the classroom should reflect this multicultural reality.

6. *It is impossible to accommodate educational approaches to the cultural needs of the many culturally different students found in any particular school system or often within a particular classroom.*

Many people do not believe that educators can accommodate their methods and techniques to the different cultural groups they work with. Some of their reasons are found in the following quotations.

"My school district, the Los Angeles County School District, has over one hundred different language/culture groups.

How can anyone be expected to know about all these different cultures, and how can anyone be expected to apply what they do know? From what I have been told during in-service training, what are appropriate teaching techniques for one group are inappropriate for another. How can I teach my Anglo students one way, my Latino students a second way, my Vietnamese students a third, my Korean students a fourth way, my Hmong, my Portuguese, etc., at the same time? Impossible!"

"Your idea of teaching all students in the style to which they are accustomed is a good one, but where will you find all those people who can walk on water?"

"The United States has an open-door policy to immigration. Refugees are pouring over our borders, legally and illegally. We should not make the classroom relevant to Hispanics and not to these other groups as well. The impossibility of training counselors, educators and psychologists to be relevant to all groups precludes a multicultural approach for all cultures thereby precluding it for Hispanics."

The argument underlying these statements is as follows: fairness and equality of opportunity are basic principles of the American way of life. If we cannot accommodate the educational system to all the different cultural groups, we should not accommodate it to any individual one. Therefore, we should continue to expect that culturally different students should adapt to the mainstream American culture.

On the surface this line of reasoning may seem to have considerable merit. However, it is based on the false assumption that it would be impossible to provide a culturally relevant education to students from different cultures simultaneously because their cultural needs are so different. It is not true that each culture can require a unique educational approach. Alternative methods of instructing students, organizing classrooms and counseling parents are limited. For example, educators can encourage or require their students to work individually or in groups; they can motivate them through the use of competitive games or cooperative settings; they can allow them to work at their own pace or encourage them to work as quickly as possible; they can attempt to develop close personal relationships with them or maintain a "professional distance"; they can correct and criticize them in front of their peers or in private; they can encourage them to discuss controversial issues and express differences of opinion or emphasize similarities of experience and opinion; they can teach abstract concepts or utilize methods which stress the concrete and learning by doing, etc.

Since counselors, educators and psychologists are always choosing between alternatives as limited as those listed above, it would be entirely possible and feasible for them to adapt their methodology to the cultural needs of their students.

7. *It is better to emphasize the similarities among people than to stress their differences?*

The following quotations express this point of view.

> "When people focus on the differences among themselves they engender conflict and hostility. Jew vs. Moslem, Moslem vs. Hindu, Catholic vs. Protestant, Missionary vs. native heathen. Religious differences have caused the human race more misery than all the solace and comfort religions have given to their adherents."

> "We are all Americans and as Americans we would do well to be blind to the differences that divide us."

> "Teachers should teach to the commonalities among their students which are much more important than any superficial differences."

The author agrees that human beings are basically the same. We all prefer success to failure, praise and recognition to criticism or condemnation, and acceptance and attention to rejection and inattention. Nevertheless, our behavior in these situations is influenced by different cultural veneers. For example, we have different criteria for success. We find different forms of praise and recognition rewarding. We differ in terms of when, where, why and how we are willing to accept criticism or condemnation and express acceptance and rejection in our own culturally determined ways.

Expecting all individuals to behave the same way or interpreting everyone's behavior from a single culturally determined point of view can also engender hostility and conflict. There is at least as much risk in treating everyone the same as there is in attempting to treat individuals as members of different cultural groups. The schools have been attempting to provide the same or similar education experience to all students, regardless of their cultural differences, without much success. Now it is time to try the opposite approach.

Differences among people are not necessarily undesirable. The participants in the study never reached 100 percent agreement that any cultural factors are actually characteristic of the Hispanic culture, nor about how professionals should modify their approaches because of these cultural factors when working with Hispanic students and their parents. These kinds of differences of opinion are to be expected. In the United States they are not only tolerated but protected by law!

One of the strengths of this study is that these differences of opinion regarding the Hispanic culture and its implications for the education of Hispanic students are quantified. Thus, the reader can judge the extent to which Hispanic professionals and non-Hispanic professionals with considerable experience working with Hispanic students agree that a particular cultural trait tends to characterize Hispanics in the United States, and the extent to which they agree about its implications for educating Hispanic students and counseling their parents.

SUMMARY

Hispanic students have had a lower rate of success in school than many other ethnic groups. While some individuals attribute this problem to an inferior Hispanic culture, many others believe it is caused by an educational system which does not provide Hispanic students with a culturally appropriate education. The purpose of this book is to help professionals to become culturally literate about the Hispanic culture in the United States by presenting the opinions of Hispanic professionals and non-Hispanic professionals with considerable experience working with Hispanic students regarding which cultural traits are characteristic of Hispanics currently living in the United States and how counselors, educators, psychologists and others can take these cultural traits into consideration when working with Hispanic students and their parents.

Providing professionals with a more accurate understanding of the Hispanic culture in the United States will decrease intolerance and prejudice and make the educational services they offer Hispanic students culturally relevant. Providing Hispanic students with a culturally appropriate education will increase their success rate in school, enable them to become more productive members of society and help them to feel better about themselves.

Chapter 2

THE STUDY

PURPOSE OF THE STUDY

As stated previously, the general purpose of the study was to provide answers to two questions:

1. What are the cultural factors which tend to characterize Hispanics living in the United States?
2. What are the specific ways in which counselors, educators, psychologists and others should modify their techniques when working with Hispanic students and their parents who demonstrate these cultural traits?

METHODOLOGY

There were at least two alternative ways of answering these questions.

1. One could actually observe Hispanics and non-Hispanics in real life or laboratory situations and determine whether there are differences between the two groups which can be attributed to culture.
2. One could ask Hispanics who have lived in the United States for a considerable period of time and non-Hispanics who have had considerable experience working with Hispanics if they have noted culture differences between Hispanics and Anglos and, if so, what they are.

The second procedure—that of asking persons who had experience in the two cultures to provide comparisons—was selected because if was felt that people with experience in the two cultures are in the best position to compare them and because this method could provide considerable data within a relatively short period of time at a relatively low cost.

QUESTIONNAIRE

Statements about which Hispanic cultural factors should be taken into account when working with Hispanic students and how specifically these factors should influence their education were collected in the following manner:

1. A letter requesting the above information was sent to Hispanic counselors, educators and psychologists.
2. The literature, both published and unpublished, in the fields of bilingual/bicultural education, multicultural education, bilingual/bicultural special education, cross-cultural psychology and Hispanic psychology was reviewed for statements by Hispanics regarding how specific Hispanic cultural factors should influence the education of Hispanic students.

The statements obtained through these two sources were compiled in a questionnaire which consisted of an introduction, directions, and 400 items divided into five sections. Four sections —instruction, classroom management, assessment and counseling—included items designed to ascertain the participants' opinion about whether certain traits are more characteristic of Hispanics in the United States than Anglos and, if so, how specifically they should be taken into account when instructing, managing or assessing Hispanic students and counseling their parents. These sections also contained subsections of items designed to query participants about whether Hispanics in the United States experience the effects of limited economic resources, limited education, stereotyping, bias and prejudice and, if so, how this should influence instruction, classroom management, assessment and counseling.

A fifth section consisted of a number of miscellaneous statements about which the opinions of the participants were solicited. It also included items designed to provide demographic data about the participants.

Relevant sections of both the introduction and the directions are reproduced below.

Introduction

"Some time ago a letter was sent to selected Hispanic professionals asking them to state what they thought others should know about the Hispanic culture in order to work more effectively with Hispanic students and their parents. This was to include:

1. Specific cultural traits with whatever qualification such as sex, geographic locations, socioeconomic status, etc.
2. How specifically these traits should influence the way the educator functions in identifying, assessing, teaching, or counseling.
3. Any bibliographic references which would be particularly helpful.

"In the letter, we stated: 'We are not looking to confirm prejudicial stereotypes. Nor do we want to present simplistic cultural descriptions. We are well aware that such factors as socioeconomic status, geography, sex, degree of identification with and acculturation to the dominant culture, etc., help determine whether an individual actually shares a particular cultural attribute. Yet given these qualifications we do believe that educators would be more effective with Hispanic students and their parents if they were more knowledgeable about and more sensitive to the cultural differences which exist in our pluralistic society.'

"The responses to this letter and the results of the review of the literature are included in this survey. We are now attempting to validate these statements by determining to what extent Hispanics and others agree with each of them.

Directions

"None of the statements included in the survey should be interpreted to mean that all Hispanics share the particular cultural trait mentioned. ALL HISPANICS ARE NOT ALIKE. In each case such factors as individual personality characteristics, degree of acculturation to the Anglo culture, sex, etc., all play a part in determining whether an individual shares the particular trait in question. The statements should be interpreted to mean that in comparison to Anglos, Hispanics are more likely to be characterized by that trait— but not necessarily so. In other words, professionals should be aware of the possibility that the Hispanics with whom they work *may be* characterized by the particular trait. For each of these traits you are being asked to state the extent to which you agree or disagree that it is *more likely* to be characteristic of Hispanics than Anglos.

"We are also interested in your comments about the statements especially if you wish to clarify, qualify or elaborate on any of your responses. If you would like to share any comments with us, please write the number of the item or items you are commenting on and your comments on a separate sheet of paper and include it when you return your answer sheets and we will certainly include your comments when we report our results."

Distribution

Information about the study was sent to members of Hispanic professional organizations; to Hispanic-surnamed members of professional organizations of counselors, educators and psychologists; to faculty members of university personnel programs in Hispanic bilingual/bicultural teacher training programs, and Hispanic bilingual/bicultural special education programs; to authors of articles about such topics as Chicano psychology and bilingual/bicultural regular education and special education; and to other individuals. In addition, announcements about the study were included in various newsletters.

Questionnaires were distributed only to individuals who specifically requested them. Therefore, the participants were self-selected and are not necessarily representative of the total population of Hispanic or non-Hispanic counselors, educators, psychologists, etc., who either were not informed about the study or who decided not to participate in the study.

Of the English version of the questionnaire, 1,112 copies were distributed to professionals who requested them for their own use and an additional 438 copies were given to agencies and individuals who offered to distribute them to interested colleagues.

However, a considerable number of these agencies and individuals subsequently reported that they had decided not to attempt to distribute them after reviewing them or had been unable to find enough colleagues who wished to participate. Therefore, it is estimated that approximately 1,336 questionnaires were received by professionals who had expressed an interest in participating in the study. Four hundred and eighty-five persons returned completed questionnaires. Of this group, 447 individuals returned usable responses and were included in the study. The responses of 17 other persons were not usable and the responses of 21 other individuals were received too late to be included.

In addition, copies of the Spanish version of the questionnaire and copies of the English version of the questionnaire were distributed to Hispanic parents or professionals or agencies who offered to give them to parents of Hispanic students. However, many of the questionnaires were not distributed by these individuals and agencies.

Only 22 of the questionnaires distributed to parents, to professionals who requested them for use with their clients, or to agencies who offered to distribute them to parents were returned. The main reasons for lack of participation by parents were:

1. The questionnaire was too long for some parents who were very busy.
2. Some parents could not read the questionnaire despite the fact that it was in Spanish because their reading ability was insufficient.
3. Some parents did not know enough about the education of their children to have opinions about many of the items.
4. Some parents did not know enough about the dominant culture in the United States to make comparisons between the Hispanic culture and the dominant culture.
5. Some parents were unwilling or unable to pay the postage to return the answer sheets.

PARTICIPANTS IN THE STUDY

The geographical distribution of the participants is described in Table I.

Participants were distributed among 19 states, the District of Columbia, Puerto Rico, Costa Rica and Ecuador.

The 469 participants consisted of 292 Hispanics, 173 non-Hispanics and four persons who did not indicate their background (Table II). Among them were 398 professionals, 31 students, 22 parents and 14 persons who did not answer this item (Table II). The group of professionals included 39 regular educators, 205 bilingual/bicultural educators, 107 special educators, 31 psychologists and 34 counselors (Table IV).

The following sections describe the Hispanic and non-Hispanic participants, respectively.

Hispanics

Among the Hispanics were 242 professionals, 20 students and 22 parents. Eight participants did not provide this information (Table III). The birthplaces of the Hispanics were as follows: Mexico, 49; Caribbean countries, 39; Central America, 12; South

TABLE I

GEOGRAPHICAL DISTRIBUTION OF PARTICIPANTS

Location	Number of Participants	Percent of Total
California	266	57
Texas	45	10
New Mexico	20	4
Arizona	19	4
Puerto Rico	19	4
Florida	16	3
New York	15	3
Connecticut	9	2
Illinois	8	2
11 other states & District of Columbia	48	10
Costa Rica and Ecudor	4	1
Total	469	

TABLE II

ETHNIC BACKGROUND OF PARTICIPANTS

Ethnic Background	Number of Participants	Percent of Total
Hispanic	292	62
Non-Hispanic	173	37
Unknown	4	0
Total	469	

TABLE III

STATUS OF PARTICIPANTS

Number of Participants

Status	Hispanics	Non-Hispanics	Total
Professional	242	156	398
Student	20	11	31
Hispanic Parent	22	0	22
Unknown	8	6	14
Total	292	173	465

TABLE IV

OCCUPATIONS OF PROFESSIONALS

Occupation	Number of Participants	Percent of Total
Educator-non Bilingual/ Bicultural	39	9
Bilingual/Bicultural Educator	205	49
Special Educator	107	26
Psychologist	31	7
Counselor	34	8
Total	416	

America, 13; non-Hispanic countries, 161. Eighteen persons did not indicate their place of birth (Table V). The family roots, that is, area of origin of the Hispanic participants, were Mexico, 173; Caribbean, 37; Central America, 14; South America, 11; Spain, 36. Twenty-one participants did not provide this information (Table VI). Thus, the Hispanic participants were overwhelmingly professionals. Over half were born in the United States; however, approximately 40 percent were born in Latin America and almost two-thirds were Mexican-American.

Non-Hispanics

The non-Hispanics included 156 professionals and 11 students. Six participants did not answer this question (Table III). Their experience working with Hispanic students and their parents was as follows: six or more years, 90; at least 3 years but less than 6 years, 35; at least 1 year but less than 3 years, 18; less than 1 year, 17; no experience, 11. Three participants did not respond to this item (Table VII). They rated their knowledge of the Hispanic culture as follows: excellent, 40; good, 72; fair, 38; poor, 17. Six participants

TABLE V

HISPANICS' PLACE OF BIRTH

Area or Country	Number of Participants	Percent of Total
Mexico	49	17
Caribbean	39	13
Central America	12	4
South America	13	4
Non-Hispanic Country	161	55
Unknown	18	6
Total	292	

TABLE VI

HISPANICS' FAMILY ORIGINS

Country or Area	Number of Participants	Percent of Total
Mexico	173	59
Caribbean	37	13
Central America	14	5
South America	11	4
Spain	36	12
Unknown	21	7
Total	292	

TABLE VII

NON-HISPANICS' EXPERIENCE WORKING WITH HISPANICS

Number of Years	Number of Participants	Percent of Total
6 years or more	90	52
3-6 years	34	20
1-3 years	18	10
Less than 1 year	17	10
None	11	6
Unknown	3	2
Total	173	

did not provide this information (Table VIII). They described their fluency in Spanish as: excellent, 53; good, 57; fair, 26; poor, 32. Five persons did not respond to this item (Table IX).

Thus, the non-Hispanic participants tended to be professionals, about half of whom had worked with Hispanic students for at least six years. Most described themselves as having at least a fair understanding of the Hispanic culture and at least fair fluency in Spanish.

TABLE VIII

NON-HISPANICS' KNOWLEDGE OF THE HISPANIC CULTURE

Familiarity	Number of Participants	Percent of Total
Excellent	40	23
Good	72	42
Fair	38	22
Poor	17	10
Unknown	6	3
Total	173	

TABLE IX

NON-HISPANICS' FLUENCY IN SPANISH

Fluency	Number of Participants	Percent of Total
Excellent	53	31
Good	57	33
Fair	26	15
Poor	32	18
Unknown	5	3
Total	173	

GENERAL FINDINGS

The specific findings of the study are included in Part II. The following section contains the findings of the study as they relate to three general questions.

Question 1: Is there a Hispanic culture in the United States?

One of the two goals of this study was to determine whether Hispanics with experience living in the United States and non-Hispanics with experience working with Hispanic students believe there is a Hispanic culture. The results regarding this question follow.

The participants (Hispanics and non-Hispanics) expressed their opinions about two statements related to the issue of whether there is a Hispanic culture or many subcultures. Their responses are reported below.

1. The cultures of the various Latin American countries are similar enough so that despite differences which exist among the countries there is still a Latin American culture which can be described.

Approximately 71 percent of the participants agreed with this statement, while 17 percent disagreed with it (Table X).

2. Although Hispanics living in the United States trace their

roots back to many Latin American countries, there is still a common denominator of Hispanic culture in the United States, especially for Hispanics in the same socioeconomic class.

Seventy-eight percent of the participants agreed with this statement as compared with 9 percent who disagreed (Table XI).

The participants' responses to these two items indicate that the majority agreed that there is a Hispanic culture.

Question 2: Are the differences between the Hispanic and non-Hispanic cultures due to socioeconomic rather than cultural factors?

The participants' opinions regarding this question were ascertained by their answers to the following item:

Most of the so-called differences between the Anglo and Hispanic cultures contained in the survey are based on socioeconomic differences rather than cultural differences.

Only 26 percent of the participants agreed with the statement, whereas 61 percent disagreed with it. Thus, it can be seen that the majority of the participants did not think that the cultural differences between Hispanics and non-Hispanics included in the study were based on socioeconomic differences.

Question 3: Did the participants think that the survey could provide the kinds of information sought?

The participants were asked to respond to two statements which bear on the issues of the usefulness of the survey.

TABLE X

EXISTENCE OF A COMMON CULTURE IN LATIN AMERICA

Responses	Percent of Individuals
Agree	71
Insufficient experience or information to judge	12
Disagree	17

TABLE XI

EXISTENCE OF A COMMON CULTURE IN THE UNITED STATES

Responses	Percent of Individuals
Agree	78
Insufficient experience or information to judge	14
Disagree	9

1. The kinds of information sought by this survey if presented in an *appropriate* manner, stressing the dangers of over-generalizations and the individual differences in acculturation, socioeconomic level, etc., among Hispanics could be very useful in preparing professionals to work with Hispanic students and their parents.

Approximately 91 percent of the participants agreed with this statement, while only 4 percent disagreed with it.

2. It would not be a good idea to present the kinds of information sought by this survey in any form because it would create stereotypes and over-generalizations which could easily lead professionals to misunderstand and misinterpret Hispanic students and their parents.

Approximately 64 percent of the participants disagreed with this statement, while 27 percent agreed with it.

Thus, it can be seen that the majority of the participants responded that the study was or could be useful.

TABLE XII

SOCIOECONOMIC FACTORS OR CULTURAL FACTORS

Responses	Percent of Individuals
Agree	26
Insufficient experience or information to judge	13
Disagree	61

TABLE XIII

USEFULNESS OF THE INFORMATION

Responses	Percent of Individuals
Agree	91
Insufficient experience or information to judge	5
Disagree	4

TABLE XIV

GENERALIZATIONS AND STEREOTYPES

Responses	Percent of Individuals
Agree	27
Insufficient experience or information to judge	9
Disagree	64

PART II
RESULTS

INTRODUCTION

The results of the study are presented in this part. Chapters 3 and 4 deal with their implications for instruction and classroom management, respectively. Chapter 5 includes those items relevant for counseling parents, especially when their children are experiencing difficulty in school. Items dealing with the assessment of students are contained in Chapter 6. While most of the items in Chapter 6 pertain to the assessment of students who are having difficulty in school, they are also relevant for the evaluation of students who may qualify for programs for the gifted or any other programs which require special skills or aptitudes. Chapter 7 consists of the participants' responses to items designed to study certain controversial issues. Chapter 8 includes comparisons between the opinions of non-Hispanics with varying amounts of experience working with Hispanic students.

The results are presented in terms of the percentage of participants who agreed or disagreed with each of the cultural traits attributed to Hispanics or the educational implications of these traits. In this way the reader can judge for himself or herself the extent of agreement among the participants. The results for the Hispanic and non-Hispanic participants are presented separately. These chapters also contain the participants' written comments about specific items which explain the bases for their opinions. Except for minor editing, these comments are quoted as they were received. In those cases in which numerous persons offered similar comments to the same item, only one example of their comments is included. For those who are interested in this factor, the ethnic background (Hispanic or non-Hispanic) of the people quoted is indicated except in the few cases in which it is unknown. The cultural traits are organized into subsections. In each subsection the cultural traits which have been attributed to Hispanics appear first. Each trait is followed by a report of the percentage of participants who agreed, disagreed or stated that they lacked sufficient information or experience to judge it.[1] The participants' comments to the item are presented lastly. A brief summary of the findings is included at the end of each subsection.

The author uses three descriptive terms in his summaries of the results which need to be defined: agree, disagree and did not agree. *Agreement* indicates that at least 50 percent of the participants either strongly agreed or agreed with the item. *Disagreement* indicates that at least 50 percent of the participants either strongly disagree or disagreed with the item. A statement that the participants *did not agree* indicates that less than 50 percent of the participants either strongly agreed or agreed with the item but less than 50 percent either strongly disagreed or disagreed with the item. This was possible because participants were also able to choose the alternative response, "lack sufficient information or experience to judge."

The reader's attention is also called to the asterisks which precede various items. Items with one asterisk are those about which the Hispanics agreed but the non-Hispanics did not agree. Items with two asterisks are those about which at least 20 percent of the non-Hispanics responded that they lacked sufficient information or experience to judge.

Finally, the reader may note that in a number of instances the percent of participants who agreed that a particular trait is characteristic of the Hispanic culture in the United States is much higher than the percent of participants who agreed with the suggested implication which accompanies it. This difference appears to reflect the fact that participants who agreed that a particular trait is characteristic of the Hispanic culture sometimes disagreed among themselves as to whether the educational system should be accommodated to the students' cultural differences or whether the culturally different students should be encouraged, required or assisted to adapt to the culture of the school as it exists.

---

[1]Because of rounding, the total percent may not always equal 100.

Chapter 3

INSTRUCTION

INTRODUCTION

"His classes are a waste of time"; "I learned more in her class than in all my other classes put together"; "All he does is assign students to make presentations"; "Read the text and don't bother to go to class"; "She's a tough teacher"; "She's an easy teacher"; "He's a good teacher"; "He's a bad teacher"; "She's an interesting teacher"; "She's a boring teacher"; "He's a good guy" are examples of the fact that students can readily perceive the differences among their instructors at all levels of education. This is a clear indication that educators do not all use the same instructional techniques. Some examples of the differences among instructors are included below.

1. Educators may employ teaching techniques which emphasize learning by doing, such as hands-on approaches, manipulatives, films, field trips, etc., or they may employ more abstract instructional methods such as learning by reading and by listening to lectures.

2. Some educators stimulate discussions of differences of opinion, while others encourage students to accept the knowledge of experts such as the authors of textbooks or the educator in charge.

3. Educators may *require* student participation by calling on those that do not volunteer, *encourage* students' participation by rewarding it, or *accept* their students' level of class participation whatever it may be.

4. While some educators prefer to advise and counsel their students and to provide them with a lot of direction and feedback about their performance in class, others encourage their students to function more independently, to learn by trial and error and to reach their own conclusions without consultation and advisement.

5. Educators may criticize and correct students in front of their peers, only in private or not at all. They may do so in a direct and frank manner or subtly and indirectly.

6. Educators can choose to assign long-term or short-term projects, provide immediate feedback or delayed feedback, allow students to work at their own pace or encourage them to work rapidly and accept assignments when they are completed, or penalize students for work handed in after a specified deadline.

7. The topics studied, the photographs in the textbooks, the holidays celebrated, etc., may reflect the interests and experiences of the majority of Americans or the instructor can develop a curriculum which reflects the pluralistic nature of American society.

These are only a few examples of the many different instructional techniques which educators have at their disposal. This chapter contains the opinions of the participants regarding both Hispanic cultural characteristics which have relevance for the instruction of Hispanic students and specific ways in which educators can modify instructional methods in light of these cultural differences when they teach Hispanic students.

RESULTS

Importance of Family, Friends, Community and Personal Qualities

Hispanics tend to experience the family as a fountain of emotional and economic security and support.

Hispanics: Agree 95% Insufficient Information 1% Disagree 5%
Non-Hispanics: Agree 88% Insufficient Information 6% Disagree 5%

"In the case of Hispanics, blood is much thicker than water." (Hispanic)

"In general the family is much more important in the Hispanic community than in the Anglo community." (Hispanic)

"Hispanic families frequently have large numbers of children; relationships extend to aunts, uncles, grandparents and in-laws often on a regular basis. Families are often split between U.S. and Mexico with some siblings living with biological parents while others may live with other relatives. All family members are expected to help meet economic needs by contributing income, help with household chores, child care, etc. As a result, as research has shown, Hispanics tend to be more cooperative and foster group rather than individualistic goals. Families also are the main source of self-worth and meet social and emotional needs of their members." (Non-Hispanic)

"The family unit of the Hispanic is no longer as strong as it once was. Families can no longer expect to stay close by. Husbands and wives may stay together but it does not necessarily mean that they are providing a secure atmosphere." (Unknown)

"I think that's the ideal—but where I teach the families are broken up and parents have disappointed their children by abandonment, drinking, too many siblings, etc." (Non-Hispanic)

"While I agree that Hispanics are more loyal to their families, I have some problems with this. In my work with junior high students, there were many family problems and I do not see the Hispanic family being as supportive as many think—on the outside, yes, but the support does not always run as deep." (Non-Hispanic)

Therefore, educators should stress the fact that Hispanic students' families will be proud of them and share the honor of their accomplishments.

Hispanics: Agree 87%   Insufficient Information 3%   Disagree 10%
Non-Hispanics: Agree 77%   Insufficient Information 12%   Disagree 11%

"The family is more important to the Hispano, but we should be careful about putting too much stress on the student." (Hispanic)

"Depends on the circumstances. It is good to say their family will be proud of them after they have accomplished things. But if we do the same thing beforehand it could mean, 'but if you fail your family will be ashamed and disappointed.'" (Non-Hispanic)

"Children should be motivated for themselves primarily." (Hispanic)

"While many do have close family ties, many other students come from troubled homes and environments and couldn't give 'two hoots' about their family being proud of them." (Non-Hispanic)

"Chicano students where I work (I have 12 years experience at this school) seem to want to be treated as independent from their family and do not like their parents bothered. This may be due to language barriers or a desire not to worry their parents or ask for things they know their parents can't afford, etc." (Non-Hispanic)

Hispanics have a strong identification with and loyalty to their family and community. They are brought up to believe that contributing to and sacrificing for the benefit of the group is more important than personal aggrandizement. As a result, Hispanic students may be highly motivated to do things that have significance for their families, friends, and community.

Hispanics:	Agree 90%	Insufficient Information	2%	Disagree	8%
Non-Hispanics:	Agree 93%	Insufficient Information	4%	Disagree	3%

"We have a stronger commitment to the group. We are more willing to go along with the group, but we also look out for ourselves. It's a question of how you do it. We would never want to appear self-centered 'egoista' while Anglos don't seem to care as much." (Hispanic)

"This is a thing of the past. Even in the past it was limited to the family and did not extend to friends and the community." (Hispanic)

Therefore, educators should include community-oriented projects in the curriculum.

Hispanics:	Agree 89%	Insufficient Information	3%	Disagree	8%
Non-Hispanics:	Agree 88%	Insufficient Information	8%	Disagree	4%

Because of their commitment to the group and other reasons, some Hispanic students may prefer to work in groups.

Hispanics: Agree 80%   Insufficient Information 9%   Disagree 11%
**Non-Hispanics: Agree 72%   Insufficient Information 20%   Disagree 9%

"Hispanic children work cooperatively rather than individually. Unfortunately this behavior is often erroneously characterized as copying or cheating." (Hispanic)

"We are a very social people. We like to work together. So working in groups comes naturally to us. It is not necessarily a matter of commitment to the group." (Hispanic)

"When I taught Hispanic students in a master's degree program at a university in Peru, students were much more group oriented than my students in the United States. If a student missed a class someone else in the group would make sure he or she got the notes and any assignment that was handed out. They almost always worked and studied together in groups. Even when it came to their masters theses all but two preferred to write them with at least one other student. It was as if who they were going to work with was more important than the topic itself since first they divided themselves into small groups and then they chose their topics. It was very difficult for me to adapt to group master's theses; however, the Peruvians on the faculty had no trouble accepting it since it was the normal way of doing things." (Non-Hispanic)

"They want to work in groups so others can do the work. No one has ideas. It's 'let George do it'." (Non-Hispanic)

Therefore, educators should emphasize or give equal time to group projects.

Hispanics: Agree 75%   Insufficient Information 10%   Disagree 15%
Non-Hispanics: Agree 72%   Insufficient Information 18%   Disagree 11%

"This helping attitude can be encouraged by working in committees. Since individualism is fostered in the dominant society, times for individual study should also be taught. Both qualities should be accepted." (Hispanic)

"Yes, give equal time to, not emphasize." (Hispanic)

"Yes, however the appropriateness of group projects may depend on the subject and the individual student." (Unknown)

"Definitely not! Don't treat them any different." (Non-Hispanic)

Therefore, educators should encourage students to ask each other for help and arrange for peer tutoring.

Hispanics: Agree 84%   Insufficient Information 5%   Disagree 11%
Non-Hispanics: Agree 85%   Insufficient Information 11%   Disagree 5%

"I agree, but not only because it is a trait of the Hispanic student. It is important to learn that group participation and involvement is important to the success of some projects and can be applied in *future* experiences." (Hispanic)

"No! Older children don't teach the younger ones. Rather, they do the work for them. They should be taught the difference between helping and doing it instead." (Hispanic)

Hispanics tend to be more interested in and dependent on the approval of others than Anglos who are more likely to be receptive to more impersonal and materialistic forms of recognition.

*Hispanics: Agree 75%   Insufficient Information 11%   Disagree 15%
**Non-Hispanics: Agree 48%   Insufficient Information 23%   Disagree 30%

"All kids like materialistic things. Fortunately our Hispanic children still value people as much as things." (Hispanic)

"It's more of a shame thing than an approval thing. What will my neighbors think, meaning bad, is more important than gaining their approval." (Hispanic)

"It's true that generally Anglo children are more materialistic. However, in my limited experience I've noticed that lower socioeconomic Hispanic children tend to want materialistic reinforcement in addition to or in lieu of personal reinforcement. This is probably due to the fact that they live in a deprived environment and they welcome any little material rewards (candy, stickers, etc.). Some are deprived of affection at home and they also want that from you. Thus, depending on the child's deprivation, materialistic or affection, he will welcome the one he needs the most." (Non-Hispanic)

"All my children have the 'gimmes' including the Hispanics." (Non-Hispanic)

Therefore, educators should use praise, hugs, pats on the back and other personal rewards with Hispanic students more than checks, gold stars and materialistic forms of reinforcement such as sweets and toys.

| Hispanics: | Agree 64% | Insufficient Information | 7% | Disagree 29% |
| Non-Hispanics: | Agree 52% | Insufficient Information | 18% | Disagree 30% |

"Yes, but only if it comes naturally to the teacher." (Non-Hispanic)

"This is true of all children, though perhaps less overt in Anglos. There has to be a personal relationship of some kind between child and teacher." (Hispanic)

"Educators should do what they feel comfortable with but explain their needs to students, expressing awareness of the students' attitudes." (Hispanic)

"My students get both. They love stickers." (Hispanic)

"This could be condescending to some Hispanic children." (Non-Hispanic)

Hispanics tend to judge people in terms of their personal qualities, who they are, rather than in terms of their accomplishments — what they are. Success, honor and prestige are attributed to good people rather than to people who have achieved a considerable amount in a material sense. As a result, some Hispanic students may not be as motivated by the work ethic to accomplish, achieve, and succeed according to the criteria utilized in the schools.

| Hispanics: | Agree 72% | Insufficient Information | 3% | Disagree 25% |
| Non-Hispanics: | Agree 66% | Insufficient Information | 15% | Disagree 19% |

"Soy lo que soy, y no lo que tengo (I am who I am, not what I have) exemplifies this." (Hispanic)

"As with many questions, this varies with social class, so it's hard to respond. Middle and upper class Hispanics are closer to Anglos in that way. But I answered 'agree' because most of our new students are not middle and upper class, and they are our clientele." (Unknown)

"This is a thing of the past. Where Hispanics do not place as much importance on accomplishments in relation to whether or not a person is good or worthwhile, Hispanic youth seeks success as much as do Anglos." (Hispanic)

"Undocumented workers from Hispanic countries are the only people in the U.S.A. who still believe in the old 'Anglo-American Protestant' work ethic. Nobody else really believes that crap any more." (Non-Hispanic)

Therefore, educators should not assume that Hispanic students who are less motivated to success academically are unmotivated in general. It may well be that their motivation is channeled into other directions by their values.

Hispanics: Agree 87%   Insufficient Information 2%   Disagree 10%
Non-Hispanics: Agree 87%   Insufficient Information 7%   Disagree 6%

Therefore, educators should modify both the curriculum and their teaching methods so that Hispanic students can achieve in those areas which they value regardless of whether these areas are highly valued by educators and the academically oriented school systems.

Hispanics: Agree 61%   Insufficient Information 8%   Disagree 32%
Non-Hispanics: Agree 50%   Insufficient Information 15%   Disagree 35%

"The key words here are academically oriented school systems. Too much of the educational pie is spent on preparing students for college which turns out to be vocational education at the professional level. More money and attention should be spent on humanistic education which has a humanistic rather than dollar sign payoff." (Non-Hispanic)

"Some modification is called for in working with non-English speaking Hispanics but competency in basic skills should not be watered down for them." (Hispanic)

"Many Hispanic students come from homes where parents do not have the knowledge as to how or in what direction to motivate them. Therefore it is the educator's duty to inform himself on these students in order to be able to help and direct him." (Hispanic)

"It is long past due that schools, educators, counselors and psychologists stop treating the Hispanic student as anything other than a human being with the same capabilities as anyone else. Our values are strong, but so are our mentalities and abilities." (Hispanic)

"Students need to learn skills to succeed in the Anglo culture." (Non-Hispanic)

"The children need to be bicultural in this regard." (Hispanic)

In comparison to the Anglo culture, the Hispanic culture emphasized people over ideas.

Hispanics: Agree 76%   Insufficient Information 12%   Disagree 13%
**Non-Hispanics: Agree 62%   Insufficient Information 29%   Disagree 9%

As a result, some Hispanic students may relate better to a person-centered rather than thing- or idea-centered curriculum.

Hispanics: Agree 75%   Insufficient Information 13%   Disagree 12%
**Non-Hispanics: Agree 68%   Insufficient Information 24%   Disagree 9%

Therefore, educators should personalize the curriculum. This can be done by having students solve math problems about people, shopping in stores rather than just numerical computational problems, teaching about human geography, how people live in different regions, rather than physical geography, etc.

Hispanics: Agree 74%   Insufficient Information 8%   Disagree 19%
Non-Hispanics: Agree 76%   Insufficient Information 14%   Disagree 10%

> "I think personalizing is better for all elementary students." (Non-Hispanic)

> "Yes, but not to the total exclusion of the existing curriculum." (Hispanic)

> "Hispanics need to learn about physical as well as human geography. The problem is that we seldom teach about the human and physical geography of Meso-America, the Southwest, etc. " (Hispanic)

> "This is really dumb! Stop treating Hispanics as if they are incapable of using their mental capacities." (Non-Hispanic)

In comparison to the Anglo culture, Hispanics are tolerant of differences of opinion within groups, "cada cabeza es un mundo" (every mind is a world in and of itself). As long as Hispanics conform to the group, they are entitled to their own beliefs and it would be a sign of disrespect to try to change someone's beliefs. Because of this, some Hispanic students may be uncomfortable with debating issues or even questioning in public the opinions of others.

*Hispanics: Agree 67%   Insufficient Information 12%   Disagree 22%
**Non-Hispanics: Agree 44%   Insufficient Information 43%   Disagree 13%

> "Debating and criticizing, I think, has to do with trust levels. When trust does not exist, there will be no debating. United States born Hispanics rarely hold back their comments if the setting is constructive." (Hispanic)

> "A good example of cultural shock. Anglo culture shows

little or no respect for differences and therefore in many cases serves to alienate students." (Hispanic)

"Muchos de nosotros no estamos acostumbrados a discutir ciertos puntos en público. Esto no se atribuye a que no nos gusta discutir. Es cierto que creemos en el concepto de 'Cada Cabeza es un Mundo,' 'Mejor solo que mal acompañado,' y en todas nuestras juntas se forman buenas 'averiguatas'. La razon por la cual no discutimos en las clases es que las personas de autoridad nos aplacan. (Many of us are not accustomed to discuss certain things publicly. This does not mean that we do not like to discuss things but that to us every mind is a world in and of itself. It's better to be alone than in bad company—together but not combined. Still we like to find out how the other person thinks in our meetings. The reason why we don't discuss things in class is that the person in charge squelches us. They come down too hard on us.)" (Hispanic)

"When I taught at universities in Latin America, I had to practically give up the use of classroom discussions of controversial issues because of my students' reluctance to participate." (Non-Hispanic)

Therefore, educators should avoid using this method with those Hispanic students who are uncomfortable with debating or criticizing opinions.

Hispanics: Agree 51%   Insufficient Information 14%   Disagree 35%
**Non-Hispanics: Agree 37%   Insufficient Information 34%   Disagree 30%

"I agree, teachers must empathize with their students. Insisting that Hispanic students learn 'your way' is definitely a 'turn off.'" (Hispanic)

"Yes, but not completely." (Non-Hispanic)

"Educators should assist students in learning the benefits of, and how to, debate. It should not be avoided. It is part of the system they will graduate into." (Non-Hispanic)

"Help the student be bi-cultural." (Hispanic)

Therefore, educators should explain to such students that while their reluctance to engage in debates is understandable, in school such procedures are considered appropriate and not impolite or improper.

Hispanics: Agree 87%   Insufficient Information 5%   Disagree 8%
**Non-Hispanics: Agree 69%   Insufficient Information 23%   Disagree 8%

"Explain but not force or require them to participate until they are ready to do so voluntarily." (Hispanic)

"Don't ever emphasize this type of instruction if it is threatening or futile." (Hispanic)

Summary: Hispanic and non-Hispanic participants agreed with the statements that family and community play a more important role in the Hispanic culture than in the mainstream American culture and that Hispanics tend to be willing to make sacrifices for the benefit of family, friends and community. The participants also agreed that these cultural tendencies should be capitalized on and accommodated when instructing Hispanic students.

Both groups agreed that Hispanics tend to judge people in terms of their personal qualities—who they are—rather than in terms of their accomplishments—what they are; that they emphasize people over ideas. They also agreed that these cultural factors should help determine both the content of the curriculum and the teaching techniques employed with Hispanic students.

The Hispanic participants agreed that Hispanic students are more receptive to personal rather than materialistic forms of recognition and more tolerant of and polite about differences of opinion within groups. The majority of the non-Hispanics did not agree with these descriptions of the Hispanic culture, and many of them described themselves as lacking sufficient information or experience to judge whether these descriptions were actually true of Hispanics in the United States.

Judging from the results obtained in this study the participants agreed in general that Hispanics in the United States maintain their characteristic methods of interpersonal relationships and that these should be taken into account when instructing Hispanic students.

Role of Children

Hispanic children are brought up to look up to their elders, especially their parents, and respect their wishes, opinions, attitudes and advice.

Hispanics:	Agree 98%	Insufficient Information 0%	Disagree 2%
Non-Hispanics:	Agree 86%	Insufficient Information 9%	Disagree 5%

Hispanic children tend to model themselves after adults whom they like, respect and admire.

Hispanics: Agree 92% Insufficient Information 3% Disagree 5%
Non-Hispanics: Agree 69% Insufficient Information 16% Disagree 16%

Therefore, educators should develop the close personal relationships with their Hispanic students which will motivate their students to seek their teachers' approval and to model themselves after them.

Hispanics: Agree 80% Insufficient Information 6% Disagree 14%
Non-Hispanics: Agree 60% Insufficient Information 18% Disagree 23%

> "It is important that the student feel that the educator is there to help." (Hispanic)

> "Even more important is being authentic with Hispanic students at all times." (Hispanic)

> "While I was in school in Mexico I felt as if my teachers, the nuns, were my friends as well as my teachers. They asked about my family and my personal life. When I came here the teachers seemed very cold and aloof. It was very hard for me to adjust to the differences. " (Hispanic)

> "I agree, but I find a need for caution so the student doesn't do things solely or constantly for the teacher's approval. We need to develop his self-motivation also." (Hispanic)

> "I agree, but only if the educator is comfortable with close personal relationships." (Hispanic)

They are much more likely than Anglo children to ask their parents and other adults for their advice and suggestions when they have to make important decisions.

Hispanics: Agree 87% Insufficient Information 5% Disagree 9%
**Non-Hispanics: Agree 61% Insufficient Information 28% Disagree 15%

As a result some Hispanic students may have difficulty when educators want them to form their own opinions and make their own decisions independently of their teachers.

Hispanics: Agree 72% Insufficient Information 8% Disagree 20%
**Non-Hispanics: Agree 61% Insufficient Information 22% Disagree 17%

> "I know for myself that can still be a problem. Due to the high respect for my parents and elders of the extended family, it was only natural to ask them for advice/suggestions on a particular problem. As part of the culture, they would tell me what they thought was best and that's what I would do. I really never questioned or doubted their answers,

because your elders are wise, and had learned from their mistakes, and you do what was told." (Hispanic)

"This is true, but it depends on the degree of assimilation ." (Non-Hispanic)

"Depends on the age of the student. It is true for elementary school students, less so for high school students." (Hispanic)

"This is so because these children tend to seek reassurance from the educator repeatedly." (Hispanic)

"One characteristic of most Mexican-American youth is their respect for authority figures who are part of the primary group. They are generally used to being told what is right with subsequent almost blind obedience to what they are told. Decisions are usually made for them." (Non-Hispanic)

"Hispanic students have opinions but many times their teachers don't wish to hear them." (Hispanic)

Therefore, educators should provide these students with the guidance and approval they need in order to make decisions in the classroom.

Hispanics:	Agree 88%	Insufficient Information 3%	Disagree 9%
Non-Hispanics:	Agree 86%	Insufficient Information 11%	Disagree 3%

"The educator needs to be aware of this and patiently help the student to understand the need to take responsibility for decisions." (Hispanic)

"Yes, but with the goal of building up the student's self-confidence to make his own decisions so he can become a more independent decision maker." (Hispanic)

Therefore, educators should try to encourage these students to be less dependent on the opinions and approval of adults so that they can begin to learn to function more independently.

Hispanics:	Agree 73%	Insufficient Information 8%	Disagree 18%
**Non-Hispanics:	Agree 62%	Insufficient Information 20%	Disagree 18%

"Expose them to an alternative way of thinking rather than encourage them to be less dependent." (Hispanic)

"A combination of the two styles would be best." (Non-Hispanic)

"This would mean eradicating an important cultural value." (Hispanic)

"Why should these students be Anglocized?" (Hispanic)

Hispanic students who are brought up to depend on the opinions of their elders may function better when adults provide encouragement and feedback about how they are doing.

| Hispanics: | Agree 89% | Insufficient Information 4% | Disagree 7% |
| Non-Hispanics: | Agree 81% | Insufficient Information 12% | Disagree 7% |

Therefore, educators should provide these students with the encouragement and feedback about how they are doing and what they require in order to work effectively.

| Hispanics: | Agree 91% | Insufficient Information 2% | Disagree 7% |
| Non-Hispanics: | Agree 86% | Insufficient Information 8% | Disagree 7% |

Therefore, educators should encourage these students to be both able to function independently when necessary and to also rely on the encouragement and feedback of adults when necessary.

| Hispanics: | Agree 90% | Insufficient Information 5% | Disagree 5% |
| Non-Hispanics: | Agree 92% | Insufficient Information 4% | Disagree 4% |

Therefore, educators should provide the approval and feedback these students seek, but only temporarily, while they are encouraging the students to function more independently.

| *Hispanics: | Agree 65% | Insufficient Information 10% | Disagree 25% |
| Non-Hispanics: | Agree 49% | Insufficient Information 14% | Disagree 37% |

Educators should not provide the approval and feedback these students seek. Instead, they should encourage the students to work more independently.

| Hispanics: | Agree 30% | Insufficient Information 7% | Disagree 63% |
| Non-Hispanics: | Agree 9% | Insufficient Information 17% | Disagree 74% |

Because these students do not function independently, educators should de-emphasize the use of trial-and-error learning, the inquiry method and other forms of independent study.

| Hispanics: | Agree 20% | Insufficient Information 15% | Disagree 66% |
| **Non-Hispanics: | Agree 16% | Insufficient Information 22% | Disagree 63% |

"These forms of independent study should be provided gradually, with guidance and encouragement from the instructor." (Hispanic)

"De-emphasize initially, but work towards independent study." (Non-Hispanic)

"No, they need to be taught to function independently." (Hispanic)

Children are taught to obey rather than to question why or disagree, to be quiet around their elders and to listen and learn rather than to speak and participate.

Hispanics: Agree 83%   Insufficient Information 4%   Disagree 13%
Non-Hispanics: Agree 75%   Insufficient Information 18%   Disagree 7%

Some Hispanic parents tend to discourage their children from showing too much initiative or independence or expressing their own ideas and opinions without consulting their elders first.

Hispanics: Agree 61%   Insufficient Information 10%   Disagree 29%
**Non-Hispanics: Agree 57%   Insufficient Information 33%   Disagree 10%

> "More true of girls." (Unknown)

> "Times have changed. It's not like this anymore." (Hispanic)

As a result, some Hispanic students may have difficulty expressing their opinions and conclusions in class.

Hispanics: Agree 79%   Insufficient Information 7%   Disagree 14%
Non-Hispanics: Agree 76%   Insufficient Information 15%   Disagree 9%

> "Hispanic children are taught to be quiet and not speak up. In the Anglo culture it is the opposite. We have to encourage children gently to express their opinions through story discussion, show and tell, perhaps starting with small groups." (Hispanic)

> "I've noticed that once someone has expressed an opinion my Hispanic students are extremely reluctant to express any disagreement." (Non-Hispanic)

> "It depends on the teacher. The presence of an acceptable adult encourages students to express their opinion. A threatening adult has the opposite effect." (Hispanic)

> "Hispanics have opinions, but many times their teachers do not wish to hear them." (Non-Hispanic)

> "Not true. I have a classroom full of very talkative Spanish-speaking kindergarteners." (Hispanic)

Therefore, educators should not over-emphasize the expression of opinions with such students until they demonstrate that they are comfortable with this role in school.

Hispanics: Agree 77%   Insufficient Information 7%   Disagree 16%
Non-Hispanics: Agree 78%   Insufficient Information 12%   Disagree 11%

Summary: Both the Hispanics and non-Hispanics agreed with all of the statements which described the relationships between

Hispanic children and adults. They also agreed with most of the implications of these cultural characteristics. They agreed that because Hispanic children are accustomed to having these roles with adults, educators should develop close, personal relationships with them and provide them with the guidance, approval, encouragement and feedback they need. Both groups also agreed, but to a lesser degree, with statements that this should be done temporarily until the students are able to function without these types of relationships with their teachers. They disagreed with the suggestion that educators should not provide approval and feedback to Hispanic students and also with the suggestion that, because Hispanic students do not function independently, educators should de-emphasize such forms of independent study as the use of trial-and-error learning and the inquiry method.

Concept of Time

Present vs. Future Orientation

Hispanics tend to be more present time oriented. Finishing a conversation now may be more important than keeping an appointment later. Living to the fullest now and enjoying what the present has to offer may be more important than saving, planning and striving for future satisfactions and security.

Hispanics: Agree 64%   Insufficient Information 8%   Disagree 28%
**Non-Hispanics: Agree 70%   Insufficient Information 20%   Disagree 10%

"This is something Anglos should learn. I see this as a positive aspect of our culture. Many uptight Anglos cannot." (Hispanic)

"The time many Mexican-Americans value most is the present. Finishing a conversation with an old friend may be more important than keeping an appointment with a doctor. Making plans for the future may be less important than living to the fullest the moment at hand. Many Mexican-Americans perceive the time-serving ways of the Anglo as a misappropriation of the present. An article in a popular journal recently asserted that the entire system of American education revolves about a ritualistic adherence to the ticking of the clock. What is the Mexican-American child's reaction to the rigid schedules and the incessant pressures to plan for the future? How does he view a reward system that is programmed to respond to him at six-week intervals?" (Unknown)

"We have also been referred to as the mañana people which makes us future oriented. We need to be very careful how we handle this present and future time orientation. 'Hay mas tiempo que vida' 'no hay mejor lecciones que las que el tiempo da' (there is more time than life; there are no better lessons than those that time teaches), etc." (Hispanic)

"It may be true of Hispanics in Latin America but not for Hispanics who have been in the United States for a few years." (Hispanic)

"Depends on the person's self-discipline." (Non-Hispanic)

"Depends on the socio-economic status of the family. It's a lower socio-economic class phenomenon." (Non-Hispanic)

"Only fits the culture of poverty." (Hispanic)

"I am sick and tired of people talking about us as if we were immature, spoiled and childish." (Hispanic)

Therefore, educators should provide Hispanic students with short-term assignments. Daily or weekly assignments would be preferable to term projects. When term projects are necessary they should be broken down into short-term objectives leading toward long-term goals.

Hispanics: Agree 64% Insufficient Information 8% Disagree 28%
Non-Hispanics: Agree 66% Insufficient Information 16% Disagree 17%

"This is also very true for Anglo students as well. In general assignments need to be broken down into more manageable parts than most teachers realize." (Hispanic)

"Depends on maturity of child, not his ethnic background." (Hispanic)

Therefore, educators should teach Hispanic students to organize and plan their time so that they can complete long-term projects.

Hispanics: Agree 85% Insufficient Information 5% Disagree 11%
Non-Hispanics: Agree 88% Insufficient Information 8% Disagree 5%

The anticipation of a large reward or satisfaction in the future may be much less motivating than a smaller satisfaction in the here and now.

Hispanics: Agree 63%   Insufficient Information 11%   Disagree 26%
**Non-Hispanics: Agree 65%   Insufficient Information 23%   Disagree 12%

Therefore, educators should provide immediate feedback, approval, recognition and reward to Hispanic students.

Hispanics: Agree 81%   Insufficient Information 7%   Disagree 12%
Non-Hispanics: Agree 80%   Insufficient Information 12%   Disagree 8%

Pace of Life

Hispanics tend to be more concerned with doing a job well, regardless of the amount of time required, than they are in finishing rapidly so they will have more time for the next task.

Hispanics: Agree 76%   Insufficient Information 10%   Disagree 14%
**Non-Hispanics: Agree 50%   Insufficient Information 30%   Disagree 20%

> "I perceive Hispanics to be more concerned about concentrating on the task at hand and finishing when it's finished." (Hispanic)

> "This mañana syndrome does not appear among Hispanics who have lived in the United States for any length of time."(Hispanic)

Hispanics tend to prefer to work at a relaxed pace even if it means taking longer to finish something.

Hispanics: Agree 72%   Insufficient Information 5%   Disagree 23%
**Non-Hispanics: Agree 61%   Insufficient Information 24%   Disagree 15%

> "True, but there are individual differences." (Hispanic)

> "The fact that we live a more relaxed life does not mean that we are slow in doing a task or that we like to do things just right, so we take longer. Field work is not slow work. It is a type of work that requires a fast pace and a constant change of gears. The difference is this: In the fields, you get up at 5:00 A.M. and you hustle to finish by 1:00 or 2:00 P.M. We are not locked into an 8:00-5:00 routine. The same applies to the packing sheds, the garment factories, etc." (Hispanic)

At home, Hispanic children are permitted to do things at their own pace without adhering to strict time schedules.

*Hispanics: Agree 60%   Insufficient Information 14%   Disagree 26%
**Non-Hispanics: Agree 46%   Insufficient Information 42%   Disagree 13%

> "This is true to a certain extent." (Hispanic)

"Not many Anglos show signs of being on tight schedules at home." (Hispanic)

"Hispanic families who have lived here seem to catch on to 'the clock' quickly." (Hispanic)

When required to rush or stop working before they have finished in order to begin the next task with their peers, they may become anxious, nervous, rebellious, etc.

Hispanics: Agree 62%   Insufficient Information 14%   Disagree 25%
**Non-Hispanics: Agree 50%   Insufficient Information 30%   Disagree 20%

As a result, Hispanic students may not complete classroom work as fast as their Anglo peers.

Hispanics: Agree 54%   Insufficient Information 13%   Disagree 34%
**Non-Hispanics: Agree 50%   Insufficient Information 28%   Disagree 23%

"Happily, some Hispanic students have not yet bought into the rush, rush, rush neurosis of Americans." (Hispanic)

"Young (K-6) students seem to catch on to the 'routine.'" (Hispanic)

"In school, we have difficulty because we are lacking in *English* and when students are lacking in *cognitive academic language skills,* of course they are going to be slow. We can't say that this is a cultural trait, however. This is in spite of the fact that in English we run and in Spanish we walk—'El reloy *anda*'—'hecha *andar* el motor.' 'Con quien andas?' (Who are you running around with?) etc." (Hispanic)

Therefore, educators should not rush Hispanic students when they are called on to answer questions in class. Nor should they assume that Hispanic students who hesitate before answering are unsure of themselves.

Hispanics: Agree 67%   Insufficient Information 7%   Disagree 27%
Non-Hispanics: Agree 68%   Insufficient Information 17%   Disagree 15%

Therefore, educators should allow Hispanic students to spend as much time as necessary to complete class assignments even though others may have already finished.

Hispanics: Agree 37%   Insufficient Information 10%   Disagree 53%
Non-Hispanics: Agree 18%   Insufficient Information 18%   Disagree 64%

"Yes, but not for Hispanics only. Educators should restructure assignments to fit the needs of all students in the class. Otherwise special privileges cause cries of unfairness and put pressure on the 'privileged' student." (Hispanic)

"To a point only. They also need to work within time limits in the real world."(Hispanic)

"I have grappled with this for years and still have no idea of what is right." (Non-Hispanic)

"Better to allow them to do the work later on their own time so as not to call attention to them." (Hispanic)

"They can finish the assignment as homework." (Hispanic)

"No! Treat all students the same—equally." (Hispanic)

Therefore, educators should help such students adjust to the time orientation which they encounter in school and which will govern their lives in the dominant culture. This should include helping them to adjust to the pressures of time limits.

Hispanics: Agree 88% Insufficient Information 3% Disagree 9%
Non-Hispanics: Agree 87% Insufficient Information 7% Disagree 6%

Punctuality

The Hispanic concept of punctuality is different than the Anglo concept. If a meeting is called for two o'clock, people are expected to arrive sometime after that. If a party or dance is set for nine o'clock, people may be expected to arrive at eleven or even later. An agreement to repair a TV for Wednesday means that it will probably be ready sometime after Wednesday.

Hispanics: Agree 66% Insufficient Information 5% Disagree 28%
Non-Hispanics: Agree 74% Insufficient Information 18% Disagree 8%

"I don't feel that there is such a thing as 'Chicano People's Time (C.P. time).' Hispanics are punctual for business appointments and casual about arriving at parties." (Hispanic)

"Another instance where it may be difficult to see beyond a prevailing stereotype. Do Hispanics miss their favorite TV shows because they turn them on at 'hora latina'?" (Non-Hispanic)

"The concept of punctuality is generally true if you're referring to Hispanics living in their native country. However, Hispanics living in the U.S. have somewhat adopted the Anglo concept of punctuality and arrive at the indicated time. I'm generalizing this point and again I'm speaking from my limited experience. Some Hispanics do arrive late for an appointment, however, it's only a matter of a few minutes (5 to 10)." (Non-Hispanic)

Therefore, educators should accommodate their schedules to the Hispanic concept of punctuality.

Hispanics:	Agree 14%	Insufficient Information 6%	Disagree 80%
Non-Hispanics:	Agree 12%	Insufficient Information 11%	Disagree 77%

"Teachers should adjust to attitudes of parents regarding when their children should arrive or hand in homework assignments." (Non-Hispanic)

"A compromise would be best." (Non-Hispanic)

"Important for them (educators) to understand the Hispanic concept of punctuality, but students may need to modify their concepts as related to school." (Non-Hispanic)

"This may cause resentment in Anglo students." (Hispanic)

"When in Rome do as the Romans. When in the U.S.A. do as the Americans." (Non-Hispanic)

Therefore, educators should inform Hispanic students that although the Hispanic concept of punctuality is fine for their homes and community, in school and other similar situations it would be best if they adapted to the dominant culture's expectations of punctuality.

Hispanics:	Agree 82%	Insufficient Information 7%	Disagree 12%
Non-Hispanics:	Agree 86%	Insufficient Information 8%	Disagree 6%

Summary: Hispanics and non-Hispanics agreed that Hispanics are more present time oriented, work at a more relaxed pace and have a different concept of punctuality. However, many individuals disagreed with the majority opinions, especially in regard to the idea that Hispanics have a different concept of punctuality. While agreeing with these descriptions of the Hispanic concept of time, non-Hispanics also tended to describe themselves as lacking sufficient information and experience to judge.

Regarding the implications of these cultural factors for instructors, a very high percentage of both Hispanic and non-Hispanics agreed with suggestions that Hispanic students should learn to function in the time frame of the school. They also agreed, but to a lesser extent, that Hispanic students should not be rushed and should be given short-term assignments. But they disagreed with suggestions that Hispanic students should be allowed to spend as

much time as necessary to complete classroom assignments and
that educators should accommodate their schedules to the Hispanic concept of punctuality.

Role of Religion and the Supernatural

Some Hispanic students may believe in the supernatural, ghosts,
magic, religion, saints, etc., more than their Anglo peers do.

Hispanics:	Agree 85%	Insufficient Information 6%	Disagree 9%
Non-Hispanics:	Agree 83%	Insufficient Information 12%	Disagree 6%

Therefore, educators should include these interests when teaching
reading, writing and oral communication skills.

Hispanics:	Agree 64%	Insufficient Information 10%	Disagree 27%
Non-Hispanics:	Agree 68%	Insufficient Information 16%	Disagree 16%

> "We know that the various forms of expressions of a given
> people, be it their legends, sayings, riddles, music, dances,
> etc., in the hands of a creative faculty can become a vital
> resource that can help us to understand our students better
> and to teach them more effectively the reality of the world
> and of the human condition in which we find ourselves. No
> one teaches us about our legends and our dichos."(Hispanic)

Quality of Work

In comparison to Anglos, quality control is not a high priority for
Hispanics. The quality of the product or the result of their effort
may be less important than accomplishing and finishing the task.

Hispanics:	Agree 28%	Insufficient Information 13%	Disagree 59%
**Non-Hispanics:	Agree 21%	Insufficient Information 29%	Disagree 50%

> "You can see this in many of the things imported from
> Mexico and other Latin American countries that are made to
> last just long enough to be sold." (Non-Hispanic)
>
> "Yuck!" (Hispanic)
>
> "Like the pyramids, right?" (Hispanic)
>
> "Lack of skills, technology, resources is not a cultural trait.
> Quality Control is Quality Control in any culture. What one
> culture learns, another culture can also learn. I would hate to
> believe that simply because I am Chicano, my Quality
> Control will not be as good as others. Teach me the skills and

you will be amazed at how well I can apply these skills with a multicultural perspective." (Hispanic)

"This is not true unless there is a great deal of time pressure." (Hispanic)

"Quality is a high priority if they are taking pride in what they are doing." (Hispanic)

Therefore, educators should adjust their expectations regarding the quality of their Hispanic students' work to the expectations of their Hispanic students.

Hispanics:	Agree 30%	Insufficient Information 10%	Disagree 61%
Non-Hispanics:	Agree 14%	Insufficient Information 12%	Disagree 74%

"The problem is that traditionally it has been the educators who have lowered their expectations for Hispanic students." (Hispanic)

"This assumes that Hispanics do not value quality work which is false." (Hispanic)

"Teachers and students expectations should correlate, but not at the expense of quality." (Non-Hispanic)

"Life doesn't adjust its expectations." (Non-Hispanic)

"No! Good educators always expect the best from *all* their students." (Non-Hispanic)

Summary: Both Hispanics and non-Hispanics disagreed with the often stated idea that quality control is not a high priority for Hispanics. Disagreeing that it is a characteristic of the Hispanic culture, they of course disagreed that it was necessary to take it into consideration when working with Hispanic students.

Learning Style

The Hispanic culture emphasizes learning by doing. As a result, some Hispanic students learn more by touching, seeing, manipulating and experiencing concrete objects than by discussing or reading about ideas.

Hispanics:	Agree 81%	Insufficient Information 5%	Disagree 13%
Non-Hispanics:	Agree 67%	Insufficient Information 19%	Disagree 15%

Therefore, educators should de-emphasize the lecture approach and emphasize direct experience with these Hispanic students.

Hispanics: Agree 73%   Insufficient Information 6%   Disagree 21%
Non-Hispanics: Agree 75%   Insufficient Information 15%   Disagree 10%

Hispanic students who have been brought up to be dependent on the opinions, values and desires of others may be more field dependent or sensitive in general. That is, they may be more dependent on and sensitive to external clues for solving problems.

Hispanics: Agree 71%   Insufficient Information 15%   Disagree 15%
**Non-Hispanics: Agree 63%   Insufficient Information 29%   Disagree 9%

> "Important for educators to know it might be true, but don't over-generalize." (Hispanic)

> "I agree that Hispanic students may be more dependent on and sensitive to other people. Yet, we must keep in mind that research has not conclusively indicated that these same 'field dependent' students are also more dependent on and sensitive to external clues for solving problems." (Hispanic)

For this reason they may perform better on tasks which require global perception rather than analysis of detail. For example, they may do better on reading tasks which require whole word sight recognition rather than phonetic analysis.

*Hispanics: Agree 51%   Insufficient Information 23%   Disagree 27%
**Non-Hispanics: Agree 36%   Insufficient Information 42%   Disagree 22%

> "Hispanic children seem to learn better when facts are not put in isolation. While this may be cultural, language considerations seem to have some import here. It may be that the children need more explanation because of the limited English." (Hispanic)

> "May be true for many, but don't over-generalize." (Hispanic)

> "Research is not conclusive in this area and, also, this is not exclusively an Hispanic trait. We have yet to clarify the concepts of learning styles. These concepts have not been expressed in terms that the average classroom teacher can understand." (Unknown)

> "Many Hispanic students do great with phonics." (Hispanic)

> "Phonics are also important." (Hispanic)

> "Ridiculous statement." (Unknown)

Therefore, educators should employ instructional techniques which de-emphasize analysis of details with such Hispanic students; then gradually provide more instruction which utilizes analytic processes.

*Hispanics: Agree 57%   Insufficient Information 16%   Disagree 27%
**Non-Hispanics: Agree 46%   Insufficient Information 36%   Disagree 17%

Summary: Both groups of participants agreed that because the Hispanic culture emphasizes learning by doing, educators should de-emphasize the lecture approach and utilize the direct experience approach with students who learn better this way. However, only the Hispanic participants agreed that Hispanic students may do better on tasks which require global perception, rather than analysis of detail, and only they agreed with the suggestion that for this reason educators should adapt their instructional techniques to this cultural difference.

Language Differences

Language Proficiency

Many Hispanic parents have considerable pride in being both Latin and belonging to "La Raza." This pride is often expressed in attempts to maintain the use of the Spanish language at home and in the community even after many years of residence in the United States.

Hispanics: Agree 90%   Insufficient Information 2%   Disagree 8%
Non-Hispanics: Agree 85%   Insufficient Information 10%   Disagree 5%

"Important to know that this can be a matter of pride—I've often heard people refer to it as ignorance, stubbornness, refusal, antagonism toward Anglo society, etc. Anyone who speaks two languages is very lucky and should be proud of their skills. Knowledge of two cultures is even more reason to be proud." (Hispanic)

"I agree, but being proud of being Spanish, Mexican, etc. and desiring to use and maintain the language does not put you in the 'La Raza' category or the 'Chicano' category. Why should we be less proud of our heritage than anyone else? Speaking English does not mean an Anglo belongs to the Ku Klux Klan any more than speaking Italian means being a member of the Mafia." (Hispanic)

"In my experience, a majority of second- and third-generation Hispanics reject their Spanish culture and language adamantly, and even believe they can't speak Spanish, although when faced with a monolingual speaker of Spanish, they really do just fine!" (Non-Hispanic)

Some Hispanic parents may have not acquired enough English to speak to their children in English because of not having lived in the United States for enough time or because of having lived in a neighborhood-barrio where English fluency was unnecessary.

Hispanics: Agree 94%   Insufficient Information   2%   Disagree 5%
Non-Hispanics: Agree 97%   Insufficient Information   2%   Disagree 1%

"Or because they do not have the time or money to study English since they are busy trying to support themselves on minimum wages." (Hispanic)

"Some parents may know a little English but not speak it for fear of being laughed at." (Non-Hispanic)

"Many Hispanics just have no interest in learning English." (Non-Hispanic)

"If we continue to print ballots in Spanish for people who are citizens and can't speak English, where is the incentive for them to learn?" (Non-Hispanic)

As a result, some Hispanic students are not fluent enough in English when they start school to profit from instruction in arithmetic, science, social studies, etc., when the language of instruction is English. Immersing them in a completely English program may cause them to fall behind their English-speaking peers in these subject areas.

Hispanics: Agree 91%   Insufficient Information   2%   Disagree 7%
Non-Hispanics: Agree 90%   Insufficient Information   2%   Disagree 8%

"It is very important to a child's self-image to be able to answer questions and present solutions to problems. For this reason alone bilingual education is indispensable. Otherwise we see too many Hispanic students who are denying their roots and 'Hungering for Memories'." (Hispanic)

"I know from personal experience of numerous cases of frustrated and angry students who became that way because they were submerged in English programs too soon." (Non-Hispanic)

"Bilingual education is for newcomers such as Mexican aliens, Cubans, Salvadorans. The student of Hispanic descent who has been born here should not need to be taught in Spanish." (Non-Hispanic)

"Non-English teaching should *not* be permitted to occupy one minute of public school classroom time, since English learning is even more vital for these students than for those of our majority background." (Non-Hispanic)

"Total immersion is *not* detrimental. Other cultures and languages work fine when they are forced by circumstances to learn. Hispanics (as well as Vietnamese) are not a 'special group.' They cling together because of numbers and ease, not ambition or ability. They readily admit that an English speaker going to Mexico (Spanish-speaking country) had better learn Spanish instead of expecting English to be spoken to them, but, while here, they (Spanish speakers) expect and demand the right to have only Spanish spoken to them and classes in that language and to 'heck' with learning English. (Not all but about 90 percent.)" (Non-Hispanic)

Therefore, such limited English proficient students should receive a bilingual education. They should be taught such subjects as math, science, etc., in Spanish while they are being helped to become proficient enough in English to profit from English language instruction in these subject areas.

Hispanics:	Agree 90%	Insufficient Information 2%	Disagree 8%
Non-Hispanics:	Agree 88%	Insufficient Information 4%	Disagree 8%

"Research clearly indicates that bilingual children who first learn to read in their own language have an easier time learning to read in English because of the transfer of basic reading skills from one language to another." (Non-Hispanic)

"If a child enters school with a different language, then of course it does not make sense to teach a child reading in English either. First, teach the child reading skills in his native tongue and at the same time teach the child oral English. When a child reaches mastery of reading in his dominant language, he is then allowed to start reading in English." (Hispanic)

"I am a Mexican-American teacher. I have a master's in bilingual education. At present, I have 22 kindergarten children—20 Hispanics and 2 Anglo. The Spanish group is made up of 1 Cuban, 4 recently moved in from Mexico, 1 from El Salvador, and 14 Mexican-American. The Mexican-Americans came in knowing more English than Spanish; some don't know any. The ones whose parents recently came from Mexico know enough English to be instructed in English. The one from Cuba had very little English but has learned enough to be able to follow oral directions. The one from El Salvador has made little progress, though he can speak a few English phrases. His Spanish is also limited. The point I am trying to make is that the earlier the child is treated simply as a 'student' and not as something different, the better off the student will be.

"To prolong Spanish instruction is to retard English. To insist on teaching the Spanish-speaking student in his language is to hinder him. He is actually being set back. To extend bilingual education to the 12th grade, as some people say it should, is the worst thing that our education agencies can do for our Spanish-speaking students. Our children deserve equal education, equal treatment, equal oportunities. Give this to them. Do not try to see them as a different specimen. They feel, love, learn, act and react just as any other cultures. They understand right and wrong, fair and unfair." (Hispanic)

"No! We do this and our Hispanic students end up two to three years behind in English reading which is the sole basis for retention. So we end up with ten-year-olds in third grade who feel like failures because they were taught to read in Spanish." (Non-Hispanic)

Even after they are proficient in English, they should be provided with enough Spanish language instruction to maintain their Spanish proficiency if they wish to do so.

Hispanics:	Agree 81%	Insufficient Information 5%	Disagree 15%
Non-Hispanics:	Agree 76%	Insufficient Information 8%	Disagree 15%

"It's not only a matter of pride, but of necessity. How else are we going to be able to relate to business people and government officials in Latin America if we don't have Americans who can speak their languages?" (Non-Hispanic)

"If this means that we should have optional bilingual classes in the upper grades for those who want them, I'm all for it." (Hispanic)

After a period of exposure to English in school and in the non-Hispanic community, Hispanic students who are exposed to Spanish at home and English in school may be Spanish dominant for words and concepts that relate to home and community and English dominant for school-related words and concepts. When educators are unaware of their students' incomplete mastery of English, they may create learning problems for such students by failing to adjust their instructional strategies and teaching materials to their students' limited English proficiency.

Hispanics: Agree 92% Insufficient Information 5% Disagree 3%
Non-Hispanics: Agree 90% Insufficient Information 8% Disagree 2%

> "Even though some students understand and speak English quite well, they do not have the necessary academic language skills to be successful in an academic setting. See research by James Cummins, Tracy Terrell, Eleanor Thonis, etc." (Unknown)

> "This is not a matter of opinion. It has been firmly established by research." (Non-Hispanic)

Therefore, educators should not automatically attribute complete fluency to bilingual Hispanic students who appear to have mastered the English taught in school, especially if Spanish is spoken in their homes. Rather, the choice of instructional techniques and materials to use with such students should be based on a thorough evaluation of their English language proficiency.

Hispanics: Agree 92% Insufficient Information 4% Disagree 4%
Non-Hispanics: Agree 94% Insufficient Information 4% Disagree 2%

> "This is so obvious that it is difficult to believe there are educators who do not realize this." (Hispanic)

> "Unfortunately, this is what most English-speaking teachers and administrators are prone to do." (Non-Hispanic)

> "I am completely in agreement that apparent oral fluency in English often does not indicate significant mastery of the written language, and that this area is a significant problem for many students and school staff. Besides a 'thorough evaluation of their English language proficiency,' there should be a thorough assessment of the student and family geographic, cultural, socio-economic, linguistic, and educational background and goals, if each student is to be genuinely served." (Non-Hispanic)

"Many Hispanic Spanish-speaking students are switched to English instructors before they are ready because their English conversation skills appear adequate. As Jim Cummins has pointed out there are two kinds of language proficiency skills, face to face conversational proficiency and academic proficiency. While it may take a non-English-speaking student a year or two to learn enough English to get by in conversations, it will probably take him four or five years to acquire the English language skills to function adequately in classes taught in English in which he has to not only answer in English, but think in English." (Non-Hispanic)

"No. If a student has enough English proficiency to perform in English, he should be instructed in English—even if he has more Spanish than English." (Non-Hispanic)

Non-English proficient Hispanic students with language disorders or serious learning problems who have difficulty learning in their primary language may find it even more difficult to learn a second language at the same time.

Hispanics: Agree 90%   Insufficient Information 6%   Disagree 3%
Non-Hispanics: Agree 91%   Insufficient Information 4%   Disagree 5%

Therefore, such Spanish dominant students should be taught exclusively in their primary language until they have either overcome their language disorders or become fluent in Spanish despite their disorders before receiving instruction in English.

Hispanics: Agree 74%   Insufficient Information 12%   Disagree 14%
Non-Hispanics: Agree 62%   Insufficient Information 16%   Disagree 22%

"This too is so obvious that it hardly seems debatable." (Hispanic)

"Oral English should continue. It seems that teaching reading simultaneously in both languages would be confusing. Most children are learning two languages orally by the mere fact they reside in the United States." (Hispanic)

"I agree in part. However, they would still need ESL orally." (Hispanic)

"This is a dilemma when you consider both the number of years it takes to overcome a language disorder and the need to survive in an English-speaking world." (Hispanic)

"It's difficult to categorically agree or disagree. Each case really has to be considered individually regarding specific needs, environment, parental concerns, etc., for each child." (Hispanic)

"I've taught not just bilingual, but other type classes. All can learn if in public schools. The 'street kids' in Tijuana can speak and understand more English in a few months because of motivation in earning a living, than 'coddled' students in school here where they expect to be kowtowed to. I'm not deriding them, I simply find that they have no need to learn English because of their environment in a totally Spanish-speaking community." (Non-Hispanic)

"Even illiterates can express themselves in another language, not necessarily written or read (witness Tijuana). If a student *wants* or *has* to learn, he will." (Non-Hispanic)

Mentally retarded monolingual Spanish-speaking Hispanic students may be unable to profit from instruction in two languages at the same time.

Hispanics: Agree 71%   Insufficient Information 15%   Disagree 14%
**Non-Hispanics: Agree 70%   Insufficient Information 21%   Disagree 10%

Therefore, instruciton should be in the language spoken at home.

Hispanics: Agree 75%   Insufficient Information 12%   Disagree 13%
**Non-Hispanics: Agree 65%   Insufficient Information 24%   Disagree 11%

"In general yes, but ESL instruction should be offered as well if the student is not severely retarded." (Non-Hispanic)

Language Style

In comparison to Anglos, Hispanics tend to use more poetic expressions and analogies when they communicate ideas.

Hispanics: Agree 78%   Insufficient Information 12%   Disagree 11%
**Non-Hispanics: Agree 54%   Insufficient Information 26%   Disagree 20%

As a result, Hispanic students may appear to Anglos to have difficulty coming to the point or thinking logically when they express their ideas.

*Hispanics: Agree 62%   Insufficient Information 16%   Disagree 23%
**Non-Hispanics: Agree 40%   Insufficient Information 30%   Disagree 30%

Therefore, educators should not insist that when Hispanic students express themselves they use an Anglo style rather than the more poetic Hispanic style.

Hispanics: Agree 65% Insufficient Information 14% Disagree 22%
**Non-Hispanics: Agree 53% Insufficient Information 25% Disagree 22%

"I agree that we are more poetic, but I am of the opinion that all students, Hispanics as well as Anglos, must learn to express themselves in different styles. If I'm addressing Hispanics, I'll use the personal analogies and poetic forms of expressions. If I'm addressing Anglos, I'll be precise and to the point, etc." (Hispanic)

"While the Hispanic 'poetic' mode of expression has much of merit and much to be encouraged, depending on age and circumstances of the student, the goal may be to help him (or them) achieve 'standard English' (or American) usage, to be able to function at the university level or in the work world." (Hispanic)

"Where are they living? In Latin America or the United States? Where are they going to live? Are they going to communicate with the rest of the world or live *only* in a world of their own?" (Non-Hispanic)

"If Hispanics are to move in the Anglo arena, then they should be familiar with the style of expression of the Anglo and assume it whenever necessary." (Hispanic)

Summary: While the appropriateness of bilingual education may be a controversial issue among some groups, a very high percentage of both the Hispanics and non-Hispanic participants agreed that students who cannot profit from instruction in English should be taught using bilingual methods until they have mastered English sufficiently. The participants also agreed that educators should be careful not to attribute fluency in English to these students too quickly. And they agreed, but to a lesser extent, that even after these Hispanic students become fluent in English they should be provided with enough Spanish language instruction to maintain their Spanish proficiency if they wish to do so. The participants also agreed that students with language disorders and mental retardation who do not speak English should be taught completely in Spanish until they have become fluent in Spanish.

Both groups of participants agreed that Hispanics use more poetic expressions and analogies and that educators should accept this style of communicating. However, only the Hispanics agreed that this may cause Anglos to think that they have difficulty coming to the point or thinking logically.

Knowledge Differences

Prior to their entrance into school, Hispanic students may be exposed to the richness of the Hispanic culture at home rather than to the many cultural concepts that are expected and valued by the Anglo school system.

Hispanics: Agree 91%   Insufficient Information 4% Disagree 5%
Non-Hispanics: Agree 91%   Insufficient Information 6% Disagree 4%

"In our home, we were taught very high values such as honesty, not lying. If we lied, it was a spanking if it was found out, and no stealing—no matter now economically deprived. And we were taught to share what we had. For example, if someone stopped by the house to visit. I don't think my Anglo colleagues were learning these things to the same extent." (Hispanic)

"Many parents are as illiterate as their children are and do not expose them to very much at all." (Non-Hispanic)

Therefore, educators should adapt their curriculum and instruction techniques to the knowledge and experiences Hispanic students bring to school. This will prevent them from being educationally behind as soon as they enter the school system.

Hispanics: Agree 86%   Insufficient Information 5% Disagree 9%
Non-Hispanics: Agree 84%   Insufficient Information 5% Disagree 11%

"Most Mexican-American children are not experientially deprived; they are rich with the experiences of their culture. but compared to more economically advantaged Anglo children, they bring a meager store of concepts valued by the Anglo school. Their curriculum should expose them to a wide variety of experiences. These students will learn least in the classroom dominated by teacher talk. They need to see and touch and smell and feel as well as listen. They need direct experience with almost every aspect of reality the school normally assumes a student has had. At the same time these students are being introduced to new experiences, they should have opportunity to use their store of concepts in learning activities. Often, social roles and institutions are studied only in terms of Anglo perceptions. The different perceptions of Mexican-Americans can become a great advantage in classrooms and their experiences should be viewed as a rich instructional resource." (Unknown)

"Amen! I get kids who come from Mexico with little or no schooling at age 10 or 11. It's really hard for them at first." (Hispanic)

"The self-concepts of our Hispanic students are contaminated because of the rigid curriculum offered them, with only Tom, Dick or Jane in mind." (Hispanic)

"We should not change the curriculum but understand the students' problems and help them to adapt to the school." (Non-Hispanic)

"Educators should adapt their teaching to the experiences of all students regardless of the cause of these differences." (Non-Hispanic)

"It is important to realize that we must prepare our children for the society in which they live. It is our responsibility to teach them and their parents what the differences are and how they cause conflicts between the child and the society, between the child and the school and between the child and the family. We must use the assets of the child's culture and teach him to function in the ways of the dominant culture, giving equal value to both." (Hispanic)

Summary: A large majority of the participants agreed that many Hispanic students begin school knowledgeable about the Hispanic culture rather than the cultural concepts expected and valued by the school systems. They also agreed that educators should adapt their curriculum and instruction to these students' knowledge and experience.

Socio-Economic Differences

Hispanic students who are raised by parents with little formal education and scant financial resources may not be exposed to the materials and experiences many middle class, educated parents provide their children. As a result they may lack some of the readiness skills expected of students in the lower grades.

Hispanics: Agree 89%   Insufficient Information   1%   Disagree 10%
Non-Hispanics: Agree 80%   Insufficient Information 13%   Disagree 7%

"It is true that these students may lack some of the readiness skills expected of students by middle class teachers, but we can't deny that the students are not void of experiences and that, in many areas of development, they are ahead of middle class children. Teachers need to know how they can assist their students to make contact with their experiences and how they can apply the skills and knowledge they already have to the classroom learning situation." (Hispanic)

"The problem is with the middle class or oriented schools, not with the low-income families." (Hispanic)

"I believe that there is definitely a 'culture of poverty.' While there may be some small differences in culture, level of aspiration, etc., among middle class majority group peoples and Hispanics, the crunch really exists between middle class majority group school personnel and poor Hispanics who are alienated from the majority power group in their own community. I think that for this reason bilingual education is important. It gives the school at least one link with the parents. We can speak the same language." (Hispanic)

These students may suffer cultural shock in school because of the differences between what is available to them at home, where they may have to wear out, make do, or do without, and what is provided by the school system. These differences may do harm to these students' self-concepts and make it difficult for these students to adjust to school.

Hispanics: Agree 73%   Insufficient Information   7%   Disagree 19%
Non-Hispanics: Agree 74%   Insufficient Information 11%   Disagree 15%

"This is true of poor Anglos as well." (Non-Hispanic)

"Educators should know this about my culture and more. I come from a patriarchal social group. I was born in the same town in Texas where my father, my grandfather, my great grandfather were born. I started working as a farm laborer at age 7 and continued until age 25. During my pre-adolescent years the only paved streets I saw were in the rich part of town. The barrio I grew up in had no paved streets.

Televisions were scarce. I didn't boast of a television in my house until 1960." (Hispanic)

"These are very negative statements. In a learning situation the room, material available, and lectures are secondary. The important aspect is, how well do we relate to our students. Let's demystify the process of learning. Children can become whatever they want to become. Our job is to assist them in this process. 'Si se puede' (Yes, you can)." (Hispanic)

Therefore, educators should take pains to reduce or eliminate those aspects of their classroom environment, teaching materials and teaching techniques which might cause cultural shock. They should make the classroom culturally relevant to these students so as to ease their entrance into the world of school.

Hispanics: Agree 71%   Insufficient Information 7%   Disagree 22%
Non-Hispanics: Agree 74%   Insufficient Information 11%   Disagree 15%

"This would help eliminate many failures that are blamed too often on the child rather than the school system." (Non-Hispanic)

"Upon entrance yes, however, students must learn to deal with the 'shock' of other cultures." (Non-Hispanic)

"The room should provide the manipulative and reading readiness skills they have missed, not culture. They didn't miss that." (Hispanic)

"We must avoid cultural shock. However, material things do not create cultural shock—language, values, religion, these can but do not necessarily create cultural shock." (Hispanic)

"It is the Anglo teaching style that is the difficulty. They probably have more difficulty adjusting to the different teacher-pupil relationships than these items." (Unknown)

"I do not agree. Educators should introduce and explain the need and uses of those aspects of their classroom environment that may be new to the students." (Non-Hispanic)

"Maybe, but they better get used to the school soon. It's the only one they'll be attending." (Non-Hispanic)

Some teenage Hispanic students whose families have serious economic problems may believe that it is more important for them to earn money to help out their families than to graduate from high school or go on to college.

Hispanics: Agree 92%   Insufficient Information 2% Disagree 7%
Non-Hispanics: Agree 90%   Insufficient Information 6% Disagree 5%

"I strongly agree here. In my case, when I graduated from high school, I was unaware of how to apply for scholarships, and I thought one would have to be a valedictorian or salutatorian (that is, the two top students of the graduating class). I did not know anything about grade point average. Although my graduating class consisted of 86 or so seniors, I found out I was ninth from the top and an honor student when it appeared in the town's newspaper. We were only three Mexican-Americans and I was the only girl. My dream was to study medicine—to work in the field of research. But, I knew my parents did not know how much tuition for a university amounted to. There were two younger sisters and a brother who still needed to complete school and I was not going to deprive them of food, clothing and other necessities or have my parents sacrifice themselves to put me through college. I never mentioned my dreams to my parents and when they asked me if I wanted to go to college or to get married (I didn't even have a boyfriend), I chose a nine-month business college so that if I ever decided to study medicine I could somehow pay my way through college. Incidentally, I enrolled for pre-med courses in the evening, then I got married. I continued for a short time but being stationed in isolated bases prevented me from realizing my dream. But I did study to become a teacher." (Hispanic)

"Unfortunately, many families are still dependent upon the economic contributions of older children. This is important for educators to understand so that they won't place pressure on students about school which might be looked at as 'disloyalty' to the family if a student were to choose school." (Hispanic)

"Family priorities will often take precedence over attendance at school functions, I.E.P. meetings, etc. This should not be interpreted by educators as lack of interest or responsibility on the part of parents regarding their child's school experience. On the contrary, especially among poor families, the necessities of the day-to-day existence such as trips to the grocery store or laundromat, emergency health needs, car trouble, etc., are of primary importance. Student school attendance is also influenced by the importance of family; in my experience, I have found that it is not uncommon for a 7- or 8-year-old girl to stay home from school to babysit for younger siblings so that Mother can go to work, for a bilingual child to be taken along as 'translator' when monolingual parents have medical or legal appointments, or for ten-year-olds to take major responsibility for preparing meals at home for 'working' family members." (Non-Hispanic)

"Family needs should come first and the self second. Independence of the family is not necessarily a good thing." (Hispanic)

"This may have been true years ago, not so much any more. Parents want an education for their children." (Hispanic)

Many of the academically oriented courses offered in the middle and secondary schools may seem irrelevant to the vocational needs of these Hispanic students.

Hispanics:	Agree 83%	Insufficient Information	6%	Disagree	11%
Non-Hispanics:	Agree 82%	Insufficient Information	8%	Disagree	11%

"This is because Hispanic students are not encouraged to take academic courses by their counselors and teachers and are sometimes prevented from doing so." (Hispanic)

"Yes, but depending on the students' needs." (Non-Hispanic)

"This is a function of socio-economic class just as for Anglos." (Non-Hispanic)

Therefore, educators should adjust the contents of the curriculum to the needs of these Hispanic students. This may include offering more vocationally oriented courses and arranging for cooperative work study programs.

Hispanics:	Agree 71%	Insufficient Information	6%	Disagree	24%
Non-Hispanics:	Agree 78%	Insufficient Information	7%	Disagree	15%

"I agree for students who choose these careers but we should not overgeneralize." (Non-Hispanic)

"Yes, but college prep shouldn't be cut back as a result." (Non-Hispanic)

"Yes, but they must not be tracked or channeled into these classes because of their race and/or their language." (Unknown)

"Rather than encouraging vocational training, etc., students should be encouraged to go on with their education whatever their goals may be." (Non-Hispanic)

"This sounds like lowering standards, like Hispanics should have mostly vocational needs." (Non-Hispanic)

"We don't need more Chicano auto mechanics. If a Chicano student is interested in auto mechanics, he should be taught how to *own* an auto repair shop." (Hispanic)

"Anglo educators have often felt that Hispanic (Mexican-American) students can only function at the vocational level. Many refuse to admit that the mentality and economic ability of the Spanish-speaking student can carry him beyond what vocational school has to offer—*give him a chance.*" (Hispanic)

Therefore, pointing out the vocational relevance of some aspects of the academic curriculum may also help to motivate Hispanic students who may be more interested in learning to make a living than in acquiring knowledge for its own sake.

Hispanics: Agree 83%   Insufficient Information   5%   Disagree 12%
Non-Hispanics: Agree 90%   Insufficient Information   4%   Disagree 4%

Summary: The participants agreed that because American schools are geared more toward middle class than lower class students, lower class students may lack readiness skills, suffer culture shock and have difficulty adjusting to school. They also agreed that educators should make classrooms more relevant to such students. However, while agreeing that the classroom environment, teaching materials and techniques should be modified, numerous participants emphasized the importance of modifying such things as teaching styles and teacher-pupil relationships as well. The participants also recognized the importance of providing more vocational education and cooperative work study programs for those students who want them. At the same time, numerous participants commented that standards and expectations for Hispanic students should not be lowered.

Prejudice

History, geography, social roles, etc., are often studied exclusively in terms of the Anglo point of view. Too often, students are taught that Columbus rather than the Native Americans discovered

America, that Ponce de Leon was a fool who was looking for a fountain of youth and that Latin Americans are lazy procrastinators who live in small underdeveloped pueblos.

Hispanics: Agree 84%   Insufficient Information   7%   Disagree 9%
Non-Hispanics: Agree 72%   Insufficient Information 11%   Disagree 18%

"All this is true, but an experience I have never forgotten as a sixth or seventh grader in Texas was when we had singing as a group. One of the songs was 'We are proud of our forefathers who died at the Alamo.' Here, as if by signal, we looked at each other, smiled, and sang as loud as we could that specific line. I don't know if in our minds we or the students meant their Mexican forefathers—or making fun of that line—who were not our forefathers. It was never mentioned in the textbook that Santa Ana's troops were caught unprepared—taking a siesta—and that Santa Ana was considered a traitor by the Mexican people." (Hispanic)

"Not only Hispanics, minorities in general, are being deprived of a knowledge of their heritage and achievements by the schools. We should let students learn about the achievements of the Mayas and the Aztecs while Europe was still in the dark and middle ages." (Hispanic)

Since Hispanic students are used to foods, music, holidays, language and customs which are very different from what Anglos are accustomed to, Hispanic students may have difficulty relating to the Anglo-oriented classroom.

Hispanics: Agree 67%   Insufficient Information 9%   Disagree 24%
Non-Hispanics: Agree 84%   Insufficient Information 5%   Disagree 11%

"Yes but they have more difficulty adjusting to the way the Anglo teachers relate to them."

"This would only be a big problem if the Hispanic students' culture is not respected." (Hispanic)

"But they better get used to it soon." (Non-Hispanic)

When their foods are not mentioned during discussions of what are good foods to eat in order to have a balanced diet, their music is not played during assemblies and music appreciation classes, etc., Hispanic students may feel that they and their culture are inferior, at least in the eyes of their teachers.

Hispanics: Agree 83%   Insufficient Information 3%   Disagree 10%
Non-Hispanics: Agree 88%   Insufficient Information 4%   Disagree 8%

"If not inferior at least not worth considering which is almost as bad." (Hispanic)

"But as John Alston stated, if you think that multicultural education is only food and dances, you'll have fat kids who can't dance." (Hispanic)

"Sometimes this occurs subconsciously and the students do not know what caused their inferiority feelings." (Hispanic)

Therefore, educators should include the Hispanic contribution in the curriculum, correct inaccurate and prejudicial stereotypes of Hispanics, and include as much of the Hispanic foods, music, language, values, etc., as possible in the daily curriculum.

Hispanics:	Agree 96%	Insufficient Information 1%	Disagree 3%
Non-Hispanics:	Agree 96%	Insufficient Information 2%	Disagree 2%

"Tell the world we came from a great culture." (Hispanic)

"Important that Hispanics be recognized and accepted." (Hispanic)

"Especially in the lower grades." (Hispanic)

"This should be a number one priority." (Non-Hispanic)

"Schools are encouraging us to lose our cultural identity. Ask any high school student to name a Mexican-American actor—he can't. Ask him to sing a complete Spanish song—he can't. Ask an elementary child why he brings his lunch to school on Mexican food day at the cafeteria—he doesn't like Mexican food! Acculturation!" (Hispanic)

"As much as possible, but not at the expense of content area emphasis." (Hispanic)

"To increase interest level, but don't overdo it." (Non-Hispanic)

"Yes, however, this should be done with respect and sensitivity." (Hispanic)

"Yes, if the class consists only of Hispanics." (Hispanic)

"When I was young two songs typified Mexico—the Mexican Hat Dance and a song by Peggy Lee which went something like

'The window she is broken
And the rain is comin in
If someone doesn't fix it

　　　I'll be soaked up to my skin
　　　But if we wait a day or two
　　　The rain may go away
　　　And we won't need a window
　　　On such a sunny day
　　　Mañana, Mañana, Mañana is
　　　Soon enough for me, etc.
　　Stereotypes like these certainly need to be corrected." (Non-Hispanic)

　　"How could anyone possibly suggest this?" (Non-Hispanic)

Summary: Participants agreed that educators should include more about the Hispanic culture and contributions in the curriculum and correct inaccurate and prejudicial stereotypes about Hispanics when they occur.

SUMMARY

The participants agreed that many descriptions included in this section are characteristic of the Hispanic culture in the United States. They also agreed with many of the suggestions about how instructional methods should be modified because of these cultural characteristics. However, as stated previously, in a number of cases the percentage of participants who agreed that these cultural differences exist was greater than the percentage of participants who agreed about their implications for instruction. For example, while 95 percent of the Hispanic participants and 88 percent of the non-Hispanic participants agreed that "Hispanics tend to experience the family as a fountain of emotional and economic security and support," only 70 percent of the Hispanic participants and 60 percent of the non-Hispanic participants agreed that "Therefore, educators should use family pride to motivate Hispanic students by saying such things as 'your family will be proud of you.'" The lower percentage of agreement in the case of some of the suggestions for modifying instructional methods appears to be due to the fact that even though the participants agreed that specific differences existed between the Hispanic culture and the Anglo (mainstream) culture in the United States, some of them believed that instructional techniques should be accommodated to these differences while others thought that the Hispanic students should be helped to adapt and acculturate to the methods commonly employed in the schools.

Nevertheless, the participants agreed that instructional techniques should be modified for Hispanic students in the following ways. They agreed that when educators are instructing Hispanic students they should:

1. Motivate them by stressing the fact that their families will be proud of them and share in their accomplishments.
2. Include more community projects, group projects, group work and peer tutoring.
3. Use more personal forms of rewards such as praise, hugs, pats on the back, etc.
4. Use a more person-centered than idea-centered curriculum.
5. Not use debating, expressing opinions, and criticizing the opinions of others with students who are uncomfortable with these techniques.*
6. Provide more guidance and feedback and maintain close personal relationships.
7. Utilize daily rather than long-term assignments while helping them learn how to organize and plan their time so as to be able to complete long-term assignments.
8. Provide them with *immediate* feedback and rewards.
9. Do not rush them if they do not answer quickly or work rapidly in class but not provide them with all the time they require to complete classroom assignments.
10. Inform them that although the Hispanic content of punctuality is fine at home and in their communities, in school and other similar situations they should adapt to the dominant culture's expectations of punctuality.
11. Include their interest in religion, saints, the supernatural, etc. when teaching reading, writing, etc.
12. De-emphasize the lecture approach in favor of a direct experience approach.
13. De-emphasize analysis of detail in favor of global perception.*
14. Utilize bilingual methods with limited English proficient students.
15. Provide additional instruction in Spanish for those students who wish to maintain their Spanish language proficiency.

---

*Only Hispanic participants agreed

16. Permit them to express themselves in the more poetic Hispanic style if they wish.
17. Base instruction in the early grades on what they know rather than what they should know.
18. Reduce or eliminate those aspects of the classroom environment which might create culture shock.
19. Provide more vocationally oriented courses for those who want them without lowering standards or expectations for those students who are more academically oriented.
20. Include more information about Hispanic contributions to society, Hispanic foods, music, customs, etc., in the curriculum.
21. Correct incorrect and prejudicial stereotypes.

Chapter 4

CLASSROOM MANAGEMENT

INTRODUCTION

Educators have many alternative management techniques at their disposal. For example:

1. Educators can utilize competition to motivate their students, mark on a curve and encourage students to work individually, or they can foster cooperation among students by rewarding the group for group achievements and by using group work, group projects and peer tutoring;

2. They can attempt to develop close personal relationships with their students or maintain a professional distance;

3. They can permit more than one person to speak at a time or insist that everyone pay attention to the one student who has the floor;

4. They can require that students decide on things by voting or allow them to reach a consensus without the formality of a vote;

5. They can insist that students acknowledge their errors and mistakes or allow them to save face by denying it, etc.

This chapter includes the opinions of the participants regarding the validity of certain Hispanic cultural characteristics and whether educators and others should employ specific classroom management techniques with Hispanic students with these cultural characteristics.

RESULTS

Interpersonal Relationships

Importance of the Group

Hispanic children are brought up to believe in the importance of the extended family; to sacrifice their own desires for the good of the family, and to expect that the family will support and aid them when they are in need.

Hispanics: Agree 88% Insufficient Information 3%   Disagree 8%
Non-Hispanics: Agree 88% Insufficient Information 10% Disagree 3%

> "This is still true today, however, this world is made up of too many people who are ready to take advantage of others. Anglos do not put others before themselves. Soon Mexican American parents learn to teach their children to look out for themselves." (Hispanic)

> "The extended family phenomenon is very evident. I am not certain that it's directly correlated to group orientation. I think there is a phenomenon known as group identity (jocks hang out with jocks, Chicanos hang out with Chicanos, etc.)." (Non-Hispanic)

> "This is a difficult statement to agree or disagree with. On the one hand I have strong recollections of Hispanic families spending Sunday's at the country club in South America. The husbands would be playing fronton, soccer or cards with their male friends, the wives would be sitting together talking about things which interested them while the children were being cared for by a niñera (maid). On the other hand I have equally strong memories of families picnicing together, playing ball together, etc. in Chapultapec Park in Mexico City. After thinking about it I would say that the lower class families tended to do a lot of things together while the upper class families tended to live much more separate lives, with many exceptions of course." (Non-Hispanic)

This upbringing tends to make Hispanic students more cooperative and group oriented than Anglo students.

Hispanics: Agree 82% Insufficient Information 8%   Disagree 10%
Non-Hispanics: Agree 73% Insufficient Information 15% Disagree 12%

As a result, Hispanic students may allow other students to copy their homework or their answers on examinations in order to show their helpfulness, brotherhood and generosity. They may not consider this to be bad behavior.

Hispanics:	Agree 65%	Insufficient Information 9%	Disagree 26%
**Non-Hispanics:	Agree 65%	Insufficient Information 23%	Disagree 12%

"When I was teaching at a university in Latin America, one of my colleagues, also from the United States, caught two graduate students cheating on the final exam. That evening he discussed the problem with me. He had already decided to either fail them for the course or ask the administration to expel them from the program and wanted my advice. I suggested he should find out how the problem was usually handled at the university and do the same thing. The next day we had a meeting with the students in the program, all of whom agreed that the correct reaction should be to have both of the students retake the exam. My colleague kept insisting that the two students should receive some kind of punishment but the rest of the students did not agree. Thinking that their suggestion was ridiculous and based on friendship for and identification with their fellow students, he refused to accept their suggestion. Instead he went to the chairman of the department who completely shocked my colleague by agreeing with the suggestion of the students." (Non-Hispanic)

"I do not see more copying among Hispanic students than among Anglo students." (Hispanic)

"We do not teach our children to copy." (Hispanic)

Therefore, educators should allow Hispanics to work on their homework together.

Hispanics:	Agree 53%	Insufficient Information 7%	Disagree 40%
Non-Hispanics:	Agree 62%	Insufficient Information 13%	Disagree 25%

"Yes, peer tutoring can be very effective." (Hispanic)

"Working together is fine—but not because they are Hispanic." (Hispanic)

"All students do, anyway." (Non-Hispanic)

"Educators should do what they feel comfortable with, but explain their needs to students, expressing awareness of the students' attitudes." (Non-Hispanic)

"Doing homework together can easily degenerate into copying from each other." (Unknown)

"The teacher needs to be unbiased in treatment of students. All students need to be aware of the cultural attitudes toward cooperative efforts, but also learn that in some cultures, at some times, only individual work is acceptable." (Non-Hispanic)

Therefore, educators should allow Hispanic students to help each other when they are called on to answer in class.

Hispanics: Agree 51%   Insufficient Information 8%   Disagree 41%
Non-Hispanics: Agree 50%   Insufficient Information 11%   Disagree 38%

"If the recipient is benefiting and not getting dependent." (Hispanic)

"Yes, but within reason." (Non-Hispanic)

"No, if the teacher wants to determine whether a student has learned something." (Unknown)

Therefore, educators *should not* prevent Hispanic students from helping each other on tests.

Hispanics: Agree 15%   Insufficient Information 8%   Disagree 77%
Non-Hispanics: Agree 4%   Insufficient Information 9%   Disagree 86%

"Take home tests are okay, but not classroom quizzes/tests of learned material." (Hispanic)

"Copying does not help students to learn." (Hispanic)

"Testing is different from the learning process and should show the individual accomplishment." (Hispanic)

"They should be able to work and study together, but testing should be individual." (Hispanic)

"I disagree with this—I think the teacher can explain that tests are to see what each individual knows and therefore answers aren't to be shared—there are times for helping each other but tests usually are not those times." (Non-Hispanic)

"Then why have a test?" (Non-Hispanic)

"At home we teach them the difference between helping and cheating." (Hispanic)

"Just what do you think Hispanic students are? Any educator who would permit students to do all these things should never be allowed to teach Mexican-American students. He should not call himself an educator." (Hispanic)

Therefore, educators should attempt to prevent Hispanic students from copying on tests but not discipline them for doing so as they might Anglo students.

Hispanics: Agree 26%   Insufficient Information 7%   Disagree 67%
Non-Hispanics: Agree 19%   Insufficient Information 14%   Disagree 67%

"Yes, but they should explain the seriousness of self-achievement." (Hispanic)

"All students should be treated equally when it comes to cheating." (Hispanic)

Therefore, educators should explain that while working on homework assignments together and helping each other when they are being evaluated may be acceptable in some cultures, it is not acceptable in the school system they are attending.

Hispanics: Agree 77%   Insufficient Information 6%   Disagree 17%
Non-Hispanics: Agree 75%   Insufficient Information 9%   Disagree 16%

In the Hispanic culture, friends are people who have proven over time to be dependable, trustworthy and worthy of respect. They are not acquaintances. Friendship is not a here today, gone tomorrow relationship. Once a friendship has been established, friends will share and make sacrifices for each other much the same as they would for their extended families. They would not do the same for casual acquaintances who in the Anglo culture may be considered friends.

Hispanics: Agree 87%   Insufficient Information 4%   Disagree 9%
**Non-Hispanics: Agree 65%   Insufficient Information 24%   Disagree 12%

"I strongly agree here. For example, as a military wife, I made many friends of different cultures and Anglos too. But I established a close friendship only when I expected it to last. As a result, the one's I keep in touch now were those who over the years we helped each other in time of need, such as taking children in the house in case of an emergency and also those whom we shared love for each other." (Hispanic)

"This would apply more to older people. Youth can change from one day to the next." (Hispanic)

Hispanic students who are asked to work in groups to which they have been assigned may be reluctant to cooperate fully if the group members are acquaintances rather than friends in the Hispanic sense of the word.

*Hispanics: Agree 52%   Insufficient Information 13%   Disagree 35%
**Non-Hispanics: Agree 38%   Insufficient Information 35%   Disagree 27%

Therefore, educators should allow Hispanic students to form their own groups of friends to work with.

Hispanics: Agree 44%   Insufficient Information 10%   Disagree 46%
**Non-Hispanics: Agree 27%   Insufficient Information 21%   Disagree 51%

"Yes, but with guidance." (Hispanic)

"Sometimes even the Chicano student may realize that his

Chicano peers might hold him back by not being as motivated as he is. Then, I think he would secretly want to be mingled with other high motivators—even if they're Anglos." (Non-Hispanic)

"Everyone has to learn to work with everybody, not necessarily to like everybody." (Hispanic)

Summary: The participants agreed that because Hispanic students are brought up to be more cooperative and group oriented, they may tend to behave this way when they do their homework and take tests without thinking that it is bad. A bare majority of the participants also agree that they should be allowed to work on their homework together and help one another when called on in class. However, the participants also agreed that educators should not allow Hispanic students to copy tests. Instead, educators should explain to them that copying on tests is not acceptable in the mainstream American culture.

The Hispanic participants, but not the non-Hispanics, agreed that Hispanic students may be reluctant to cooperate fully if the members of the groups to which they are assigned are acquaintances rather than friends. But neither group of participants agreed that educators should allow Hispanic students to form their own groups of friends to work with in the classroom.

Cooperation vs. Competition

Hispanics tend to believe that it is bad manners to try to excel over others in the group or to attempt to be recognized for their individual achievement. To be called sofisticado—acting as if you are better than others—is an insult.

Hispanics: Agree 56% Insufficient Information 8% Disagree 36%
**Non-Hispanics: Agree 52% Insufficient Information 23% Disagree 25%

"This has been clearly demonstrated in research studies. Mexican children do better than Anglo children in cooperative games while Anglo children score higher than Mexican children in competitive games. Mexican-American children score in between Mexican and Anglo children. This indicates that they are partly but not completely acculturated in this respect." (Non-Hispanic)

"To be pretentious is offensive to Anglos as well as Hispanics. And Hispanics do value achievement and recognition as a result of their effort. However, success coupled with good manners is much more esteemed by Hispanics than Anglos. (Hispanic)

"This is generalizing. It depends on the social, economic and educational background of the individual's family." (Hispanic)

"The Hispanic student is becoming less and less 'field sensitive' every day. They want to excel as much as anyone else—and it starts in kindergarten." (Hispanic)

"My male students are more competitive than I'd like them to be." (Non-Hispanic)

As a result, many Hispanic students will avoid competing with their peers for fear of being criticized or rejected by them.

*Hispanics: Agree 56%   Insufficient Information 7%   Disagree 37%
**Non-Hispanics: Agree 45%   Insufficient Information 23%   Disagree 31%

"Yes, but fear is not of being criticized or rejected so much as hurting someone's feelings." (Hispanic)

"Unlike the Anglo child, the Mexican-American will tend to look down on overt competition because of his fear of arousing the envy and destructiveness of peers." (Unknown)

"Once they experience the competitive pressures in the Anglo schools, they change and compete." (Hispanic)

"Recognition, academic or otherwise, is just as important to Hispanics. The manner in which the teacher deals with high achieving students in a classroom is more influential in promoting criticism or rejection problems." (Hispanic)

Therefore, educators should de-emphasize competition and stress cooperation when attempting to motivate some Hispanic students.

Hispanics: Agree 64%   Insufficient Information 8%   Disagree 28%
Non-Hispanics: Agree 71%   Insufficient Information 16%   Disagree 13%

Therefore, educators should utilize group participation as a motivational technique and play down individual achievement with Hispanic students who are responsive to this approach.

Hispanics: Agree 66%   Insufficient Information 6%   Disagree 28%
Non-Hispanics: Agree 75%   Insufficient Information 10%   Disagree 15%

"Good idea for all students." (Hispanic)

"This would not prepare the student to a realistic way of life. He will have to make it alone at some point in his life." (Hispanic)

Therefore, educators should praise and reward students for cooperative behavior as much as for individual achievement.

Hispanics: Agree 94%   Insufficient Information 1% Disagree 5%
Non-Hispanics: Agree 90%   Insufficient Information 6% Disagree 10%

"A good example of not doing this is marking on the curve in college. This causes students to compete and can create problems between them. Why shouldn't we promote cooperation among students and give them the grades they earn without making comparisons?" (Non-Hispanic)

"The issue of cooperation vs. competition is an important one. Competition should be positive and constructive. The U.S. school system infrequently uses cooperation as a motivation technique. My feeling is that Hispanics, like everyone, should have cooperative skills as well as competitive." (Hispanic)

"Both are needed and should be enjoyed by *all* students." (Hispanic)

Because of their belief that it is bad manners to try to excel over others, Hispanic students may resist being singled out in front of their peers for praise and awards.

Hispanics: Agree 47%   Insufficient Information 9% Disagree 44%
**Non-Hispanics: Agree 55%   Insufficient Information 20% Disagree 26%

"I see this in some cases where a child receives an award he/she may not want to go in front of a group." (Hispanic)

"While they may appear to be embarrassed they also love to be singled out if its done properly." (Hispanic)

"I think they love it as long as you mention his group also, i.e. 'Carlos from the blue group did an excellent job.'" (Hispanic)

"This I haven't noticed, as long as praise/reward is done with sensitivity and understanding." (Hispanic)

Therefore, educators should be sensitive to the needs of those Hispanic students who prefer not to be singled out in front of the group and recognize their achievements in a less public manner. One way of doing this would be to communicate their praise to their students' families.

Hispanics: Agree 75%   Insufficient Information 6%   Disagree 19%
Non-Hispanics: Agree 82%   Insufficient Information 11%   Disagree 8%

"When I was a student I was tremendously embarrassed any time I was singled out. I would have preferred my recognition in private." (Hispanic)

"Assess students' reactions and react accordingly." (Hispanic)

"School life is an extention of family life, therefore, public recognition is important especially with peers." (Hispanic)

Because of their belief that it is bad manners to try to excel over others, some Hispanic students may not volunteer answers or they may even pretend not to know the correct answer when called upon.

Hispanics: Agree 52%   Insufficient Information 10%   Disagree 38%
**Non-Hispanics: Agree 54%   Insufficient Information 20%   Disagree 26%

"This is true of some Mexican-American students even though it may be difficult for non-Hispanics to believe." (Hispanic)

"This is more true in rural rather than urban settings." (Non-Hispanic)

"Unfortunately, I have heard adolescents pressuring their peers by saying 'don't be a square' and things of that sort to students who do well in class." (Hispanic)

"I have heard and read this so often that I almost believe it, but I haven't really seen it very much in my classroom." (Non-Hispanic)

"My kids are eager to respond. They will wave their hands, shout 'oo oo oo' and do anything they can to get my attention." (Non-Hispanic)

"Some Hispanics want to compete but avoid it because they lack competitive skills." (Hispanic)

"This is a personality not a cultural problem." (Unknown)

Therefore, the educator should not assume that these students do not know the answers when they do not volunteer them.

Hispanics: Agree 77%   Insufficient Information 6%   Disagree 17%
Non-Hispanics: Agree 76%   Insufficient Information 12%   Disagree 7%

Therefore, educators should be sensitive to the needs for anonymity of some of their Hispanic students and avoid using the question-and-answer technique with them.

| Hispanics: | Agree 50% | Insufficient Information | 9% | Disagree 41% |
| Non-Hispanics: | Agree 54% | Insufficient Information | 16% | Disagree 30% |

"Until they have had sufficient appropriate practice answering questions in a non-threatening format." (Hispanic)

"No! They have to learn how to function in the Anglo world." (Hispanic)

Summary: The statements which described Hispanic students as non-competitive were extremely controversial. A bare majority of both the Hispanic and non-Hispanic participants agreed with most of the statements regarding the fact that Hispanic students believe that it is bad manners to try to excel over others and therefore they may avoid competing, resist being singled out in front of the group for their achievements, and not volunteer answers or even pretend not to know the correct answer. However, in each case, a large minority of participants disagreed that these statements were true. And in two cases, a majority of either the Hispanics or the non-Hispanics did not agree that the statement was true.

The participants also agreed that in general educators should accommodate their teaching styles to the non-competitive tendencies of their Hispanic students. Specifically, they agreed that educators should de-emphasize competition, utilize group participation, praise and reward students for cooperative behavior, not single out these students for their individual achievements and not assume that students who do not volunteer answers or compete in academic games do not know the answers. The participants also agreed that teachers should avoid using the question-and-answer method of instruction with these students, but a large minority of the participants disagreed with this idea.

Giving and Sharing with Others

Hispanics are generous with their belongings with friends and family. They practice the dictum "it is better to give than to receive." Hispanic children are also taught to share their belongings with others.

| Hispanics: | Agree 88% | Insufficient Information | 6% | Disagree 6% |
| **Non-Hispanics: | Agree 67% | Insufficient Information | 27% | Disagree 6% |

"I have told my daughter if she does not want to share what she is eating with anyone (like candy, etc.), not to eat in front of her friends. The people used to say that you might get a little sore on your tongue or mouth for not sharing. If someone would come by unexpectedly, my father would invite him or her or them to join us at the table. He would tell mother to put another plate on the table. He would always say, 'there is always room for one more.' And at the same time we knew in our hearts that we had to eat a little bit less so that there would be food for the visitor. Now, these high values, I have passed to my own children." (Hispanic)

"These statements *are* probably more true of Hispanics than we Anglos." (Non-Hispanic)

"When I lived in Peru there was a family living across the street from us in a shell of a house that was being constructed. As a watchman, the father earned less than a dollar a day. The little children often came to the door to ask for something to eat. After a while we regularly saved them milk and other foods for the children. As poor as they were, we often saw them feeding others from what we gave them. The same was true in Guatemala. In general, the poor people seemed very willing to share with others. The wealthy less so which seemed strange because they had so much more." (Non-Hispanic)

"Having spent time in the Peace Corps and seen the beggars trying unsuccessfully to secure a little charity from passersby, this is hard to believe." (Non-Hispanic)

As a result, Hispanic students are quick to share their things with their peers and they expect their peers to reciprocate. When Anglo students do not, Hispanic students may take their refusal as a rejection.

Hispanics: Agree 74% Insufficient Information 10% Disagree 16%
**Non-Hispanics: Agree 61% Insufficient Information 20% Disagree 10%

When educators attempt to resolve sharing difficulties among students by explaining the rights of owners—emphasizing private property or what's mine is mine and what's yours is yours, Hispanic students may feel bewildered, confused or even rejected and insulted.

Hispanics: Agree 57% Insufficient Information 13% Disagree 31%
**Non-Hispanics: Agree 50% Insufficient Information 34% Disagree 16%

Therefore, educators should stress the importance of sharing with others rather than respect for the rights of owners when working with mixed groups of Anglo and Hispanic students.

*Hispanics: Agree 55%   Insufficient Information 11%   Disagree 33%
**Non-Hispanics: Agree 38%   Insufficient Information 21%   Disagree 41%

> "Children must be taught not to 'help themselves' . . . taking without asking." (Non-Hispanic)

> "I agree, except that Anglo students' rights should not be sacrificed. Anglos should learn to share more and Hispanics to respect the property of others." (Hispanic)

Therefore, educators should help Hispanics learn to respect the rights of owners and Anglos to become better sharers.

Hispanics: Agree 83%   Insufficient Information 9%   Disagree 8%
Non-Hispanics: Agree 87%   Insufficient Information 9%   Disagree 4%

Hispanic students may give gifts to, or offer to do favors for, their teachers and their peers in order to express their "amistad" (friendship, good feeling).

Hispanics: Agree 91%   Insufficient Information 4%   Disagree 6%
Non-Hispanics: Agree 79%   Insufficient Information 15%   Disagree 5%

> "Not so much amistad but to show gratitude. I always share—food, clothing, drinks, etc.—with my co-workers." (Hispanic)

> "I haven't seen Hispanic students doing this more than Anglos." (Non-Hispanic)

Therefore, educators should not view such gifts and favors as bribes to buy affection or special privileges.

Hispanics: Agree 90%   Insufficient Information 4%   Disagree 7%
Non-Hispanics: Agree 88%   Insufficient Information 10%   Disagree 2%

Anglos expect that people who are working together will all share the load equally and think that a group member who does not is a loafer, an idler, or a person who is taking unfair advantage of the efforts of others. However, Hispanics tend not to be upset by a group member who does not do his or her share of the work because he or she is less qualified, less motivated, or less interested.

Hispanics: Agree 41%   Insufficient Information 14%   Disagree 45%
**Non-Hispanics: Agree 35%   Insufficient Information 43%   Disagree 22%

> "They may be too polite to show their resentment, but they feel it." (Hispanic)

"You should hear my Hispanic students complain because someone in their group won't work." (Non-Hispanic)

Therefore, educators should not insist that all Hispanic group members share equally in the work if the group members themselves do not mind if some do not.

Hispanics: Agree 29% Insufficient Information 10% Disagree 61%
**Non-Hispanics: Agree 26% Insufficient Information 20% Disagree 54%

"At least initially." (Hispanic)

"Students must learn to assume their group responsibilities." (Non-Hispanic)

Summary: Both Hispanic and non-Hispanic participants agreed that Hispanic students are taught to share with others, that if their peers do not reciprocate they may feel rejected and when educators attempt to resolve difficulties among children regarding sharing by emphasizing the rights of owners, the Hispanics may feel bewildered, confused or even rejected and insulted. Both groups of participants agreed that educators should help Hispanic students learn to respect the rights of owners and Anglo students become better sharers. A slight majority of the Hispanic participants also agreed that educators should stress the importance of sharing with others rather than respect for the rights of owners when working with mixed groups of Anglo and Hispanic students. However, non-Hispanic participants did not agree with this suggestion.

The participants agree that Hispanic students may give gifts to teachers and offer to do favors for teachers and their peers to express their friendship and, therefore, educators should not view such gifts and favors as bribes. They did not agree that Hispanics are not upset by group members who do not do their share of the work.

Expressing Unwillingness or Disagreement

Hispanics are less likely to state their disagreement with others or their unwillingness to do what others ask or expect from them. This is especially true of children and adolescents who are taught to respect their elders.

Hispanics: Agree 82% Insufficient Information 8% Disagree 10%
**Non-Hispanics: Agree 74% Insufficient Information 20% Disagree 6%

"Working as a bilingual educator I have developed friend-
ships with quite a few Latins. We often made plans to go out
dancing, to listen to music or to eat out on the weekends and
almost as often the plans fell through. It took me quite a few
years to realize what had been happening. I was invariably
the one to suggest that we get together and they almost
invariably agreed. However, if they said they would call me
to arrange the time and place, they almost never called.
When I called them to confirm, we usually got together.
Finally, I realized that they couldn't tell me 'no' to my face.
Telling me that they would call me to arrange things was
tantamount to saying "no thank you.' So I learned that it
wasn't that they weren't dependable. It was more that I didn't
understand the way they said, 'thanks, but no thanks.'"
(Non-Hispanic)

"When Latinos get together for planning sessions they need
to set aside more time than Anglos because they can only
express their disagreement with the previous speaker in very
indirect ways such as stating all the ideas they agree with and
then adding one new one which is different. To just come
out and state a different point of view is unusual. Its not the
polite way of doing things (mal educado)." (Non-Hispanic)

"This is true of the lower socio-economic class, not of the
middle and upper classes." (Hispanic)

"This could be more associated with attitudes towards
school and school personnel because of what they are taught
about teachers at home, and less so regarding other adults,
even parents." (Hispanic)

"While they don't express it verbally, you can see it in their
demeanor if you look for it. There are polite and impolite
ways of expressing such things." (Hispanic)

"I agree that they are less likely to express unwillingness, but
they will express disagreement." (Hispanic)

"Hispanic adolescents born and raised in the United States
are very rebellious and questioning like their Black and
Anglo counterparts." (Hispanic)

"We are no longer a docile population to be manipulated.
'La Raza' has awakened us and we are demanding our
rights." (Hispanic)

Therefore, educators should not assume that because Hispanic students have verbally acquiesced to their expectations or demands, they either agree with them or plan to carry them out. Instead, educators should take into consideration the vast array of non-verbal communications that some Hispanic students use to express their disinclination or disagreement.

Hispanics:	Agree 82%	Insufficient Information	7%	Disagree	8%
Non-Hispanics:	Agree 82%	Insufficient Information	12%	Disagree	6%

"Educators need to develop 'checking systems' to read their reticent students." (Non-Hispanic)

"This seems to be saying that you must always consider that the child may not be saying what he means—a switch from the Anglo emphasis on and expectations of telling the 'truth.' If this is true, shouldn't we teach Hispanic students to express their feelings about things instead of hiding them?" (Non-Hispanic)

Therefore, educators should not be surpised when some Hispanic students fail to complete contracts even though they verbally agreed to them.

Hispanics:	Agree 59%	Insufficient Information	13%	Disagree	28%
Non-Hispanics:	Agree 66%	Insufficient Information	19%	Disagree	15%

"I disagree. This is a matter of responsibility and it should be met." (Hispanic)

"If the student agrees to finish a contract, the educator should have made very clear to the student the importance and responsibility of the task." (Non-Hispanic)

Summary: The participants agreed that Hispanics are less likely to state their disagreement and unwillingness and that educators should be sensitive to the non-verbal ways in which these students express their feelings. They also agreed to a lesser extent that because of this reluctance to express disagreement or unwillingness verbally, some Hispanic students may fail to complete contracts which they verbally agreed to.

Personal vs. Impersonal Motivation

Whereas, in the United States, Americans have professional and business relations with people who may occasionally become their personal friends, Hispanics tend to look to persons with whom they already have personal relationships when they do business or require professional help. If this is not possible they tend to expect that the business or professional relationship will turn into a personal relationship.

Hispanics: Agree 63%   Insufficient Information 16%   Disagree 21%
**Non-Hispanics: Agree 50%   Insufficient Information 40%   Disagree 11%

This applies to educators who are expected to be personally involved with students and their families.

Hispanics: Agree 59%   Insufficient Information 10%   Disagree 22%
**Non-Hispanics: Agree 50%   Insufficient Information 36%   Disagree 15%

For this reason Hispanic students may be much more willing and able to accept criticism, direction and discipline from educators with whom they have a close personal relationship.

Hispanics: Agree 76%   Insufficient Information 13%   Disagree 12%
**Non-Hispanics: Agree 70%   Insufficient Information 25%   Disagree 6%

> "This is true if and when the personal relationships lead to more trust and mutual respect." (Hispanic)

> "It seems to me that there is a contradiction between telling us Anglos that Hispanic students may be more comfortable with formal relationships in the class and in the same breath to tell us that they may function better if they also have close personal relationships with us." (Non-Hispanic)

Therefore, educators should not maintain an impersonal, objective, aloof or distant relationship with Hispanic students.

Hispanics: Agree 75%   Insufficient Information 10%   Disagree 17%
Non-Hispanics: Agree 73%   Insufficient Information 18%   Disagree 10%

Therefore, they should strive to become their students' friends by sharing their feelings, attitudes, opinions and personal lives with them.

*Hispanics: Agree 58%   Insufficient Information 10%   Disagree 33%
Non-Hispanics: Agree 49%   Insufficient Information 17%   Disagree 34%

> "This can be very effective in establishing trust, but being friends without clear role distinctions can cause a lot of trouble." (Hispanic)

> "If the teacher feels comfortable with that." (Hispanic)

> "Educators should not do this. They are the students' teachers, not their peers." (Hispanic)

> "I would never be able to do this with my students, nor do I feel I should." (Non-Hispanic)

What motivates Hispanics to be punctual are not impersonal reasons such as it is efficient for everyone to arrive at the same time and begin at the same time. Hispanics may feel that the meeting or work could have started without them if necessary. On the other hand, personal relationships do concern them. For example, they may be very concerned that their lack of punctuality not be interpreted as a sign of disrespect or a lack of courtesy toward others and arrive on time to make sure they do not seem disrespectful.

Hispanics: Agree 76%   Insufficient Information 13%   Disagree 12%
**Non-Hispanics: Agree 64%   Insufficient Information 30%   Disagree 6%

> "While I agree with the statement, I do not feel that Hispanics would interpret lack of punctuality as a sign of disrespect. Making someone wait who has arrived on time, that could be seen as disrespectful." (Hispanic)

> "I have noticed this especially during parent meetings." (Non-Hispanic)

Therefore, when educators find it necessary to reprimand Hispanic students for tardiness or to encourage them to be punctual, they should focus more on the interpersonal than the impersonal results of their lateness. Such statements as "if you respect your classmates, you will get here when we need you" may have more effect than statements such as "we could not finish on time" or "we wasted fifteen minutes because we had to wait for you."

Hispanics: Agree 75%   Insufficient Information 12%   Disagree 12%
**Non-Hispanics: Agree 70%   Insufficient Information 20%   Disagree 10%

> "Yes, but in private, not in front of their classmates." (Hispanic)

> "This plays on guilt. I do not think making children feel guilty is a good way to discipline them." (Non-Hispanic)

Summary: The participants agreed that Hispanics have or develop personal relationships with the people with whom they do business, professionals from whom they seek help and educators. Both groups of participants agreed that for this reason educators should not maintain an impersonal, aloof or distant relationship with their students and that they should focus more on the personal rather than the impersonal reasons why their Hispanic students should conform to the expectations of the school authorities. However, only the Hispanic participants agreed that educators should try to become their students' friends. While the majority of the non-Hispanics agreed with the statements mentioned above, many of them stated that they lacked sufficient information or experience about these aspects of the Hispanic culture.

Sensitivity to Others' Feelings and Needs

Hispanics are expected to be sensitive to the needs, feelings and desires of others so that it is unnecessary for others to be embarrassed by asking for help or understanding or to be left alone.

  Hispanics: Agree 75%   Insufficient Information 12%   Disagree 13%
**Non-Hispanics: Agree 50%   Insufficient Information 39%   Disagree 12%

> "This was often a problem for me with Anglo teachers who had to be told things they could not figure out for themselves." (Hispanic)

> "This is part of what is meant by Ramirez and Castaneda who say that Chicanos are field sensitive." (Non-Hispanic)

> "This is not part of the Hispanic culture alone. All types of people have trouble communicating their needs." (Hispanic)

> "This statement is too general and very stereotypic. It needs to be more specific."(Hispanic)

> "I really don't know anything about this, I am embarrassed to admit." (Non-Hispanic)

Males especially may rely on the sensitivity of others and express their needs only in indirect and subtle ways.

  *Hispanics: Agree 79%   Insufficient Information 12%   Disagree 9%
**Non-Hispanics: Agree 50%   Insufficient Information 33%   Disagree 10%

Therefore, educators should be tuned into these subtle expressions of need. They should not assume that because Hispanic students have not expressed a need for help or understanding in a direct and forthright manner, they do not need special attention or consideration.

  Hispanics: Agree 93%   Insufficient Information 4%   Disagree 4%
  Non-Hispanics: Agree 86%   Insufficient Information 11%   Disagree 3%

Summary: Both Hispanics and non-Hispanics agreed that educators should be sensitive to the indirect manner in which Hispanics may express their need for help or understanding because

Hispanics tend not to express such needs in a direct manner. While agreeing with this, many non-Hispanic participants described themselves as lacking sufficient information or experience about this cultural characteristic.

Physical Contact and Physical Space

Hispanics tend to show affection and acceptance through touching. Friends are likely to kiss when they meet. Males are likely to hug each other or pat each other on the back as well as shake hands. And it is not unusual for people to hold others by the arm or place their hands on their shoulders when conversing.

Hispanics: Agree 93% Insufficient Information 2% Disagree 6%
Non-Hispanics: Agree 90% Insufficient Information 7% Disagree 3%

"When I first lived in Latin America I felt very uncomfortable with all the kissing and back patting and it really bothered me when someone held me by the arm when he talked to me. It felt like he was trying to make sure I wouldn't go away. It was like I was a captive audience." (Non-Hispanic)

"Maybe that's part of being Latin." (Hispanic)

"This often surprises tourists when they visit Latin America." (Hispanic)

"This is not true of Americanized Hispanics." (Hispanic)

"It's necessary to be careful with this idea. There are Hispanic students who will not tolerate physical contact." (Hispanic)

Therefore, educators should utilize physical contact when expressing approval and acceptance of their Hispanic students, especially the young ones.

Hispanics: Agree 80% Insufficient Information 4% Disagree 17%
Non-Hispanics: Agree 81% Insufficient Information 11% Disagree 8%

"This really works with the young ones." (Non-Hispanic)

"If the educator has the rapport and is comfortable with this approach." (Hispanic)

"As long as it's sincere." (Hispanic)

"Children can detect insincere behavior. Educators should use whatever means of behavior is comfortable and profes-

sionally appropriate to provide positive reinforcement."
(Hispanic)

"This is generally untrue. It depends on the student—
Hispanics are not all alike." (Hispanic)

Hispanics tend to stand closer together when talking or relating.

Hispanics:	Agree 83%	Insufficient Information 6%	Disagree 11%
Non-Hispanics:	Agree 80%	Insufficient Information 15%	Disagree 5%

"My theory is that English-speaking people keep a greater
distance because of our aspirated /p/ and /t/ we might get a
shower of saliva. Whether true or not, it helps my students
understand this cultural difference." (Non-Hispanic)

When people back away from them they may feel rejected.

Hispanics:	Agree 71%	Insufficient Information 10%	Disagree 19%
**Non-Hispanics:	Agree 70%	Insufficient Information 22%	Disagree 8%

Therefore, educators should try to not back away from Hispanic
students when they stand too close for comfort.

Hispanics:	Agree 66%	Insufficient Information 12%	Disagree 22%
Non-Hispanics:	Agree 72%	Insufficient Information 18%	Disagree 11%

"If this happens often, explain space preference and where
you feel comfortable, find a comfortable space." (Non-
Hispanic)

"Educators should not try to be who they aren't. If they try to
do what they are not comfortable with, this discomfort will
show. Better to be oneself." (Non-Hispanic)

Summary: The participants agreed that Hispanics show affection
and acceptance through physical contact and stand closer together
when talking, etc. They also agreed that educators should try to do
the same in their relationships with Hispanic students.

Formal Relationships

Hispanic children tend to have formal respectful relationships
with adults. This is reflected in their use of the "usted" form when
they address adults.

Hispanics:	Agree 93%	Insufficient Information 3%	Disagree 4%
Non-Hispanics:	Agree 83%	Insufficient Information 11%	Disagree 7%

"The special educator who plans to work with someone like
myself should know that I respect older people, women and

people who have a professional title and am inclined to address them formally with usted rather than the tu." (Hispanic)

"This is definitely true. Even the United States Hispanic children will feel disrespectful using the informal form and even adults will use the formal form with teachers." (Hispanic)

"It depends on their 'educators' upbringing." (Hispanic)

"Less true today than in the past." (Hispanic)

"A lot of my first graders don't even know the usted form." (Non-Hispanic)

"One can be respectful without being formal. Formal and respectful are not synonymous. That was a puritanic Victorian concept of relationships." (Non-Hispanic)

As a result, they may be uncomfortable with the less formal relationships usually observed between Anglo teachers and Anglo student.

Hispanics:	Agree 76%	Insufficient Information 6%	Disagree 17%
**Non-Hispanics:	Agree 63%	Insufficient Information 21%	Disagree 17%

"This is true for some." (Hispanic)

"Most students are adaptable and assimilated enough to adjust to this." (Hispanic)

"As a student, I preferred a closer relationship with my teachers but a more formal one." (Hispanic)

"Anglo teachers are not informal with students, neither are we standoffish." (Non-Hispanic)

Therefore, educators should tell Hispanic students that although formal relationships may be appropriate at home, a less formal relationship is more typical of the classroom.

Hispanics:	Agree 62%	Insufficient Information 11%	Disagree 28%
Non-Hispanics:	Agree 55%	Insufficient Information 18%	Disagree 28%

"I agree. Students can adapt to this very quickly." (Hispanic)

"They should be allowed to choose the kinds of relationships they are most comfortable with." (Hispanic)

"Depends on the individual style of the teacher." (Hispanic)

Therefore, educators should not attempt to develop informal

relationships with their Hispanic students who are not comfortable with such relationships.

Hispanics:	Agree 59%	Insufficient Information	6%	Disagree 36%
Non-Hispanics:	Agree 55%	Insufficient Information	14%	Disagree 31%

Summary: Participants agreed that Hispanic children tend to have more formal relationships with adults and therefore may feel uncomfortable with the less formal relationships between teachers and pupils in the school. They also agreed but to a lesser extent that educators should explain to Hispanic students that less formal relationships are more typical of the classroom. But they also agreed that educators should not attempt to develop informal relationships with Hispanic students who are not comfortable with such relationships.

Group Processes

In the Hispanic culture it is not impolite for more than one person to speak at a time during group discussions. Multiple conversations may be carried out simultaneously without anyone being considered rude or discourteous.

Hispanics:	Agree 66%	Insufficient Information	11%	Disagree 23%
**Non-Hispanics:	Agree 62%	Insufficient Information	31%	Disagree 7%

> "This allows everyone to have his or her say." (Hispanic)

> "I've often seen three or four people in a group of six speaking all at once even though one of them is speaking without an audience as if he were sure sooner or later someone would tune into him." (Non-Hispanic)

Therefore, educators should not insist that Hispanic students adhere to the rule of only one person speaking at a time.

Hispanics:	Agree 23%	Insufficient Information	7%	Disagree 70%
Non-Hispanics:	Agree 11%	Insufficient Information	15%	Disagree 75%

Therefore, educators should explain to Hispanic speakers that while it may be alright for more than one person to speak at a time at home, in school students are expected to wait their turn before speaking.

Hispanics:	Agree 81%	Insufficient Information	5%	Disagree 14%
Non-Hispanics:	Agree 86%	Insufficient Information	9%	Disagree 5%

When a group of Hispanics disagree, they may resolve the issue by continuing to discuss it until it becomes apparent that a consensus has been reached without polling the group or calling for a vote.

*Hispanics: Agree 63% Insufficient Information 20% Disagree 18%
**Non-Hispanics: Agree 47% Insufficient Information 47% Disagree 6%

> "This is much better than bringing out the differences of opinion among people by requiring them to take a stand—stand up and be counted, show which side you're on, etc. This can increase conflict and often does." (Hispanic)

> "We are better able to let go of an issue once it becomes clear what the majority feels." (Hispanic)

Therefore, when working with groups of Hispanic students, educators should allow them to arrive at a consensus in whatever manner is most comfortable for them. Educators should not insist that decisions be made by voting.

Hispanics: Agree 51% Insufficient Information 12% Disagree 37%
**Non-Hispanics: Agree 54% Insufficient Information 27% Disagree 20%

Summary: The participants agreed that in the Hispanic culture it is not impolite for more than one person to speak at a time. But they disagreed that students should be allowed to do this in class. The Hispanic participants also agreed that Hispanics tend to resolve issues by arriving at an apparent consensus without calling for a vote. Many of the non-Hispanic participants had insufficient information or experience regarding this characteristic. However, both groups agreed that Hispanic students should be allowed to arrive at a consensus in whatever way is most comfortable for them without necessarily requiring them to vote.

Disciplining Children

Disciplinary Techniques

Some Hispanic parents tend to use physical punishment rather than deprivation of love and affection when disciplining their children.

Hispanics: Agree 84% Insufficient Information 7% Disagree 9%
**Non-Hispanics: Agree 66% Insufficient Information 26% Disagree 9%

> "This is not totally accurate. There are many Hispanic parents from all economic stratas who practice and don't practice this form of punishment." (Hispanic)

Moreover, once they have punished their children, they tend to forgive them rather than to remain angry, resentful, or to hold a grudge.

Hispanics: Agree 87% Insufficient Information 8% Disagree 6%
**Non-Hispanics: Agree 65% Insufficient Information 29% Disagree 6%

Because of this, when educators deprive Hispanic students of attention and affection in order to discipline them, these students may feel that they have been rejected rather than justly punished.

Hispanics: Agree 72% Insufficient Information 10% Disagree 10%
**Non-Hispanics: Agree 65% Insufficient Information 30% Disagree 6%

Therefore, educators should not use deprivation of affection to manage Hispanic students.

Hispanics: Agree 65% Insufficient Information 13% Disagree 22%
**Non-Hispanics: Agree 58% Insufficient Information 28% Disagree 14%

> "This can work if the educator explains the reasons for his/her behavior." (Hispanic)

> "No parent or teacher should ever use this technique." (Hispanic)

Hispanic parents tend to speak more politely and indirectly when they criticize or discipline their children. In the United States, educators are much more gruff and direct with students.

*Hispanics: Agree 55% Insufficient Information 16% Disagree 29%
**Non-Hispanics: Agree 37% Insufficient Information 37% Disagree 27%

> "Maybe—parents tell their children how much their behavior has affected them." (Hispanic)

> "The English language sounds more gruff and direct simply as a result of the tone variety that exists." (Non-Hispanic)

> "I have seen some of my Hispanic students humiliated by the parents—some of them are even beaten." (Non-Hispanic)

Some Hispanic students, especially males, may interpret the gruff or more direct manner of Anglos as an indication that educators do not consider them worthy or deserving of a proper relationship. When educators speak to them in a matter-of-fact or authoritarian manner, they may feel insulted, angry or resentful and lose respect for these educators and the desire to cooperate or conform.

*Hispanics: Agree 68% Insufficient Information 16% Disagree 17%
**Non-Hispanics: Agree 49% Insufficient Information 38% Disagree 13%

> "I would advise Anglo educators to speak to the child in a warm and friendly manner instead of using or stressing

harsh English language sounds all the time, i.e. Clean your desk, etc., in an authoritarian mood which would alienate the child's cooperation and instill rebellious attitudes to an alien authority." (Hispanic)

"This is more characteristic of secondary school age males when treated in such a manner by female instructors in particular." (Hispanic)

"American teachers aren't more gruff and direct. It's a linguistic difference. We choose other words for saying the same thing. For example, we have no 'tú' form." (Non-Hispanic)

Therefore, educators should be indirect rather than direct and frank, and respectful rather than disrespectful when reprimanding or disciplining Hispanic students.

*Hispanics: Agree 64% Insufficient Information 11% Disagree 26%
**Non-Hispanics: Agree 49% Insufficient Information 34% Disagree 18%

"True, but I still feel the key is being constructive and confidential." (Hispanic)

"These are good techniques that should be used for *all* students." (Non-Hispanic)

"You can be frank and still be courteous and direct and still respectful." (Hispanic)

"No! Direct, but never disrespectful!" (Hispanic)

"I think it is important that the educator will be always frank and direct. At the same time he/she could be respectful and will not offend any type of student." (Hispanic)

"Latin students are used to being addressed very directly and immediately when engaging in inappropriate behavior." (Unknown)

The participants agreed that because Hispanic parents tend to use physical punishment rather than deprivation of affection to discipline their children, Hispanic students may feel they have been rejected rather than justly punished when educators use deprivation of attention and affection to discipline them. They also agreed that educators should not do this with Hispanic students. If and when Hispanic parents suggest that educators also use physical punishment with these children, the participants agreed that they should not do so nor think that these parents are cruel and rejecting. Rather, they should explain to the parents that although physical punishment may be alright at home, it is against school policy.

Hispanics agreed that Hispanic parents speak more politely and indirectly when disciplining their children; that Hispanic students, especially adolescents, may interpret the more direct manner of Anglo teachers as a sign of disrespect and feel angry or insulted; and that, therefore, educators should be indirect when disciplining Hispanic students. Non-Hispanics tended to describe themselves as lacking sufficient information and experience about these statements.

Male versus Female Authority Figures

Because the Hispanic culture tends to be patriarchal, some Hispanic male students, especially adolescents, may have difficulty complying with female authority figures.

Hispanics: Agree 73%   Insufficient Information 6%   Disagree 22%
Non-Hispanics: Agree 74%   Insufficient Information 14%   Disagree 12%

"Educators who want to work with people like me should realize that I came from a patriarchal family where the men's decisions were law." (Hispanic)

"Without stereotyping, one should be conscious of a male Chicano's lack of understanding in trying to take orders from a female teacher. He will really look up to or listen with better interest if an adult male is talking to him. This youngster is accustomed to following the authoritative rules of a male household figure." (Hispanic)

"This is true, but only for some adolescents." (Hispanic)

"This is not true in general, but it can occur." (Hispanic)

"Because of the increase in single-parent families among Hispanics born in the United States, in many families it is the mother who is the authority figure nowadays." (Hispanic)

"It depends on the woman. Some of my colleagues have problems, but I do not." (Non-Hispanic)

"My experience has been that 'la maestra' (the teacher) commands respect regardless of gender." (Non-Hispanic)

Therefore, when it is necessary to discipline such students, it may be more effective for the discipline to be administered by a male even when the classroom teacher is a female.

Hispanics: Agree 37%   Insufficient Information 9% Disagree 55%
Non-Hispanics: Agree 32%   Insufficient Information 17% Disagree 60%

> "This is true of secondary school age students, less so of younger ones." (Hispanic)

> "This may be possible, I don't know, but the students (all) should learn to accept discipline from the classroom teacher on the basis of respect." (Non-Hispanic)

> "Students must learn to relate to females as well. Discipline does not have to be inhumane. It can be a personal talk with the student." (Hispanic)

> "This is a sexist statement. In my experience female disciplinarians are often more effective just because they use non-authoritarian techniques to discipline their students." (Hispanic)

Therefore, female educators should stress non-authoritarian methods such as requesting rather than ordering for managing the classroom behavior of these Hispanic male students.

Hispanics: Agree 55%   Insufficient Information 8% Disagree 37%
**Non-Hispanics: Agree 52%   Insufficient Information 22% Disagree 27%

Summary: Both groups of participants agreed that male Hispanic students, especially adolescents, may have difficulty accepting the authority of female educators. However, they disagreed that because of this, discipline should be administered by a male. Rather, they agreed that females should discipline their own students utilizing non-authoritarian methods.

Children's Roles

Hispanic children often have a very active role to play in the family. They may be responsible for helping to take care of the younger children and may have many chores to do. When their parents do not speak English, they may be required to serve as translators when the adults have to meet with doctors, agencies, businessmen, etc.

Hispanics: Agree 98%   Insufficient Information 1% Disagree 1%
Non-Hispanics: Agree 98%   Insufficient Information 1% Disagree 1%

"In our family it was taught that when the parents were not around, the oldest was responsible in disciplining the younger ones and to look up to the oldest with respect and to obey him and her. And if anything happened to the parents, the oldest was expected to take care of the youngest ones. It's almost like an unwritten code or law. The oldest is just two years older than myself and the oldest was given more things in the way of special gifts in comparison to the rest for special occasions. In other words, our sister kept us in line when our parents weren't present. Also, if one misbehaved, all were punished. So, in another way, we all kept any of the members of the family from getting out of hand." (Hispanic)

"This certainly has been my experience with my Hispanic students." (Non-Hispanic)

"For the past few years my family and I have been sharing a house with a Hispanic woman and her teenage daughter who have become like a second mother and sister to my young daughter. Sometimes I find myself getting angry with my Hispanic 'daughter' when she tells her 'sister' what to do and what not to do. From my Anglo point of view she seems to be butting in, especially when I and my wife are around. However, in her case she is just doing what an older sister would do in any Hispanic family—that is, take care of the younger ones." (Non-Hispanic)

When these responsibilities interfere with the students' attendance at school or homework and study time, Hispanics tend to view the students' responsibilities to the family as more important than their responsibility to the school.

Hispanics: Agree 88%   Insufficient Information   3%   Disagree   9%
Non-Hispanics: Agree 91%   Insufficient Information   5%   Disagree   4%

"A large family might work for today's needs rather than think about sending their children to college for the future. To a teacher it might appear that the parents don't care about their children's education. On the contrary they care very much, but they need to care for their immediate needs first." (Hispanic)

"I have observed that family priority occurs more among Hispanics and school priority among Anglos." (Non-Hispanics)

"While this is a very important cultural difference, socio-economic realities affect their attitudes as much as culture." (Non-Hispanic)

"This is no longer true." (Hispanic)

Therefore, when Hispanic students miss school or come unprepared, educators should determine when conflicting family responsibilities are the cause and accommodate their expectations and teaching methods to the students' and parents' realities.

Hispanics: Agree 68% Insufficient Information 6% Disagree 26%
Non-Hispanics: Agree 71% Insufficient Information 10% Disagree 19%

"Usually, the oldest brother or sister is interpreter and babysitter. That is, there is added pressure on this sibling. So, if he/she did not finish his/her assigned homework, ask for the explanation and find out if it is laziness related or family emergency related. It could very well be he/she had to go to the doctor's office with his Spanish-speaking mother to translate the doctor's diagnosis for his mother and/or family." (Hispanic)

"This is extremely important. Educators need to be more sensitive to this and adjust to it." (Hispanic)

"I agree. It is always possible for students to make up the work at other times." (Non-Hispanic)

"We need to be more lenient and flexible with due dates with these students." (Non-Hispanic)

"Educators should systematically teach Anglo values while recognizing and supporting Hispanic values so that children can learn to 'make it' in both systems." (Hispanic)

"No, they should help the parents change their attitudes." (Hispanic)

Therefore, educators should not pressure students to choose between their responsibilities to their families and the school by insisting that they attend school and complete assignments even when family responsibilities interfere. However, they should talk with the Hispanic parents and try to help them to shift their priorities somewhat so that the students' responsibilities at home do not interfere with their success in school.

Hispanics: Agree 88% Insufficient Information 2% Disagree 10%
Non-Hispanics: Agree 86% Insufficient Information 5% Disagree 9%

"In our school we have a visiting teacher whose responsibility is to do things like this." (Hispanic)

"They should accept this temporarily and help the parents and students to understand the importance of school attendance." (Hispanic)

"At least become familiar with possible resources for families or develop alternative study plans for students." (Hispanic)

"Only if it doesn't happen too often. Otherwise this right can be very abused." (Non-Hispanic)

Therefore, educators should not lower course grades or punish Hispanic students in other ways when family responsibilities prevent them from completing assignments, arriving on time, or attending class.

*Hispanics: Agree 51%   Insufficient Information 9%   Disagree 40%
 Non-Hispanics: Agree 47%   Insufficient Information 11%   Disagree 42%

"If family problems interfere with schooling, teachers can provide alternatives for the motivated students. Example: make-up assignments, different test format on the same material, tutoring before or after school, etc." (Hispanic)

"If it's an occasional responsibility, but the family and student must both understand that a grade cannot be given for intentions. As far as possible, students need to make up work." (Hispanic)

"However, some type of compromising should be done." (Hispanic)

"While they shouldn't be punished, etc., the problem should not be ignored, especially if it is very severe." (Non-Hispanic)

"Sometimes, students use this as an excuse. When it is difficult to determine whether there is a real legitimate conflict or not, it's best to treat them as you would treat any other student." (Non-Hispanic)

"Disagree. They should be treated in school like they will be treated in real life. On the job if they come to work late or don't finish a job within a specified time, there will be consequences, so why not in school, too?" (Non-Hispanic)

"Policies and implementation thereof need to be uniform and consistent for *all* students, not resulting in the appearance or implementation of special privileges for one group. Individualized adjustments need to be arranged to avoid creating a counter-productive attitude of 'prejudice' for or against *any* group." (Non-Hispanic)

Summary: Almost all the participants agreed that Hispanic children often have many responsibilities at home. Most of the participants also agreed that when conflicts occur between their children's responsibilities to the family and the school, Hispanic parents tend to give priority to their children's responsibilities to the family. They also agreed that when these conflicts occur, educators should not pressure students to fulfill their obligations to the school—instead, they should try to convince the parents to change their priorities. The suggestion that educators should not lower course grades or punish students in these circumstances was not as well received. Only a slim majority of the Hispanics agreed with it and almost as many non-Hispanic participants disagreed with it as agreed with it. There appears to be an inconsistency in the responses of the non-Hispanics—on the one hand they agreed that students should not be pressured to fulfill their obligations to the school when they are caught in these kinds of conflict situations. Yet, they did not agree that the students should not receive lower grades or punishment if they fulfill their obligations to their families rather than their schools in these situations.

Sex Role Differences

Hispanic families often have different expectations for their sons and daughters. Despite women's liberation and the non-sexist attitudes currently prevailing in the United States, many Hispanic parents have different expectations for their sons and daughters. They still protect girls and expect them to be mothers' helpers and to eventually marry, have children and focus their energies in the home. On the other hand, boys are expected to grow up to be more independent, to be more involved in activities outside the home and to be breadwinners. Thus, some Hispanic girls may not be highly motivated to succeed academically, to go to college, or to complete vocational learning programs.

Hispanics:	Agree 75%	Insufficient Information	4%	Disagree	21%
Non-Hispanics:	Agree 89%	Insufficient Information	6%	Disagree	5%

"This is still true to some degree today. In my experience many Hispanic women like myself are placed in situations of serious conflict when they attempt to pursue career goals." (Hispanic)

"Among Mexican-American families, in my experience, I have seen considerable difference in the way families treat sons and daughters. Expectations for boys include 'machismo,' independence and freedom beyond the home as well as higher aspirations for academic achievement than for girls. Girls tend to be more protected, are expected to serve as 'mother's helper' and to eventually marry and have children. Despite 'liberated' attitudes regarding male/female differences among Anglo and middle class Mexican-Americans, lower class Hispanic families, in general, have not assimilated these new values. These factors are particularly important as they relate to parents' involvement in planning for their children's special needs, their attitude regarding students dropping out of school, and their attitudes toward problems of adolescence." (Non-Hispanic)

"This is generalizing too much. It depends on the social, economic and educational background of the Hispanic family. Middle class parents are now encouraging daughters to go on to college." (Hispanic)

"When students are recent arrivals from Mexico, boys seem more motivated to achieve in school than girls. In contrast, among Chicanos born here, more girls seem to have higher academic aspirations." (Hispanic)

"This is less true for Mexican-Americans today. Even newcomers from Mexico are feeling the economic need for a housewife to get out and work and this changes the old expectations for girls and women." (Unknown)

Therefore, educators should base their expectations of their Hispanic students on the goals and aspirations of the individuals with whom they work.

Hispanics:　　　　Agree 67%　Insufficient Information　8%　Disagree 25%
Non-Hispanics:　Agree 59%　Insufficient Information 10%　Disagree 31%

"They should be allowed to be themselves. They should not be pushed to become what we think is best for them." (Hispanic)

"They should motivate them to be what they are capable of. But they should not be too pushy." (Hispanic)

"Students have a mind of their own." (Non-Hispanic)

"Teachers should present alternatives but not push too much." (Hispanic)

"Both males and females should be made more open to non-sexist roles." (Hispanic)

"Teachers should try to be consistent with the attitudes of the students' parents regarding this, since the parents not the teachers should have the most to say." (Non-Hispanic)

Therefore, educators should explain to their female students that while the differences between the roles of the sexes may be appropriate for those who are comfortable with such differences, nowadays women can perform the roles and functions which in the past were traditionally assigned to men.

Hispanics: Agree 95% Insufficient Information 2% Disagree 4%
Non-Hispanics: Agree 87% Insufficient Information 6% Disagree 7%

"Explain yes, but not push. The difference is very important." (Hispanic)

"This is good but with care not to 'put down' traditional roles." (Non-Hispanic)

"I am uncomfortable with contradicting parents' wishes." (Hispanic)

Hispanic boys are taught to be protective of their sisters and other girls, escorting them to and from school, protecting them from other boys, handling their money, etc., in general performing a macho role; Hispanic girls are encouraged to assume a submissive role toward brothers and other boys. As a result, both sexes may feel uncomfortable when they are required to work and play together as equals.

Hispanics: Agree 70% Insufficient Information 6% Disagree 24%
Non-Hispanics: Agree 71% Insufficient Information 17% Disagree 12%

"This was definitely true about me while I was growing up, and I bring my children up the same way. My son is taught to protect the girls, although they are not brought up to be as submissive to him as much as my sisters were." (Hispanic)

"I agree about how they are brought up at home. However,

despite this, in school they do not feel uncomfortable when required to work and play together as equals." (Hispanic)

"Not anymore." (Hispanic)

Hispanic students prefer to work in school in groups of their own sex. They may feel uncomfortable when well-meaning egalitarian non-sexist Anglo educators require that the sexes work or engage in athletic activities together.

Hispanics: Agree 65%   Insufficient Information 12%   Disagree 24%
**Non-Hispanics: Agree 56%   Insufficient Information 30%   Disagree 14%

For these reasons, some Hispanic girls may react negatively when they are expected to compete with boys or to perform as their equals.

Hispanics: Agree 69%   Insufficient Information 8%   Disagree 23%
Non-Hispanics: Agree 73%   Insufficient Information 18%   Disagree 11%

"Important for teachers to know so won't place unrealistic or embarrassing expectations on students or be angry when students respond as per statement." (Hispanic)

"Times are changing. This applies to only some girls." (Hispanic)

Therefore, educators should respect the wishes of Hispanic students by not requiring that the sexes work and play together if specific individuals are not inclined to do so.

Hispanics: Agree 43%   Insufficient Information 12%   Disagree 45%
Non-Hispanics: Agree 32%   Insufficient Information 18%   Disagree 50%

"Depends on the activity—the only spanking I got was for refusing to dance with a boy in the third grade." (Hispanic)

"At least not all the time. There should be a balance between the schools expectations and the children's wishes." (Hispanic)

"Si se refiere a Educacion Fisica estoy de acuerdo. Pero no en la parte academica (I agree regarding physical education but not regarding academic classes)." (Hispanic)

"All students need to be helped to try to learn to accommodate to differing roles so as to be able to deal with the world beyond secondary school." (Non-Hispanic)

Summary: Hispanics and non-Hispanics agreed that parents have different expectations for the sons and daughters and that this may make it difficult for girls to compete with boys or perform as their equals. While both groups agreed that educators should adapt their expectations to the goals and aspirations of these Hispanic students, they agreed even more with suggestions that female students should be motivated to fulfill non-sexist roles and roles that have been traditionally assigned to males. The participants also agreed that because Hispanic boys and girls are brought up to fulfill different roles, they may not feel comfortable engaging in some activities together. However, the non-Hispanic participants disagreed with the suggestion that educators should not require them to work and play with the opposite sex if they did not want to. The opinions of the Hispanics regarding this suggestion were almost equally divided between agreement and disagreement.

Modesty

Because Hispanics, especially females, tend to be modest about exposing their bodies, some students may feel very uncomfortable about wearing shorts to physical education classes, showering in the presence of others and being examined by doctors or nurses.

Hispanics: Agree 85%   Insufficient Information   5%   Disagree 10%
**Non-Hispanics: Agree 65%   Insufficient Information 24%   Disagree 11%

"In the Hispanic culture the women are more modest in dress and behavior. For instance, Lupita, a little girl in my first grade classroom, was completely uncooperative during P.E. She was limited in English and could not express herself to her teacher. After discussing the problem with Lupita, I discovered that she did not want to play the games because she was wearing a dress. After explaining to her and to her mother that she could wear jeans, etc., on P.E. days, Lupita did not have any problems after that. I find that Hispanic girls usually wear frilly dresses and inappropriate shoes for the active role expected of them in American schools."
(Hispanic)

"Modesty is a moral, which many Anglos do not practice, especially when it comes to nakedness. There should never be a need to expose one's body in front of others, other than a physician. No amount of persuasion should be used."
(Hispanic)

"This statement seems to apply to highly unassimilated Hispanics. In my experience, even kids of migrant workers from Mexico came to summer school in shorts and halters." (Non-Hispanic)

Therefore, Hispanic students should not be required to wear shorts to physical education classes or to shower in the presence of others.

Hispanics: Agree 30%   Insufficient Information 14%   Disagree 56%
**Non-Hispanics: Agree 23%   Insufficient Information 23%   Disagree 54%

"VERY TRUE! P.E. is the hardest subject for Mexican students to pass because of this and related reasons. With a little understanding, they can be taught to dress for P.E., but inflexible rules put them so far behind that they give up." (Unknown)

"However, true for *any* child from *any* culture with *any* reticence." (Non-Hispanic)

"Other options for dress should be given, i.e. long pants or sweats." (Hispanic)

"Shorts are one thing, showers another. Perhaps they should be excused from showering in public, but shorts should not cause much embarrassment." (Non-Hispanic)

"Shorts—okay. To shower in the presence of others—*No*." (Hispanic)

"Don't you think showers are necessary after physical exertion?" (Non-Hispanic)

Summary: The participants agreed that Hispanic students, especially females, tend to be modest. However, they disagreed that this was sufficient reason not to require them to wear shorts to physical education classes or shower in the presence of others.

Acknowledgement of Errors, Mistakes and Inability

Hispanics are less likely to verbally acknowledge responsibility for mistakes and errors or to apologize when they have wronged someone.

*Hispanics: Agree 53%   Insufficient Information 12%   Disagree 34%
**Non-Hispanics: Agree 48%   Insufficient Information 32%   Disagree 19%

Instead of blaming themselves for errors, they frequently attribute it to adverse circumstances. They didn't miss the bus because they arrived too late. Instead, they blame the bus for leaving before they arrived. They did not get drunk because they chose to drink too much. They got drunk because too much liquor was served at the fiesta.

Hispanics: Agree 60% Insufficient Information 10% Disagree 30%
**Non-Hispanics: Agree 61% Insufficient Information 28% Disagree 11%

"Our language is an expression of our culture. It is true that we can't blame ourselves—'me dejo el avion' (the plane left me), 'se me durmio el gallo' (the rooster made me sleep), 'se me subieron les tragos' (the drinks did me in), etc. (Hispanic)

"I don't buy that old theory about the Spanish reflexive indicating a lack of responsibility. That's carrying Whorf's hypothesis a little too far." (Unknown)

"Too literal an interpretation. Hispanics accept as much responsibility for their actions as anyone else. We are just less likely to admit it to others." (Hispanic)

"This is an insulting stereotype." (Hispanic)

"This sounds too old and too corny! Have you heard of 'The Generation Gap'—the 'Gap' did away with all of this, if in fact it ever existed." (Hispanic)

"This happens with all ethnic groups, especially adolescents. I don't believe that this statement is totally accurate and particular to Hispanics." (Hispanic)

Therefore, educators should not assume that Hispanic students who do not "own up" to their errors, mistakes and wrongdoings are either unaware of them or too rebellious and recalcitrant to admit them and apologize for them.

Hispanics: Agree 67% Insufficient Information 12% Disagree 21%
**Non-Hispanics: Agree 65% Insufficient Information 23% Disagree 12%

Therefore, educators should not shame Hispanic students by requiring them to make verbal acknowledgements of their mistakes and wrongdoings in ways which are culturally unacceptable to them.

Hispanics: Agree 71% Insufficient Information 8% Disagree 22%
Non-Hispanics: Agree 67% Insufficient Information 19% Disagree 14%

"Educators should not shame anyone." (Non-Hispanic)

"The issue is not whether they should be shamed or not. The issue is whether they learn to acknowledge their mistakes. I believe they must learn what's acceptable for the Anglo culture they live in." (Non-Hispanic)

Hispanics, especially males, tend not to admit to not knowing something or being unable to do something.

Hispanics: Agree 73%   Insufficient Information 11%   Disagree 16%
**Non-Hispanics: Agree 70%   Insufficient Information 20%   Disagree 10%

Therefore, educators should not assume that Hispanic students who have not said that they do not understand something or cannot do something or have not asked for help actually understand their lessons and can do their assignments without help. Rather, educators should be sensitive to the subtle clues which indicate that they are in need.

Hispanics: Agree 89%   Insufficient Information 5%   Disagree 7%
Non-Hispanics: Agree 88%   Insufficient Information 8%   Disagree 4%

The notion that Hispanics are less likely to verbally acknowledge their errors and mistakes proved to be very controversial. A bare majority of the Hispanics agreed with it and slightly less than half of the non-Hispanics agreed with it. The idea that they tend to blame adverse circumstances rather than themselves for their errors and mistakes was almost as controversial, although a small majority of both groups of participants agreed with it. Taking these cultural facts into consideration, the participants also agreed that educators should not require Hispanic students to acknowledge their mistakes and wrongdoings, nor assume that if they do not do so it is because they are unaware of them or too rebellious to admit them. The theme of acknowledgement of mistakes and errors in the Hispanic community was one about which many non-Hispanic participants described themselves as lacking sufficient information or experience.

Summary: The idea that Hispanic students also tend not to admit that they do not know something or cannot do something was not as controversial. The participants agreed both that the description was true and that educators should be sensitive to the subtle clues which their Hispanic students use to express these facts about themselves.

Spontaneity

Hispanics tend to react spontaneously and impulsively to life. When faced with problems they tend to look for immediate solutions without reflecting on their implications for the future.

Thus, some Hispanic students may be more impulsive and less reflective than their Anglo peers when asked to solve problems or answer questions in school.

Hispanics: Agree 62%   Insufficient Information 7%   Disagree 31%
**Non-Hispanics: Agree 47%   Insufficient Information 28%   Disagree 24%

> "While I agree that this is a true statement, I do not like the way it is stated so negatively. A better way to have said this would have been, 'Hispanics tend to react to life in terms of the present, to enjoy what the moment offers. Don't put off to tomorrow what you can enjoy today.'" (Hispanic)

> "This is more true of poor Hispanics who have to struggle to survive in the present and can't afford the luxury of long range planning." (Hispanic)

Therefore, educators should use teaching strategies which minimize the likelihood that such students will respond impulsively to questions and problems while teaching them how to be more reflective in their problem-solving approaches.

Hispanics: Agree 77%   Insufficient Information 8%   Disagree 15%
**Non-Hispanics: Agree 65%   Insufficient Information 23%   Disagree 12%

Hispanics tend to be more spontaneous in their actions. They are not as concerned about hiding their feelings or acting on them. They are less likely to reflect first or ask themselves, "how will it look, or will it turn out alright?" before acting on an impulse. They have what some call a "Latin temperament."

*Hispanics: Agree 58%   Insufficient Information 9%   Disagree 32%
**Non-Hispanics: Agree 45%   Insufficient Information 30%   Disagree 25%

> "One of the things I like about Latins is the fact that they are not uptight about enjoying themselves, laughing, joking, dancing, having a good time in general. When I go to a party with Latins I expect a lot of dancing and partying. An Anglo party too often is a polite talkathon." (Non-Hispanic)

> "This is an untrue and negative stereotype used to keep Hispanics 'in their place.'" (Hispanic)

> "They are very much peer/group oriented and do care about what others think." (Hispanic)

> "This statement is a gross generalization. In certain areas of behavior I would agree but in others Latins are very concerned about 'el que dirá la gente' (what will people say?)." (Hispanic)

Therefore, educators should not assume that when Hispanic students express their joy or anger in class it will lead to even more acting-out behavior and they should not feel obliged to "nip such problems in the bud" or to stop them before they occur.

Hispanics: Agree 51%   Insufficient Information 13%   Disagree 36%
**Non-Hispanics: Agree 54%   Insufficient Information 21%   Disagree 25%

Therefore, educators should expect and accept a certain amount of so-called acting-out behavior from Hispanic students. Just because Anglo students are less likely to act out their anger, joy, or sadness, educators should not require the same degree of control from Hispanic students.

Hispanics: Agree 39%   Insufficient Information 8%   Disagree 53%
**Non-Hispanics: Agree 27%   Insufficient Information 28%   Disagree 51%

"This question is difficult to answer—do you mean emotion control or behavior control? Hispanics tend to be more generous in showing their emotions, but this is not necessarily the same as 'acting-out' behavior." (Hispanic)

"Within the limitation of not disrupting the class." (Hispanic)

"They should be able to begin expecting (not requiring) control after a period of time." (Hispanic)

"It would be difficult justifying to the Anglo students why the behavior is acceptable for Latins and not for them. May encourage more resentment." (Hispanic)

"Educators should demand the same decent behavior from all of their students." (Non-Hispanic)

"Children who respond physically to a situation by hitting should be taught other ways to solve problems—whatever their cultural background." (Non-Hispanic)

Therefore, educators should help Hispanic students to become more reflective in their approach to both interpersonal and academic tasks.

Hispanics: Agree 69%   Insufficient Information 10%   Disagree 22%
**Non-Hispanics: Agree 65%   Insufficient Information 21%   Disagree 15%

Summary: By a small majority Hispanic participants agreed with the descriptions of Hispanics as more spontaneous in their reactions to life; however, a considerable number of them did not agree. Non-Hispanics did not agree with this description and many of them stated that they lacked sufficient information or experience to judge its validity. Regarding the ramifications of these cultural characteristics, participants agreed that educators should help Hispanic students to become more reflective but disagreed that educators should allow Hispanics a certain amount of uncontrolled spontaneous acting-out behavior in the classroom.

Names

Hispanics, like other people, are very proud of their names.

| Hispanics: | Agree 93% | Insufficient Information | 3% | Disagree | 4% |
| Non-Hispanics: | Agree 86% | Insufficient Information | 9% | Disagree | 4% |

Therefore, educators who have difficulty remembering or pronouncing their students' names should not Anglicize José to Joe or Maria Teresa to Mary.

| Hispanics: | Agree 90% | Insufficient Information | 5% | Disagree | 5% |
| Non-Hispanics: | Agree 91% | Insufficient Information | 4% | Disagree | 5% |

"Emphatically agree. I am shocked every time I hear that this practice continues still in 1982." (Non-Hispanic)

"It really bothers me when I hear people Anglicize a name." (Non-Hispanic)

"This is a subtle way of conveying to a student that they are not okay the way they are." (Hispanic)

"I think it is more accurate to say that educators should not try to conform students to be 'good Americans' by Americanizing Hispanic names." (Hispanic)

"Depends on how long the student has been in the United States. Even kindergarten children come in as Frank, Robert or Mary, rather than Francisco, Roberto or Maria because their parents have given them non-Hispanic names." (Hispanic)

"Older students get a kick out of using Anglicized names when these are used in a stress-free humorous setting. They're going to get Anglicized anyway and it's best to let them pick out a name they like. You're doing Margarito no favors by postponing his inevitable name change." (Unknown)

Therefore, addressing younger students with diminutives such as

Juanito and Manuelita is a good way of expressing both affection for students and respect for their culture.

Hispanics: Agree 75%   Insufficient Information   3%   Disagree 22%
Non-Hispanics: Agree 69%   Insufficient Information 16%   Disagree 16%

"This works well with younger children, but it would not be appropriate in the upper grades." (Hispanic)

"With girls, yes, but the boys like to be 'older' and disdain 'nicknames.'" (Non-Hispanic)

"Depends on the student and when." (Hispanic)

"It's not what you say, it's how you say it—and culture could be the farthest thing from your mind when you say Juanito— it's just a name." (Hispanic)

"I wouldn't suggest doing that unless the teacher knew Spanish and related well to the student. I'd hate to see a teacher who knew nothing of the culture or language get wind of that practice and overuse it or use it at the wrong time!" (Hispanic)

"I was aware of this for showing affection, but not as a means of showing respect—I would think it might be taken as an affront if used with a child I didn't know—my ignorance, I guess." (Non-Hispanic)

Acculturation

Many Hispanic youth are faced with the necessity of surviving in two cultures—the Latino culture at home and in the community and the Anglo culture at school. When they find that they can neither be "All American" or "Todo Latino," they may identify with a youth culture like the Low Riders, Vatos Locos, or Guardian Angels. This may lead them to dress, speak and walk differently than the other students in school.

Hispanics: Agree 75%   Insufficient Information   9%   Disagree 16%
Non-Hispanics: Agree 82%   Insufficient Information 12%   Disagree 6%

"Because of their orientation towards cooperation, the Latin American adolescent even more than the Anglo adolescent is a loyal group member. When his group dresses differently etc., he too wants to show unity and pride. If he does not he may be called a 'vendido' (sold out) or a 'coconut' (brown on the outside and white in the middle) and ostracized from the rest of his peers." (Hispanic)

"I did it when I was a teenager and my teachers didn't like it. Now I'm the teacher and I understand my students. I have no problem with them. However, many of the others do." (Hispanic)

"Latino youth are faced with the reality of surviving within two cultures—home-Hispanic and school/establishment-English. Both cultures demand that the youngster succeed effectively. More often than not, one is short-changed. The pressure of competently living in both systems is tremendous." (Hispanic)

"Peer pressure is tremendous and adolescence is a time of 'identity crisis.' Latino youth know they are right in the middle. Namely, they want to be 'All American,' but society won't let them. Those that want to be 'Todo Latino' (completely Latin) can't either because we live in an English dominant society. They (and we) need more Chicano counselors as models with some guidance suggestions alternatives." (Hispanic)

"In describing the present day Chicano, one can say that 'he ceases to deny traits that heretofore caused him great anxiety. His new perception of himself means that he has developed new understandings about the sufferings inflicted upon him and his forebears and he is more acutely aware and intolerant of present affronts of his human dignity.' Chicanos are intolerant of, and hostile toward, whites who approach them with the usual racist stance in terms of language, attitudes and behavior. Because of their new self-perception, they are apt to cause whites, particularly those who harbor residuals of racism, a great deal of anxiety. Therefore, the educator who is unable or unwilling to acknowledge the new concept of this group is apt to be ineffectual in realting to them." (Hispanic)

"Gang membership is determined not so much by culture but by SES (poor Anglos, Blacks, Latinos belong not only in the United States but have become increasingly common in Latin America among lower classes). Upper classes would tend to join clubs, fraternities and other 'positive' social groups. Gangs are negative groupings not only to Anglos but for the parents of the youngsters who are members—regardless of ethnic/racial origin." (Hispanic)

Educators who are unaware of the value of this kind of group identity may mistakenly believe that these youth are delinquent or dangerous.

Hispanics:	Agree 87%	Insufficient Information	6%	Disagree	7%
Non-Hispanics:	Agree 86%	Insufficient Information	8%	Disagree	7%

"Children are still sent home just because they dress differently." (Hispanic)

"A trip through the Mission or L.A. should convince anyone that all these people can't be dangerous criminals." (Non-Hispanic)

Therefore, educators should welcome the development of such group loyalty and they should use it when they manage their classes.

*Hispanics:	Agree 55%	Insufficient Information	18%	Disagree	27%
**Non-Hispanics:	Agree 49%	Insufficient Information	29%	Disagree	23%

"Cultural conflicts between home and school cause youth to either choose one or the other. This causes conflicts in personality, adjustment, etc. He needs to act one way at school and gets home, uses a different language and a different set of cultural values. If the school allowed him to be himself, he wouldn't have the problem." (Hispanic)

"The Vato Loco,' as well as his predecessors, is the individual of Mexican descent that has refused to lose his Chicano identity. He is a Chicano, where not all Chicanos are Vatos Locos. The Vato Loco has his own patterns of speech, dress and a distinctive walk. He also has tattoo markings on his face, hands and arms. He is aware that the Anglo society is trying to impose its culture on him, but he is also aware of the vendido—the Chicano that becomes a part of the establishment and refuses to help his people. The vendido is ashamed of his Mexican ancestry and the Vato Loco will not accept that shame. The Vato Loco is an individual who has grown up in the barrio, a low socio-economic area which demands toughness for survival. Due to the tough Vato hero ideal, acts of violence and destruction will occur, which legally can be termed delinquent. However, the Vato Loco is not inherently delinquent. For the most part, his behavior is the consequence rather than the cause of what he is and represents. He is basically neither abnormal or disturbed but rather a product of poverty and social discrimination. The Vato Loco has great knowledge of barrio life. He is the Vato de la Calle, and it is the streets within his barrio that have been the greatest influence on him. His potential for positive involvement in his community should be developed. He could be valuable in the community in the fight against drugs, in working with Chicano youth groups, and in community educational programs. Some former Pachucos who have become leaders in the Chicano Movement are Cesar Chavez, with his work for the farm workers, and Corky Gonzales, who established the first all-Chicano School in Denver, Colorado. Both men have shown great sensitivity in understanding and working to alleviate the plight of the Chicano. There are many Vatos Locos in every barrio with the potential to help their people also. Educators will have a difficult time relating to the Vato Loco unless he can accept him as a unique individual and has a deep understanding of his cultural background and his environment." (Hispanic)

"I feel such groups somehow need to be oriented towards positive goals because during adolescence there definitely exists the potential of negative group behavior, and we are naive to believe otherwise." (Non-Hispanic)

"This can backfire. Students can see through manipulation." (Hispanic)

Educators should not evaluate Hispanic behavior patterns which are different than what they are accustomed to in such terms as right and wrong, good and bad, or acceptable and unacceptable. Such conceptualizations are prejudicial and can lead to biased classroom management procedures. Instead, they should evaluate these behaviors in terms of such concepts as same and different or efficient and inefficient.

Hispanics:	Agree	85%	Insufficient Information	7%	Disagree	8%
Non-Hispanics:	Agree	87%	Insufficient Information	8%	Disagree	5%

Summary: The participants agreed that some Hispanic youth may resolve their identity crises by identifying with groups of Low Riders, Vatos Locos or Guardian Angels. Both groups of participants agreed that educators should not make the mistake of believing that these groups are delinquent or dangerous, nor should they evaluate the different behavior patterns such students demonstrate in class with judgmental terms like good and bad, right and wrong, etc. However, only the Hispanics agreed that educators should welcome the development of such group loyalty and use it to manage their classes.

SUMMARY

The participants agreed with twenty-nine suggestions for modifying classroom management techniques when working with Hispanic students. They agreed that educators should:

1. allow them to work on their homework together and to help each other when they are called on in class but not to copy from each other on tests;
2. de-emphasize competition, utilize group participation and reward students for cooperative as well as competitive behavior;
3. not assume that students who do not volunteer answers or answer correctly during academic games do not know the answers;
4. do-emphasize the question-and-answer approach;
5. help them accept the fact that some students may not be as willing as they are to share their things with others while helping Anglo students become better sharers;
6. not assume that when they give gifts or do favors for teachers or their peers they do so to bribe them or to buy their affection;
7. be sensitive to the non-verbal indirect ways in which they express disagreement and unwillingness;
8. not assume that when they say they are willing to do something they actually intend to do it;
9. not maintain impersonal, aloof or distant relationships with their students;
10. stress personal rather than impersonal reasons when explaining why they should conform to the expectations of school officials:
11. be sensitive to the indirect manner in which they may express their need for help and understanding;

12. utilize physical contact when expressing approval and acceptance;
13. stand close to them when talking or relating to them;
14. explain that while formal relationships may be appropriate at home, less formal relationships are more typical of the classroom without attempting to develop informal relationships with students who are not comfortable with such relationships;
15. not permit multiple conversations during class discussions even though Hispanics tend to do so in meetings;
16. allow them to arrive at a consensus in whatever way is most comfortable for them without necessarily requiring that they vote;
17. not use deprivation of attention and affection to discipline them;
18. be indirect, rather than direct and frank, and respectful rather than disrespectful when reprimanding or disciplining them;*
19. use non-authoritarian methods when female educators discipline male students, especially adolescents;
20. not pressure them to fulfill their obligations in school if they have obligations at home which interfere;
21. not lower their grades or punish them in other ways when family responsibilities prevent them from completing assignments, arriving on time or attending class;*
22. motivate female students to fulfill non-sexist roles and roles traditionally assigned to males;
23. require males and females to work together even though they may feel uncomfortable about doing so;
24. neither assume that when they do not admit their mistakes or wrongdoings it is because they are unaware of them or too rebellious to admit them, nor insist that they verbally acknowledge them;
25. be sensitive to the subtle and indirect ways in which they communicate that they do not know something or cannot do something;
26. utilize teaching strategies which help them to become less impulsive and more reflective in their problem-solving approaches;

---

*Only Hispanic participants agreed

27. not Anglicize their names—for example, Joe for José or Mary for Maria Teresa—and use diminutives, such as Juanito for Juan, to express affection for their students and respect for their culture;

28. not be threatened by students who join groups of Low Riders, Vatos Locos, Guardian Angels, etc., nor evaluate the behavior of such students in terms of prejudicial concepts like good and bad, right and wrong, acceptable and unacceptable;

29. welcome the development of such group loyalty and use it to manage their classes.*

---

*Only Hispanic participants agreed.

Chapter 5.

COUNSELING

INTRODUCTION

This chapter includes the opinions of the participants about suggestions for making the counseling process more culturally relevant to Hispanic parents. The first section is concerned with suggestions which apply to counseling all Hispanic parents, while the second deals specifically with counseling parents of handicapped students.

GENERAL PRINCIPLES

Interpersonal Relationships

Importance of Family and Community

The family is the most valued institution in the Hispanic culture. The individual owes his primary loyalties to the family. When one has a family, one is never alone or without help in time of need.

Hispanics:	Agree 95%	Insufficient Information 3%	Disagree 2%
Non-Hispanics:	Agree 91%	Insufficient Information 7%	Disagree 2%

Therefore, counselors should be aware that a sense of responsibility to their family might cause Hispanics to change their behavior when they otherwise would not do so. When appropriate, counselors should appeal to their counselees' sense of responsibility to their family in order to motivate them to change their behavior.

Hispanics: Agree 87%   Insufficient Information 5%   Disagree 8%
Non-Hispanics: Agree 81%   Insufficient Information 12%   Disagree 8%

Therefore, counselors should be aware that the family may provide more support to a Hispanic counselee in need of support than the counselor is able to offer. And counselors should enlist the family's assistance when necessary.

Hispanics: Agree 94%   Insufficient Information 3%   Disagree 2%
Non-Hispanics: Agree 92%   Insufficient Information 6%   Disagree 1%

Therefore, counselors should consider the possibility that group counseling which might include representatives of both the immediate and extended families could prove more effective than merely meeting with one or both of the parents.

Hispanics: Agree 80%   Insufficient Information 6%   Disagree 14%
Non-Hispanics: Agree 83%   Insufficient Information 15%   Disagree 2%

"In counseling the exceptional Mexican-American child, a special educator should be aware of the importance of the nuclear family in the Mexican heritage. If you are having problems at school with this child, get in contact with the parents, especially the father or head of household, and have a personal and candid conversation. Usually, you will see positive results on the part of the child and his behavior." (Hispanic)

"The family unit of the Hispanic culture is very strong. The counselor must commit himself to work with the entire family to be more effective. A good method is outreach counseling, where the child is counseled in his surroundings. Also, there is a family group consultation where two or three families (up to 20 people) are counseled with three counselors. A counselor must be aware of many methods of counseling. The family unit can be very effective in the counseling of a client in the family or a detrimental aspect— depending on how it's handled." (Non-Hispanic)

"Counselors should be aware of the possible importance of the family and consider the possibility of doing family counseling that might include aunts, uncles, cousins, etc., that are living in the house instead of doing individual counseling. Also, when the situation is understood, an extended family is able to offer support to a person experiencing emotional problems. A sense of responsibility to the family might cause a person to change his behavior where he would not do so just for himself. A counselor should also be aware that the wife or the child might not feel comfortable going against the wishes of the father." (Hispanic)

"In working with Hispanics, the counselor should consider ways in which he can assist the whole family in some form of education. Also, writing an IEP for the child will enable the family to get involved in his education." (Hispanic)

"Depends on the counselee and how willing he/she is to have other family members present." (Hispanic)

Hispanics have a sense of belonging to a community (La Raza) which is very distinct from the dominant culture. When programs are developed for them by Anglos at the national, state, or even local level without their input and participation, they may experience them as irrelevant and unresponsive to their needs and may not utilize their services.

Hispanics:	Agree 95%	Insufficient Information 4%	Disagree 11%
Non-Hispanics:	Agree 79%	Insufficient Information 17%	Disagree 4%

"This is why CETA didn't work. It was not a grassroots program." (Hispanic)

"Unless they are introduced to these programs very diplomatically, they may reject them." (Hispanic)

"It has been claimed that Hispanics do not take advantage of community mental health center services because they believe in curanderos and witchcraft. That is false. The true reason is that these programs are irrelevant to us." (Hispanic)

Therefore, counselors should actively encourage the participation of the Hispanic community in the planning and implementation of programs.

Hispanics:	Agree 95%	Insufficient Information 2%	Disagree 3%
Non-Hispanics:	Agree 94%	Insufficient Information 5%	Disagree 2%

Formal vs. Informal Relationships

Because one of the ways in which Hispanics demonstrate their respect for each other is through the maintenance of certain formal conventions like the use of the formal usted rather than the informal tú in conversation, Hispanics may mistake an Anglo's less formal approach to interpersonal relationships as a sign of disrespect.

Hispanics:　　　　　Agree 81%　Insufficient Information　9%　Disagree 11%
**Non-Hispanics:　Agree 76%　Insufficient Information 20%　Disagree　4%

"The Anglo's informal, to-the-point frankness in dealing with people differs from the very courteous and formal style of the Mexican-American. The Chicano, for example, typically engages in small talk before business-like discussions. The business-like, informal discussion between teacher and parent about a child's problem may easily offend the Mexican-American and can cause the Mexican-American to avoid visiting the school and create a negative attitude toward it." (Unknown)

"When counseling the Hispanics I have learned to let them lead. If they tú me, I tú them. Until they do I use the usted form and maintain as formal a relationship with them as they do with me." (Non-Hispanic)

"It really depends on individuals, warmth and how much they do things in other culturally appropriate ways." (Non-Hispanic)

"Any Hispanic who's been here six months understands the Anglo manner. It's the Anglos who don't understand the Hispanics." (Hispanic)

Therefore, counselors should respect the cultural expectations of the Hispanic parents with whom they work by maintaining a formal relationship with them until the parents indicate otherwise.

Hispanics:　　　　Agree 91%　Insufficient Information　3%　Disagree　7%
Non-Hispanics:　Agree 85%　Insufficient Information 14%　Disagree　1%

Therefore, when counselors believe that it is necessary to put such parents at ease, to relax them, make the situation seem less formidable, etc., they should not use informality in their relationships as a technique. Such an unfamiliar unexpected relationship may make Hispanic parents even more uncomfortable and uneasy in the situation.

Hispanics:　　　　Agree 84%　Insufficient Information　7%　Disagree 10%
Non-Hispanics:　Agree 83%　Insufficient Information 16%　Disagree　2%

"This is important during the first few sessions." (Hispanic)

"I haven't found this—I think the key is to be sensitive to the individual situation." (Non-Hispanic)

Communication Styles

One area in which Anglos and Hispanics are likely to be markedly disparate is the area of manners, courtesy, interpersonal relations. Anglos are taught to value openness, frankness, and directness. They are much more likely to express themselves simply, briefly, and frequently bluntly. The traditional Hispanic approach requires the use of much diplomacy and tactfulness when communicating with another individual. Hispanics often find themselves in difficulty if they disagree with an Anglo's point of view. To them, direct argument or contradiction appears rude and disrespectful. On the surface they may seem agreeable, manners dictating that they do not reveal their genuine opinion openly unless they can take time to tactfully differ.

Hispanics: Agree 85%   Insufficient Information 8%   Disagree 7%
Non-Hispanics: Agree 81%   Insufficient Information 17%   Disagree 3%

"I agree here. Many times I agreed with my fellow teachers' opinions, but out of courtesy, on the surface, deep down I disagree. Perhaps because there isn't another Hispanic to support my idea or opinion and so as to keep that person's friendship." (Hispanic)

"This would be true of unacculturated Hispanics." (Hispanic)

"In the late 1960s the children of a number of paraprofessionals whom I worked with had difficulty in school. The typical response of their parents was to ask me to visit the school to find out what it was that their children were doing wrong. These were the days before bilingual cross-cultural education programs. Usually, the problem was that the children, who spoke little English, did not understand their teachers, who spoke even less Spanish. On three different occasions the school authorities wanted to place the children in special education programs. It took a tremendous amount of counseling on my part to get their parents to question the school's decision even though at home their children behaved perfectly normal. It was obvious that to these parents the idea of questioning the decisions of educators was next to unimaginable. (Non-Hispanic)

Therefore, counselors should encourage Hispanic parents to ask questions when they do not understand and express their opinions when they disagree. Moreover, counselors should not interpret polite acquiescence on the part of Hispanic parents to mean that they truly agree with what they have merely acquiesced to.

Hispanics: Agree 95%   Insufficient Information 1%   Disagree 4%
Non-Hispanics: Agree 94%   Insufficient Information 4%   Disagree 2%

"Many Hispanics hold the belief that a teacher, doctor, or other professionals 'know best' and are unaccustomed to being asked to share their opinion about their child's education and much less take an active part in it. This would especially affect a child for whom extra attention and tutoring were necessary due to a learning disability. For most Hispanics, their exposure to any form of special education would be limited or none at all. This could also explain the confusion of many parents when confronted with a team of professionals at a meeting where, often without previous explanation of any kind, a parent is presented with materials he/she doesn't understand for a purpose he/she does not understand. It is for this reason that it would be important for the counselor to meet with the parents more than once in order to enable the parents to discuss the information alone and return with questions or doubts for further clarification by the counselor." (Non-Hispanic)

"In many of my home visits, I have found on several occasions the clients will listen politely and seemingly agree with what is being discussed. They seldom ask questions about methods or information given. The counselor or teacher may misinterpret this by thinking that the clients understand and really agree with everything discussed, when, in reality, they do not. It is a sign of respect not to disagree verbally." (Non-Hispanic)

"Many parents won't speak out because they are illegal and afraid.!" (Non-Hispanic)

Among Hispanics, conducting business or meetings in general is somewhat of a social affair. Digressions from the topic at hand make for a more personal, relaxed atmosphere. Counselors who have an Anglo "let's get down to business" or "let's stick to the point" approach may misperceive these digressions as avoidance or resistance.

Hispanics: Agree 81%   Insufficient Information 9%   Disagree 10%
Non-Hispanics: Agree 80%   Insufficient Information 17%   Disagree 4%

Therefore, when counseling Hispanic parents, counselors should not immediately call the parents back to the issue or point at hand.

Hispanics: Agree 73% Insufficient Information 6% Disagree 21%
**Non-Hispanics: Agree 68% Insufficient Information 20% Disagree 12%

> "Digressions is a loaded word. Hispanics are as capable of taking care of business as anyone else. The difference is in how you travel, not if you get there. (Non-Hispanic)

> "Only to an extent. Overloaded counselors may not have time for a lot of digressions." (Hispanic)

Therefore, when counseling Hispanic parents counselors should plan for sufficient time to accomplish their goals even if it takes more time or many more sessions.

Hispanics: Agree 90% Insufficient Information 4% Disagree 6%
Non-Hispanics: Agree 83% Insufficient Information 12% Disagree 5%

> "Great in theory, difficult for over-worked counselors to do in practice." (Hispanic)

> "Counselors often do not have the luxury of appropriating more time. The school counselors I have to come to know must carry a tremendous workload." (Non-Hispanic)

Hispanics maintain less physical distance between themselves when conversing than do Anglos.

Hispanics: Agree 82% Insufficient Information 7% Disagree 11%
Non-Hispanics: Agree 80% Insufficient Information 17% Disagree 3%

Therefore, counselors who are not accustomed to being in such close proximity to others when they speak may be tempted to increase the distance between themselves and the Hispanic parents they are counseling by sitting behind a desk, etc. However, counselors should allow their Hispanic counselees to determine the distance between them in order to make their counselees more comfortable in the counseling session.

Hispanics: Agree 81% Insufficient Information 7% Disagree 12%
Non-Hispanics: Agree 83% Insufficient Information 14% Disagree 4%

Attitude Toward Authority

Many Hispanics come from cultures which emphasize respect for authority. This is especially true of those whose families have not been a part of the power structure. They are generally used to being told what is right by government officials, priests, educators, etc., and to obey.

Hispanics: Agree 88%   Insufficient Information 6%   Disagree 6%
Non-Hispanics: Agree 84%   Insufficient Information 11%   Disagree 4%

"The Hispanic culture emphasizes respect for authority. Children and youth are taught respect for their parents, priests and ministers, and teachers. Although urban experiences have taught many Mexican-Americans to mistrust authority figures such as police, immigration officials, etc., it can be generally stated that this factor of respect for authority is still present in the counseling process. (Non-Hispanic)

"Although not all Latin Americans are the same, they tend to have authoritarian if not dictatorial governments." (Hispanic)

Coming from countries where citizens are expected not to question the law but to trust in the authorities, they may have difficulty participating in the educational decision-making process as described by PL 94-142. Unaccustomed to the concept of parents' rights in general and unaware of their specific rights under the law, it may be difficult to fulfill the role ascribed to them by PL 94-142, especially when it is in their children's best interest that they demand that school systems respect their rights or those of their children.

Hispanics: Agree 85%   Insufficient Information 8%   Disagree 7%
Non-Hispanics: Agree 82%   Insufficient Information 14%   Disagree 4%

In the counseling situation, where counselees are supposed to assume responsibility for the outcomes or decisions, this attitude will make the process more difficult. Out of respect for teachers and school authorities, parents may accept imposed decisions rather than exercise their rights or act out their disagreement.

Hispanics: Agree 87%   Insufficient Information 7%   Disagree 7%
Non-Hispanics: Agree 85%   Insufficient Information 11%   Disagree 4%

Therefore, counselors should emphasize their role as partners rather than authorities in the counseling process. They should make an effort to encourage parents to participate fully. Counselors should emphasize the role of receiving, accepting, understanding, clarifying, and supporting; they should avoid manipulating, commanding, or otherwise taking advantage of the client's tendency to "go along with" counselors out of respect for their authority alone rather than a personal commitment to change.

| Hispanics: | Agree 95% | Insufficient Information | 3% | Disagree | 2% |
| Non-Hispanics: | Agree 95% | Insufficient Information | 4% | Disagree | 1% |

> "I have found many of the parents I have talked with very trusting. They take what you say as if it were the truth, without questioning it. The counselor must promote independence within his relationship with his client. He must develop skills of reasoning and critical thinking. The clients must be taught that they do have a choice, and that they don't have to accept what they receive." (Non-Hispanic)

> "I agree. Without a personal commitment to change on the part of the parent, what is achieved is little more than lip service." (Non-Hispanic)

Therefore, counselors should inform Hispanic parents of their rights and responsibilities and those of their children and prepare, train and encourage them to exercise these rights and responsibilities during the educational decision-making process.

| Hispanics: | Agree 98% | Insufficient Information | 2% | Disagree | 1% |
| Non-Hispanics: | Agree 94% | Insufficient Information | 5% | Disagree | 1% |

Some Hispanic parents come from cultures where they are taught to be wary of signing documents. When they are asked to sign forms necessary for their evaluation of their children or the provision of special education services, they may be reluctant to do so.

| Hispanics: | Agree 80% | Insufficient Information | 9% | Disagree | 12% |
| **Non-Hispanics: | Agree 65% | Insufficient Information 27% | Disagree | 8% |

> "Especially if the documents are in English or... if the document is in Spanish but the parent does not know how to read." (Hispanic)

> "I haven't had this happen. It's more that they go along with it because the school is trusted." (Non-Hispanic)

Therefore, counselors should inform these Hispanic parents about the need for the evaluation and services and relate to them in ways which earn their trust. This can best be accomplished by understanding their special needs and relating to them as advocates rather than adversaries.

| Hispanics: | Agree 94% | Insufficient Information | 2% | Disagree | 4% |
| Non-Hispanics: | Agree 94% | Insufficient Information | 5% | Disagree | 1% |

The participants agreed with all of the following suggestions:

- Because family and community play important roles in the Hispanic culture, counselors should include family and community participation in the planning and provision of counseling services and should use the family as a motivating factor.
- Counselors should maintain formal relationships with Hispanic parents until they indicate otherwise.
- Counselors should read between the lines for hints of disagreement, reluctance, etc., when counseling Hispanic parents because the Hispanic approach requires much more diplomatic and tactful communication in such situations.
- Because of this and the fact that Hispanic parents may expect a certain amount of social intercourse during counseling sessions, counselors should allot more time than usual to accomplish their goals.
- Counselors should encourage Hispanic parents to play a more active and responsible role in the counseling process even though these parents may not be used to questioning the authorities in the countries from which they came. They should also actively attempt to earn their clients' trust because Hispanics who have been brought up in Latin America may be wary of signing documents.

Attitude Toward Counseling

Hispanics are proud and self-reliant. When they need assistance they tend to go to their families rather than public agencies for support. Many of them come from countries where public welfare type programs are virtually non-existent. Because of their pride and previous experience, they may be reluctant to accept free services for themselves or their children from public agencies.

| Hispanics: | Agree 85% | Insufficient Information | 4% | Disagree 11% |
| Non-Hispanics: | Agree 72% | Insufficient Information | 14% | Disagree 14% |

"Most Anglos don't realize this because all they can see is those who are receiving public support. They aren't aware of how many Hispanics will do almost anything to survive on their own, nor do they take into account how terrible many

Hispanics who receive public assistance feel about doing so." (Hispanic)

"Maybe for moral support but most are more than willing to accept financial support." (Hispanic)

"And some have no trouble at all accepting, or even asking for, free services (and some that might not necessarily be deserved)." (Non-Hispanic)

Therefore, counselors should be sensitive to this possibility and when necessary assure these parents that they are entitled to these services, have paid indirectly for them and in no way is it demanding to accept them.

| Hispanics: | Agree 96% | Insufficient Information | 0% | Disagree | 4% |
| Non-Hispanics: | Agree 89% | Insufficient Information | 8% | Disagree | 3% |

Hispanics who are accustomed to seeking the help of family members with their personal problems may not feel the need to discuss things with strangers regardless of their professional qualifications.

| Hispanics: | Agree 88% | Insufficient Information | 4% | Disagree | 8% |
| Non-Hispanics: | Agree 86% | Insufficient Information | 10% | Disagree | 5% |

"One of the most important pieces of cultural information for the counselor is probably the fact that most Hispanics will have never worked with a counselor before and feel quite uncomfortable talking of their personal lives and feelings with someone who is most likely neither a relative nor a close friend." (Non-Hispanic)

They may even experience the counseling process as an invasion of their privacy by a stranger.

| Hispanics: | Agree 87% | Insufficient Information | 5% | Disagree | 9% |
| Non-Hispanics: | Agree 83% | Insufficient Information | 12% | Disagree | 5% |

"Especially a non-Hispanic who doesn't understand their cultural make-up." (Hispanic)

"Families will not feel comfortable discussing family problems with a stranger. They would more likely discuss problems with a sister, aunt, uncle, or other family member. They would be resistant to 'open up' for a stranger. Counselors should really warm up to families, really work up to establishing rapport, etc., before getting down to clinical work." (Hispanic)

Therefore, counselors should spend a great deal of time building rapport and establishing trust, etc., before getting to the heart of the matter.

Hispanics:	Agree 90%	Insufficient Information	4%	Disagree	7%
Non-Hispanics:	Agree 91%	Insufficient Information	8%	Disagree	2%

Since Hispanic parents who do not perceive a need to speak to professional counselors will not seek out their services, counselors cannot wait passively for the initial contact to be initiated by them. Instead, they should actively offer their services, keeping in mind the importance of developing rapport and establishing trust before beginning to deal with important issues.

Hispanics:	Agree 95%	Insufficient Information	3%	Disagree	2%
Non-Hispanics:	Agree 87%	Insufficient Information	9%	Disagree	4%

Summary: Both Hispanic and non-Hispanic participants agreed that because Hispanics may be too proud to accept free services, counselors should actively offer their services to Hispanic parents. If the services are free, they should assure them that they are entitled to them. They also agreed that because some Hispanics may not feel comfortable talking to a counselor regardless of his or her professional qualifications, counselors should spend a great deal of time building rapport and trust with their counselees before getting to the heart of the matter.

Sex Role Differences

In traditional Hispanic families the male and female roles are very distinct. Among other differences the father tends to function as the authority and decision-maker while the mother is the nuturer and comforter.

Hispanics:	Agree 95%	Insufficient Information	1%	Disagree	4%
Non-Hispanics:	Agree 88%	Insufficient Information	8%	Disagree	4%

"The old command the young and the males command the females. Latino society rests firmly on a foundation of family solidarity and the concept of male superiority." (Hispanic)
"While this is still often true, times are changing especially for the single parent." (Hispanic)

"Even in traditional Hispanic families the mother (often) is the authoritative figure." (Hispanic)

"Studies are beginning to show that this dichotomy is stated too simply. Women in Hispanic families are often the ones who determine how the family income is spent. A study done for the purpose of developing effective recruitment techniques at the community college level has indicated that it is the mother in Hispanic families who decide who will go to college." (Non-Hispanic)

Therefore, counselors may find that *who* they see makes a big difference. If they want authority, they may want to counsel the father. If they want supportive treatment for a child, they may want to counsel the mother.

Hispanics: Agree 83%   Insufficient Information   4%   Disagree 13%
Non-Hispanics: Agree 84%   Insufficient Information 13%   Disagree   4%

"The Hispanic culture holds a different view of the traditional male/female roles. The male holds extensive power to make final decisions. This is considered to be his right and his responsibility. The female is seen as more pliant and supportive. Thus, any attempt to resolve a problem through a mother may be thwarted because she holds no decision making power. On the other hand, if some leeway in permitted behavior is desired, the mother may be the perfect person with whom to deal." (Hispanic)

"I don't think you want to perpetuate sexism." (Non-Hispanic)

Since in many traditional Hispanic families the members would not act contrary to the wishes of the father, counselors should avoid encouraging family members to change their behavior or attitudes until the father agrees.

Hispanics: Agree 63%   Insufficient Information 10%   Disagree 28%
**Non-Hispanics: Agree 62%   Insufficient Information 22%   Disagree 16%

"The male head of the family is often the most influential member of the Latino family and trying to change family dynamics without the dominant male's cooperation is unlikely in a traditional family. The counselor should be very sure that any techniques used will not violate a person's sense of being master of his own destiny and leader of his family." (Hispanic)

"This should be done on an individual basis only when the family fits this description."(Hispanic)

"That depends on the father! With some fathers, they would never change their views, and as a counselor your first concern is the child's survival. Sometimes you can reason with the father, sometimes not." (Unknown)

"The ideal male role is primarily defined by the concept of machismo. The women who suffer under this dominance are naturally resentful. Fewer and fewer women are willing to accept the traditional role assigned to them according to traditional values. Why should they? The counselor may find himself fulfilling the role of a psychiatrist. The Latino must understand that belittling others does not make a person superior. If we grow strong and secure in ourselves, we would not need to look down on and dominate others. We must respect and take care of our old people, but leadership and authority should be in the hands of the most able and the wise." (Hispanic)

"This has become less true, especially in third- and fourth-generation families." (Hispanic)

Summary: Although the participants agreed that in Hispanic families the roles of mother and father are still quite distinct, many of them expressed the opinion that these role differences are no longer as sharp. Believing that these role differences continue to persist, at least to some degree, the participants also agreed that when counselors want parents to exert more authority over their children, they should look towards the fathers, and when they want parents to be more nurturing and supportive, they should seek this from the mothers. They also agreed but to a lesser degree that counselors should avoid encouraging family members to change until the father who tends to have the authority in the family has changed.

Concept of Time

The Hispanic concept of punctuality is different than that of the Anglo. As a result, Hispanic parents may not arrive "on time" for meetings and counseling sessions when "on time" is defined in Anglo terms.

Hispanics:	Agree 73%	Insufficient Information 4%	Disagree 23%
Non-Hispanics:	Agree 84%	Insufficient Information 12%	Disagree 4%

"This is true of Hispanics who have not yet acculturated to

the American concept of time. However, these unacculturated parents are not aware that they are arriving late. As soon
as they become cognizant of the way school officials operate,
they adapt." (Hispanic)

"I've heard this but haven't seen it here. Occassionally, a
parent will agree to meet and won't show up, but usually
they are on time." (Non-Hispanic)

"Breaking Hispanic rules of punctuality is as offensive to a
Hispanic community as breaking Anglo rules is in an Anglo
one." (Non-Hispanic)

Therefore, counselors should neither assume Hispanic parents
will arrive promptly for meetings nor interpret their lateness to be
a sign of resistance to or disinterest in the counseling process.

Hispanics: Agree 74% Insufficient Information 6% Disagree 20%
Non-Hispanics: Agree 80% Insufficient Information 13% Disagree 7%

Language Differences

Because many Hispanic parents are not fluent in English,
counselors should not assume that the Hispanic parents of
bilingual students are also bilingual. Since these parents are
unable to participate in counseling meetings and other school
activities when only English is spoken, communication in the
form of notices, etc., should be sent to the homes in Spanish as
well as English and counseling sessions, meetings, and confer-
ences should be conducted in Spanish, if possible, or a Spanish-
speaking interpreter should be utilized.

Hispanics: Agree 98% Insufficient Information 1% Disagree 1%
Non-Hispanics: Agree 97% Insufficient Information 2% Disagree 1%

"Mexican-American parents tend to have limited understanding in English communication. Among the bilingual
special educators this may seem overly obvious, but I have
included it because in my experience monolingual English
speakers in the school setting have been particularly insensitive to these needs. Counselors and special educators should
not assume that once children have become bilingual that
their parents are also bilingual. Parents often live in
neighborhoods, work at jobs, and attend social functions

where there is no need or opportunity to learn English. Economic needs often make attendance at night school English classes impossible. Parents often have limited education in their native language as well, so self-taught English programs are not always effective either. In order for counseling with lower socio-economic Hispanics to be effective, counselors and certificated school personnel must be bilingual. All I.E.P. planning meetings should include at least one bilingual professional. Translators are often inadequate at I.E.P. meetings, since professional expertise and knowledge of educational 'jargon' in Spanish is often prerequisite to effective communication. In counseling and therapy sessions the knowledge of the client's native language and local vocabulary is also critical. Without these skills mistrust and misunderstanding is sure to be the result." (Non-Hispanic)

"The level of English fluency will affect the ability to interact and exchange information. Words that are commonly known here, such as educational jargon, are not familiar to the Hispanic. Schools frequently try to improve the communication by providing notices that have been translated. If these translations are poorly done, they serve only to increase the strain and distance between the family and the mainstream as well as casting doubts on the credibility of the school. Lastly, language can affect the accessibility of a number of important community resources." (Hispanic)

"It is highly recommended that a counselor with Hispanic clientele be able to speak the Spanish language rather fluently. It is most imperative that the counselor be able to *communicate* in the style of the level of the counselee if he is to be effective. He should be aware of the subcultural language in the barrios and their colloquialisms." (Hispanic)

"According to statistics there are about four million Spanish-speaking people in the Southwest. For many of them, English is a second language. The counselor should be aware that some parents may feel ashamed of their poor command of English and may therefore be reluctant to communicate with the school or be receptive to home visits by school personnel. If the counselor is non-Spanish speaking, he should have an interpreter to facilitate the counseling session." (Hispanic)

"Beware the Tex-Mex or Angeleno Spanglish school communication which confounds more than clarifies. In my experience, it is the rule not the exception." (Unknown)

"Parents are here by choice, not coercion. They should learn English or have someone from home translate—not all should be done for them at school." (Unknown)

"In my school district, we are probably more aware of this problem than any other district, as we have more Hispanics *in proportion* than any other district in the state. Therefore, my answers may be totally different than others who do not teach in a city whose ethnic make-up is over 50 percent Hispanic. The problem in doing such counseling is time and language. In a district where Hispanics number in the low hundreds, it's one thing. In our district, we number in the thousands. Unfortunately, there are not enough bilingual and/or bicultural personnel available. (We also have an unprecedented number of Asians with some of the same and totally different problems.)" (Unknown)

Many Hispanic parents who have learned English as a second language have not been exposed to the educational jargon used by educators and other school officials. As a result, when jargon is used they may misunderstand what is being communicated or they may decide to avoid contact with school altogether.

Hispanics:	Agree 93%	Insufficient Information 3%	Disagree 4%
Non-Hispanics:	Agree 90%	Insufficient Information 6%	Disagree 4%

Therefore, counselors should avoid using educational jargon when communicating with Hispanic parents.

Hispanics:	Agree 88%	Insufficient Information 4%	Disagree 9%
Non-Hispanics:	Agree 91%	Insufficient Information 5%	Disagree 5%

Summary: The participants agreed that counselors should not assume that the parents of Hispanic students who speak English are also fluent in English. They also agreed that counselors and other school officials should communicate in Spanish with non-English speaking Hispanic parents and avoid the use of educational jargon with parents who have learned English as a second language.

Acculturation

Like many other people with roots in more than one country or culture, Hispanics have many alternative ways of viewing who they are. They may identify with the country and culture in which they or their families originated and conceive of themselves as Spaniards, Mexicans, Puerto Ricans, Cubans, Chileans, etc. They may identify with both their original and current cultures and think of themselves as Cuban-Americans, Puerto Rican-Americans, Mexican-Americans, Chicanos, Spanish-Americans, etc. Or they may identify themselves solely in terms of their current residence and consider themselves to be Americans.

Hispanics:	Agree 93%	Insufficient Information 1%	Disagree 6%
Non-Hispanics:	Agree 88%	Insufficient Information 8%	Disagree 4%

Therefore, counselors should be aware of the cultural and national terms within which Hispanic parents define themselves and they should address the parents appropriately.

Hispanics:	Agree 95%	Insufficient Information 1%	Disagree 3%
Non-Hispanics:	Agree 91%	Insufficient Information 8%	Disagree 2%

> "At a very basic level, the counselor must desire to get to know the client and find out as much as possible about him/her." (Hispanic)

> "Unrealistic. It would be too difficult to achieve." (Non-Hispanic)

Hispanics who are affected by cultural pluralism may have difficutly resolving the conflicting cultural pressures and demands. Those who assimilate or acculturate rapidly may experience less pressure than those who try to either maintain their original culture or satisfy both cultures.

Hispanics:	Agree 77%	Insufficient Information 8%	Disagree 15%
Non-Hispanics:	Agree 73%	Insufficient Information 19%	Disagree 8%

> "It is more important to know the implications of living in two cultures than to know all the factors involved in each culture. Bridging two cultures often creates internal conflicts in what it means to be a successful individual, what one should do with his time, what directions one's life should take and what role in society is desirable. A Latino's problem may be caused by these conflicts, the difficulty or implausibility of acculturation. He has to deal with a different color, a

different language, a different culture and sometimes a different socio-economic level. The Latino may have difficulty establishing and maintaining his identity balancing between two cultures (i.e. competitiveness vs. cooperativeness, extended vs. nuclear family, demands at school vs. demands at home and/or peer group, etc.)." (Hispanic)

"Fabrega and Wallace (1968) found that among Mexican-American patients hospitalized for psychiatric care, those more marginally acculturated had the highest number of hospitalizations, in comparison to those who were either traditional or highly acculturated. The counselor needs to be aware that a client who is only marginally acculturated may be subject to more conditions causing psychological stress. He or she may not feel part of any group and thus seek group identity in a gang or club and may be very unsure of their self-identity." (Hispanic)

"Cultural conflict and difficulty in adjusting is when assimilation is the goal of the professional and not the goal of Hispanics." (Hispanic)

Therefore, knowing how Hispanic parents have resolved their cultural conflicts may provide counselors important information about how to relate to them, what techniques to use with them and what kinds of solutions they will be able to accept for their problems with their children.

Hispanics:	Agree 94%	Insufficient Information	3%	Disagree	3%
Non-Hispanics:	Agree 89%	Insufficient Information	9%	Disagree	2%

"The degree of acculturation has an effect upon several areas. Firstly, the male/female roles are changed by the degree of acculturation. Secondly, well-meant questions that seek helpful information may be viewed as an invasion of privacy in a less acculturated family. Thirdly, the poorly acculturated individual may not know *how* to go about using community resources. Fourthly, those who are not highly acculturated may suffer from a lack of self-esteem and confidence. Fifthly, those newly arrived from other countries may have dealt with authoritarian governments. They may fear that any questioning of institutions or protection of legal rights may result in deportation. Some families may react to expressions of concern as interference with family values and not appropriate for outsiders meddling. Lastly acculturation may affect the willingness to enter into the counseling process. Hispanic culture values the extended family and may feel that problems should be dealt with at home." (Hispanic)

"This is difficult to achieve. This is a very sensitive topic and Hispanic parents may not be willing to consider or discuss this with counselors. They may not even think about themselves in these terms." (Hispanic)

Summary: A high percentage of participants agreed that when counseling Hispanic parents, counselors should use techniques which are appropriate for the way their counselees have resolved their cultural identity problems.

Limited Economic Resources

Hispanic families with limited economic resources in need of counseling are often in a double bind if counselors cannot be flexible in scheduling appointments and availability of services. Typically, jobs which lower-economic people have are not flexible regarding work hours, absenteeism, etc. Parents often cannot leave work to attend daytime appointments. If counseling facilities are far from neighborhoods, parents often find it a hardship to arrange transportation, provide for babysitters, etc. Special treatments, counseling fees for private therapy, etc., are often impossible to include in the family budget. Time to attend regular counseling sessions, even if they are scheduled during non-working hours, is often not possible due to family obligations of housework, meal preparation, child care. Family priorities must often take precedence over attendance at school functions, meetings, etc. Among poor families, the necessities of day-to-day existence such as trips to the grocery store or laundromat, emergency health needs, car trouble, etc., are of primary importance.

Hispanics: Agree 95% Insufficient Information 3% Disagree 3%
Non-Hispanics: Agree 92% Insufficient Information 4% Disagree 4%

"In the educational field there are often attempts to involve parents through community projects and get-togethers.

Families may view this as an unfair demand on their time and resources. Lastly, since low-income families often rely on welfare or food stamps to supplement their income, they may view the school or counselor with the same enmity with which the social worker is greeted." (Hispanic)

"Many parents bring their children along because they don't want to leave them with sitters or anyone except close relatives or friends. They take their children everywhere." (Hispanic)

"Isn't this true for all poor people?" (Unknown)

Therefore, counselors should adapt to the needs of these parents by seeking financial assistance for long-term therapy, providing areas for children to play while parents attend counseling, and by being available informally at youth functions, etc.

Hispanics:	Agree 92%	Insufficient Information	4%	Disagree	5%
Non-Hispanics:	Agree 89%	Insufficient Information	8%	Disagree	3%

Therefore, counselors should offer to work with the family in its natural environment, at home, rather than expecting the family to visit the school, especially when it requires expenditures for car fare, babysitting or loss of time at work.

Hispanics:	Agree 89%	Insufficient Information	5%	Disagree	7%
Non-Hispanics:	Agree 83%	Insufficient Information	8%	Disagree	9%

"I have found that I accomplish more during one home visit than a year's worth of sending home letters and notices in Spanish and parent-teacher conference days." (Non-Hispanic)

If it's possible." (Non-Hispanic)

"Priorities? Parents take children out of school for a whole day for a half-hour appointment with a doctor, dentist, etc., that is *after* school hours. Parents pull students out of school so the parents can go 'shopping,' to Los Angeles, etc., but parents never have time to talk to counselors during or after school, return teacher's calls, etc. I very often have a hard time talking to parents after *their* working ours—student answers, says parent is not home, etc. I do find the parents very cooperative when I do reach them. Students generally are doing something they don't want their parents to know. (Anglos are no different.)" (Non-Hispanic)

At times there may be significant differences between the parents' values and those of the school, e.g., parents may feel it is more important that a daughter help out at home or a son earn money than attend school. At such times these parents may feel that the school system is interfering in their lives or even trying to take control of their children.

Hispanics: Agree 84%   Insufficient Information   5%   Disagree 12%
Non-Hispanics: Agree 87%   Insufficient Information 10%   Disagree 3%

> "The high dropout rate of Hispanics is not indicative of their educational aspirations. On the contrary, they come from families that stress and emphasize the value of education." (Hispanic)

> "I have never known Hispanic parents to feel that the school was trying to take control of their children." (Non-Hispanic)

> "I feel that most importantly the teacher should always keep in mind that although the parents of minority children may not always present a model of what they would like their children to become when they grow up, they nonetheless have the same expectations for their children as all other parents. They want their children to become responsible, self-sufficient (as much as possible) members of society." (Hispanic)

Therefore, when these conflicts exist counselors should respect the values of the parents. Instead of trying to change them, counselors should provide the parents with the additional information necessary for the parents to evaluate whether their values are appropriate for their current situation. Then they should abide by the parents' wishes to the extent that it is legally possible to do so.

Hispanics: Agree 77%   Insufficient Information   4%   Disagree 19%
Non-Hispanics: Agree 77%   Insufficient Information 11%   Disagree 13%

> "How about offering the parents alternatives or even home tutors for a period of time if the youth's income is important for the subsistence of the family?" (Hispanic)

Therefore, while acknowledging that the parents' values might have been valid for their situations, counselors should inform them their children live in other circumstances and require other values.

Hispanics: Agree 79% Insufficient Information 6% Disagree 16%
**Non-Hispanics: Agree 56% Insufficient Information 21% Disagree 23%

> "Their child does not require other values but appropriate behavior for each social situation. This is a less threatening way to explain the problem." (Hispanic)

> "Hispanic parents would readily agree that their children live in other circumstances, but they would consider it an insult that an outsider would suggest that their children *require other values.*" (Hispanic)

Hispanics who have serious economic problems often justifiably attribute the cause of their frustrations, anger, etc., to the social and economic situation around them.

Hispanics: Agree 82% Insufficient Information 8% Disagree 10%
**Non-Hispanics: Agree 65% Insufficient Information 26% Disagree 9%

> "Not as often as we should. Unfortunately, we often blame ourselves even though there is little we can do about the oppression we experience." (Hispanic)

They may prefer concrete action on the part of counselors as opposed to talking in the resolution of their problems and concerns. They want action-oriented counselors who can be change agents, who will do their best to change the situation which is causing the problem rather than counselors who think they should adjust to or adapt to these conditions.

Hispanics: Agree 81% Insufficient Information 14% Disagree 6%
**Non-Hispanics: Agree 56% Insufficient Information 37% Disagree 7%

> "The lower socio-economic youth wants the counselor to be his advocate. He wants to not only see social change but also be a part of this social change. He wants more than just a discussion about his problems, he wants active methods of counseling which should be employed to give the youth means (effective) of affecting social change, without becoming negative or violent." (Non-Hispanic)

Summary: The participants agreed that when Hispanic parents with limited economic resources find it difficult to avail themselves of the counseling services offered them, counselors should assist them to do so by obtaining financial assistance when necessary, arranging for child care, making home visits, etc. They agreed that when these parents permit their economic necessities to take precedence over school requirements, counselors should help parents re-evaluate their values. Both groups of participants agreed that when Hispanics justifiably perceive that the cause of their frustrations and anger is the social or economic situation around them, they prefer counselors who will help them correct these situations as opposed to counselors who think they should adjust to these situations. However, many non-Hispanics reported that they lacked sufficient information or experience to judge the validity of these statements.

Prejudice

Some Hispanics have lost their trust and respect for Anglo institutions because of the prejudicial treatment they have received from employers, landlords, real estate agents, neighbors, welfare case workers, indifferent school officials, etc. This lack of trust may extend to counselors even when counselors do not merit such mistrust.

Hispanics: Agree 88%   Insufficient Information   6%   Disagree   6%
Non-Hispanics: Agree 86%   Insufficient Information 13%   Disagree   1%

"Unfortunately, I have encountered quite a few counselors who do merit the parents' mistrust, particularly those counselors who, for fear of losing their jobs, adhere strictly to school policies and attitudes, some of which can be very prejudicial." (Hispanic)

"The Anglo image of Latin Americans is very similar to that of the Chicano. Both are seen as foreign and inferior. When our children start school they are made to feel inferior merely because they are different from the Anglos. So we learn to look at our brothers and sisters that way. How else are we brainwashed? All through life, we are divided inside ourselves personally and among ourselves as a people. This is why, in the last few years, the Latinos have been talking about an 'identity problem.' This is why many Chicanos are now asking, Who am I? Who are we? What shall I call myself? Many of our people are confused. There are those who call themselves Hispanis or Spanish. But we have to be careful that when we say we are Spanish, we are not trying to deny our mestizo origins and culture. We must develop a feeling of group pride instead of self-hatred, unity instead of division. It means that we will build upon the history and culture that are ours. We must pay tribute to our ties with Mexico or Latin America and recognize our cultural roots. The history of America includes all races and should mean an absolute rejection of racism. If we are all races, then no one race can be superior. We are human beings and we have the same hopes as the Anglos, the same fears, the same drives, same desires, same concerns, same abilities. In the America of today, we can have justice and freedom and the same chance as the Anglos to become individuals, but we must find a national identity and throw off the sense of inferiority." (Hispanic)

"Many Hispanics have had bad experiences at counseling services due to discouraging institutional policies, long waiting lists, inflexible hours, irrelevant services, no transportation, services not centrally located and counselors who do not speak Spanish or know the Hispanic culture. The people responsible for setting up special service programs should study the area and find out the needs of the people being served. In this way the program will be more efficient and will reach more Hispanics in the community." (Non-Hispanic)

These Hispanic parents may also assume that counselors share the prevalent stereotype of Hispanics, such as they are disinterested in their children's school performance, lazy, stupid, dishonest, procrastinators, etc.

Hispanics:	Agree 84%	Insufficient Information	7%	Disagree	9%
**Non-Hispanics:	Agree 76%	Insufficient Information	20%	Disagree	4%

Those dependent on social welfare programs and undocumented aliens may be unwilling to confide in counselors for fear that the information might be used against them.

Hispanics:	Agree 95%	Insufficient Information	3%	Disagree	2%
Non-Hispanics:	Agree 90%	Insufficient Information	8%	Disagree	2%

"The correct label is undocumented worker, there is nothing alien about Hispanics." (Hispanic)

"I have found that many Mexican immigrants who do not have legal documentation to be in this country often: are unwilling to question any educational practice, are afraid and/or unable to come to school, think of themselves as inferior to school personnel because of the inability to speak English fluently and/or socio-economic class, are reluctant to answer questions about their family or give any information they think could lead to deportation (almost any question could be in this category), don't want assistance because they've never experienced the schools taking a personal interest in one of their children, will give and say they understand an educational assessment even when they don't." (Hispanic)

"The statments seem logical/possible. Luckily, perhaps, this has not been the case in my experience." (Non-Hispanic)

"Quite simply, a telephone call to the parents and a fair explanation of the situation/problem. You would get the support of Latino parents as opposed to the current middle class strategy that 'you don't touch or yell at my kid, he has his rights'." (Hispanic)

Therefore, counselors should try to empathize with the feelings of distrust of these parents. They should educate themselves about the extent of discrimination against Hispanics in the United States.

Hispanics: Agree 90%   Insufficient Information   6%   Disagree   5%
Non-Hispanics: Agree 90%   Insufficient Information   8%   Disagree   3%

"A counselor should be aware that most Mexican-Americans find themselves to be the object of prejudice at times and may feel anger, depression, decreased self-confidence, suspicion, or loss of self-esteem as a result. These are reactions to reality and should be dealt with as such." (Hispanic)

"The school system and society as a whole are incongruent in empathizing with unique cultures and characteristics. The counselor can break this chain of not understanding by permitting verbalization, by himself being a good listener. When the Latino client has confidence in you, he will confide in you like a true 'compañero.'" (Hispanic)

Therefore, counselors should act as advocates for Hispanic parents when they are confronted by discrimination.

Hispanics: Agree 85%   Insufficient Information   6%   Disagree   9%
Non-Hispanics: Agree 84%   Insufficient Information 10%   Disagree   5%

"Temporarily and not patronizingly. However, in the long run they should prepare Hispanic parents to advocate for themselves." (Hispanic)

"Where are we to find these guardian angels?" (Non-Hispanic)

Therefore, counselors should build bridges to the Hispanic community on a daily basis rather than to wait until crises develop and there are problems to be solved and issues to be resolved before contacting the community. In this way, they will already have established relationships of mutual respect, understanding and confidence on which to base their counseling relationships when the necessity arises.

Hispanics:	Agree 96%	Insufficient Information	2%	Disagree	2%
Non-Hispanics:	Agree 94%	Insufficient Information	5%	Disagree	2%

"Is this counselor going to walk on water, too?" (Non-Hispanic)

Therefore, counselors should point out to members of the dominant culture as well as the Hispanics with whom they work that respect and acceptance of other cultures and values is part of living in the United States.

Hispanics:	Agree 97%	Insufficient Information	1%	Disagree	2%
Non-Hispanics:	Agree 91%	Insufficient Information	7%	Disagree	2%

"I like the idea that it's not only the Hispanics but the Anglos as well who need to be educated. Too often all the responsibility for change is placed on our shoulders." (Hispanic)

"Ideally, this is so. But in real life, I feel that we are *striving towards* equality. Equality is certainly *not* a part of living in the United States, and all minority peoples are aware of this." (Non-Hispanic)

Therefore, counselors should attempt to correct stereotypes and myths about Hispanics.

Hispanics:	Agree 96%	Insufficient Information	3%	Disagree	2%
Non-Hispanics:	Agree 93%	Insufficient Information	5%	Disagree	2%

Therefore, counselors should explain that Hispanics are culturally different, not culturally deprived.

Hispanics:	Agree 96%	Insufficient Information	2%	Disagree	2%
Non-Hispanics:	Agree 91%	Insufficient Information	6%	Disagree	3%

Summary: The participants agreed that when counseling Hispanic parents counselors should take into account the prejudicial and discriminatory treatment Hispanics often experience and the mistrust this engenders in them. Specific ways in which counselors should adapt their techniques to these realities include building bridges to the Hispanic community, trying to empathize with their counselees' feelings of mistrust, advocating for them when they are discriminated against, correcting the stereotypes of Hispanics which are held by others, etc.

COUNSELING PARENTS OF HANDICAPPED STUDENTS

Beliefs about Handicapping Conditions

Some Hispanics believe that mental retardation, blindness, emotional problems, etc., can be caused by mal de ojo (bad eye), brujeria (witchcraft), alcohol abuse, looking at the moon at the wrong time, etc. As a result, they may prefer to rely on prayer, curanderismo, herbs, brujas and other methods as ways of alleviating their children's difficulties rather than the services offered by the schools and other agencies.

Hispanics: Agree 74%   Insufficient Information 12%   Disagree 14%
**Non-Hispanics: Agree 69%   Insufficient Information 28%   Disagree 3%

"I am an educated Hispanic who believes in the power of prayer as well as the value of certain medicinal herbs. Does that make me superstitious? Only if my religion is different than the person who is evaluating me. Miracles have occurred since time immemorial and will continue to occur despite the skepticism of modern man." (Hispanic)

"More likely to be true of Hispanics who have immigrated from rural areas and fairly recently and first generation." (Hispanic)

"Not the rule but generally true." (Hispanic)

"I suppose—though the people I've met seek help in other ways." (Hispanic)

"Not in the United States. My parents take their kids to the clinics." (Non-Hispanic)

"OVERGENERALIZATION!!!! You would have all people believe that all Hispanics believe in some kind of 'quackery.' While some people do believe in spiritualism and herbal curing, it is unfair to say that 'looking at the moon at the wrong time' would be considered a cause of mental retardation in the Hispanic community. " (Hispanic)

Some Hispanics believe that drinking too much, looking at the moon at the wrong time, leading a bad life, etc., may cause the birth of handicapped children. Holding themselves personally responsible for their children's disabilities, they may feel so guilty and ashamed that they may attempt to hide their children from others in the community.

Hispanics: Agree 66%   Insufficient Information 14%   Disagree 20%
**Non-Hispanics: Agree 57%   Insufficient Information 35%   Disagree 8%

"This is very typical of rural areas in Latin America, less so in the cities and only occasionally true of Hispanics living in the United States." (Non-Hispanic)

Therefore, while being respectful of their beliefs, counselors should educate parents about the actual causes of handicaps.

Hispanics: Agree 92%   Insufficient Information 4%   Disagree 4%
Non-Hispanics: Agree 91%   Insufficient Information 7%   Disagree 2%

"Yes, we need to counsel parents about the actual causes of handicaps; but there are some causes that we are not aware of ourselves, and the parents' views are just as authentic as ours." (Hispanic)

Therefore, while respecting the parents' beliefs and communicating this respect to the parents, counselors should attempt to persuade them to accept the services offered by educators, psychologists, doctors, social workers, etc., as well as the traditional herbalists, curanderos, etc.

Hispanics: Agree 80%   Insufficient Information 8%   Disagree 12%
Non-Hispanics: Agree 79%   Insufficient Information 15%   Disagree 6%

Therefore, when counseling parents who believe fervently in these methods, counselors should consider working in conjunction with people in the community such as priest, curanderos, herbalists, who provide these kids of treatments.

Hispanics: Agree 63%   Insufficient Information 13%   Disagree 23%
**Non-Hispanics: Agree 66%   Insufficient Information 22%   Disagree 12%

"Right! This may be the only effective method with them."
(Hispanic)

"Curanderos—come on!" (Non-Hispanic)

Therefore, counselors should not utilize the counseling relationship as a vehicle to encourage Hispanic parents to change from their own cultural frame of reference to the reference of the majority or dominant culture at the expense of their own desires and identity even if counselors believe that it would be to the advantage of the parents or their children to do so.

Hispanics: Agree 71% Insufficient Information 9% Disagree 20%
**Non-Hispanics: Agree 60% Insufficient Information 24% Disagree 16%

"Strongly agree. This is a counseling session not an acculturation session." (Hispanic)

"*Good!* In other words, respect the *differences.*" (Hispanic)

"This is an extremely important principle which Anglo counselors should be aware of." (Hispanic)

"Maybe not changing their frame of reference but certainly changing behaviors which are self-defeating, for example; defending the child even when he is wrong." (Hispanic)

"Can we maintain a democracy and our freedom without a common culture?" (Non-Hispanic)

Some Hispanics believe that their misfortunes are inflicted on them by God as punishments for their sins. They may believe that their handicapped children are the crosses God has given them to bear. As a result they *may be* reluctant to attempt to thwart God's will by trying to change the condition of their children.

Hispanics: Agree 65% Insufficient Information 11% Disagree 24%
**Non-Hispanics: Agree 62% Insufficient Information 30% Disagree 8%

"Some families may fear that trying to ameliorate a problem is somehow going contrary to the will of God. The degree of acculturation is important to the seriousness with which religion is viewed." (Hispanic)

"Padres de niños retardos no culpan al niño por su afliioń, si no se culpan ellos mismos. El niño es recibido por todos los de la familia porque el niño no tiene la culpa que ha nacido. Los padres lo reciben con cariño y ven los que ha sucedido como algo que les ha venido a ellos por su naturaleza, por algo que deben, o un castigo. Por eso es dificil hacerlos ver que es posible darles ayuda, no es porque no quieren ayudarle al niño. Es su cruz, y la llevarán o se cargará con paciencia. (Parents of retarded children blame themselves not their children for their offspring's afflictions. They are accepted by all of the members of the family since their condition is beyond their control. Their parents treat them with great affection and believe what has happened to them is the result of a punishment the parents deserve. That is why it is difficult to help the parents realize that their children can be helped, not because they do not want to help them. It is their cross and they will bear it patiently." (Hispanic)

"Whereas they may feel that it is a cross to be born, most parents want to help their children in any way that they can." (Hispanic)

"This is a very individual matter and is less true for Hispanics living in the United States." (Hispanic)

"This is a function of socioeconomic status and religious fervor, *not ethnicity.* (Hispanic)

"Whereas I agree with the first two sentences of the statement, I disagree with the last sentence." (Hispanic)

"Haga uno lo que haga, todo es lo que Dios quiere" (Do what we will, everything is in the hands of God) is a saying that sums up the fatalistic philosophy of many Hispanics. Believing that God rather than man controls the events of their lives, many Hispanics try to accept and appreciate what Anglos try to control and overcome. This may make it difficult for some Hispanics to believe that their handicapped children can be helped.

Hispanics:	Agree 70%	Insufficient Information 9%	Disagree 22%
Non-Hispanics:	Agree 77%	Insufficient Information 17%	Disagree 7%

"What the Anglo tries to control, the Latino tries to accept. Misfortune is something the Anglo tries to overcome and the Latino views as fate. Acceptance and appreciation of things as they are constitute primary values of La Raza. Since God, rather than man, is viewed as controlling events, the Latino lacks the future orientation of the Anglo and his passion for planning ahead. He lives for today instead of creating a blueprint for the future. Latinos must be taught to realize that an attitude of resignation is not acceptable. We shape our destiny by our efforts and action. It may be that we will fail in spite of our efforts, but we cannot hope to succeed if we don't even try." (Hispanic)

"Although Mexican-American families do not necessarily attend church regularly, religion generally has an effect on their life philosophy. In my experience I have seen that most lower socio-economic Mexican-Americans have a fatalistic attitude towards life. They tend to accept their poverty, their inability to change their lives, or their children's, as God's will. Among migrant families, future plans are seldom discussed without inclusion of the phrase 'Si Dios Quiere' (God willing). They will often accept a handicapped child in the family for what he is and so may not seek maximum services for the education of that child. The intellectual abilities of their children often are limited when parents make statements such as 'Pobre Martin! El es bien burro' (he's really stupid) or 'Mi hija es muy mensa' (my daughter is very stupid). This attitude toward a child by its parents may become a self-fulfilling prophecy. Families are not always able to recognize their child's potential to 'change' or improve conditions through counseling or education. Counselors should try to demonstrate the validity of the counseling process as a way to change or 'undo' existing conditions." (Non-Hispanic)

Therefore, when counseling Hispanic parents who have such fatalistic attitudes toward their handicapped children, counselors should be respectful and tread lightly on their beliefs about what *should* be done to help their handicapped children. At the same time, counselors should make every effort to inform these parents about what *could* be done to help these children. When the parents are aware of what could be done, they may be more able to change their attitudes about doing it.

Hispanics:	Agree 94%	Insufficient Information	4%	Disagree	2%
Non-Hispanics:	Agree 94%	Insufficient Information	4%	Disagree	2%

"As a professor of special eduction, I have found that many of my students are very skeptical about this and are rather intolerant of these parental attitudes." (Non-Hispanic)

"Since religion is very strong, I use the statement 'God helps those who help themselves' a lot in my counseling sessions for these situations." (Hispanic)

"Maybe not change their attitudes, but maybe more receptive to suggestions to help their children." (Hispanic)

"I've never met any Hispanic family that didn't want their handicapped child helped." (Unknown)

The parish priest may be an effective ally in this endeavor.

Hispanics: Agree 81%   Insufficient Information 9%   Disagree 10%
Non-Hispanics: Agree 78%   Insufficient Information 19%   Disagree 3%

"I can personally attest to this." (Hispanic)

"The Catholic religion and religious beliefs are an important part of the Mexican-American culture. Priests carry a great deal of power and respect within the community. When counseling a particularly resistant family, it might be very helpful to consult the priest of the parish and build a good rapport with him. With the priest's help it might be easier to develop a better rapport with the family, thus being more effective in counseling the family or client." (Non-Hispanic)

"Hardly any of my Hispanic students go to church or even know very much about God or Jesus." (Non-Hispanic)

"A recent study in my area shows that there is no such thing as a parish priest for Hispanics." (Non-Hispanic)

Hispanic parents who believe that their children's handicaps are the will of God tend to be more accepting and protective of their children who are seen as "los benditos de Dios."

Hispanics: Agree 78%   Insufficient Information 12%   Disagree 10%
**Non-Hispanics: Agree 68%   Insufficient Information 29%   Disagree 3%

"This is one reason why fewer severely handicapped people are institutionalized in Latin America even when services are available." (Non-Hispanic)

"Some parents have come here to get help from other countries in Latin America where services are limited or non-existent." (Hispanic)

"Some parents accept but do not protect. Accepting and protecting are totally different things." (Non-Hispanic)

Therefore, when counseling such parents counselors should capitalize on their positive attitudes toward their children's difficulties.

Hispanics: Agree 92%   Insufficient Information 3%   Disagree 5%
Non-Hispanics: Agree 87%   Insufficient Information 12%   Disagree 1%

In comparison to Anglos, Hispanics are more likely to believe that behavior is controlled on a conscious level through will-power rather than unconscious intro-psychic motivation.

*Hispanics: Agree 68%   Insufficient Information 24%   Disagree 8%
**Non-Hispanics: Agree 40%   Insufficient Information 50%   Disagree 11%

As a result, some Hispanic parents may believe that their children's misconduct or learning problems are caused by laziness and stubbornness rather than emotional, psychological or neurological problems beyond their control.

Hispanics: Agree 81%   Insufficient Information 6%   Disagree 12%
**Non-Hispanics: Agree 66%   Insufficient Information 28%   Disagree 7%

> "This is exactly true of the parents of my students." (Non-Hispanic)

Therefore, when necessary, counselors should educate Hispanic parents regarding the true cause of their children's problems in school so that they will understand why their children would benefit from appropriate special education services.

Hispanics: Agree 96%   Insufficient Information 3%   Disagree 1%
Non-Hispanics: Agree 91%   Insufficient Information 7%   Disagree 2%

When the difficulties of handicapped children are caused by or aggravated by emotional problems or unconscious conflicts, educators should explain these facts to their parents. And they should explain why the children are *unable* rather than *unwilling* to fulfill the expectations their parents and others have for them. When the parents have accepted these explanations, counselors can suggest non-behavioral techniques to the parents.

Hispanics: Agree 91%   Insufficient Information 7%   Disagree 2%
Non-Hispanics: Agree 85%   Insufficient Information 11%   Disagree 4%

Therefore, if Hispanic parents resist or reject counselors' suggestions that their children's behavior or their own behavior is based on unconscious motivation, counselors should distinguish when this resistance is based on cultural beliefs rather than defensive reactions and proceed accordingly.

Hispanics: Agree 87%   Insufficient Information 7%   Disagree 6%
Non-Hispanics: Agree 81%   Insufficient Information 18%   Disagree 1%

Believing that behavior is subject to conscious control, Hispanic parents are more likely to utilize behavior modification techniques in order to control their children's behavior than techniques which are designed to change their children's dynamics or resolve their problems.

*Hispanics: Agree 70%   Insufficient Information 18%   Disagree 11%
**Non-Hispanics: Agree 46%   Insufficient Information 44%   Disagree 10%

Hispanics tend to utilize corporal punishment more and deprivation of love and affection less when disciplining their children. Thus, when counselors report that the school is having difficulty with their children, some Hispanics may respond that they will hit them.

Hispanics: Agree 86%   Insufficient Information 4%   Disagree 10%
**Non-Hispanics: Agree 75%   Insufficient Information 22%   Disagree 3%

Therefore, if this occurs, counselors should respond by saying something like, "thank you for your support. I agree with you that we need to be very firm. At home parents can hit their children if they wish. However, in school we have to use other means of disciplining them."

Hispanics: Agree 74%   Insufficient Information 6%   Disagree 20%
Non-Hispanics: Agree 68%   Insufficient Information 14%   Disagree 18%

> "I could never say 'at home parents can hit their children if they wish.' That would be condoning it. This practice, in my opinion, is related strongly to social class and/or educational background—it is *not* true of all." (Hispanic)

> "This is just as bad as encouraging corporal punishment." (Non-Hispanic)

Therefore, counselors who disagree with the use of corporal punishment should not criticize Hispanic parents who use it, nor perceive them to be ineffective or abusive parents because they hit their children.

Hispanics: Agree 77%   Insufficient Information 6%   Disagree 17%
**Non-Hispanics: Agree 69%   Insufficient Information 21%   Disagree 10%

> "I'm not Hispanic, but when I was bad my mother made me take off my strap and hit me with it. I'd hate to tell you how many times this left red marks where she hit me on my bare behind, but I learned what to do and what not to do and I never thought she was cruel. She did the same to my sister and we both love her. It hurt for the moment but left no psychological aftereffects." (Non-Hispanic)

> "It is better to hit a child for being bad than to act like you no longer love him." (Hispanic)

> "We have to respect each others' child-rearing practices." (Hispanic)

"But they should not use statements which encourage corporal punishment either." (Non-Hispanic)

"Disagree. Interference is necessary when done to protect children." (Non-Hispanic)

"However, some Hispanic parents really beat them black and blue and we are reluctant to enlist their support in discipline." (Non-Hispanic)

"Child abuse can be a problem—especially with drinking parents—and parents should be encouraged to use new approaches." (Non-Hispanic)

Believing that behavior is consciously controlled, Hispanic parents tend to view their children's behavior as a reflection on the family and their ability as parents. They may become defensive when their children's misbehavior is brought to their attention.

Hispanics:	Agree 81%	Insufficient Information 5%	Disagree 15%
**Non-Hispanics:	Agree 70%	Insufficient Information 20%	Disagree 11%

"True, but have you ever spoken to an Anglo parent who wasn't the same way?" (Hispanic)

Therefore, counselors should avoid presenting children's behavior problems to their parents in ways that will make them defensive.

Hispanics:	Agree 86%	Insufficient Information 3%	Disagree 11%
Non-Hispanics:	Agree 88%	Insufficient Information 8%	Disagree 4%

Hispanics who believe that behavior is controlled on a conscious level may not have a great deal of faith in psyhchological counseling as a problem-solving approach and are more likely than Anglos to resist the use of these approaches with their children or themselves.

Hispanics:	Agree 81%	Insufficient Information 10%	Disagree 9%
**Non-Hispanics:	Agree 58%	Insufficient Information 36%	Disagree 7%

They may believe that psychological counseling is only suitable for the very disturbed or crazy.

Hispanics:	Agree 81%	Insufficient Information 7%	Disagree 10%
**Non-Hispanics:	Agree 63%	Insufficient Information 30%	Disagree 8%

"One of the many reasons why mental health centers fail to attract Hispanic clients." (Hispanic)

"Yes, but a lot of unsophisticated Anglos believe this too." (Hispanic)

Therefore, when working with such Hispanic parents, counselors should make referrals for psychological counseling using tact and compassion and other techniques so that it does not appear that they believe that either the parents or their children are crazy.

Hispanics: Agree 94%   Insufficient Information 4%   Disagree 3%
Non-Hispanics: Agree 85%   Insufficient Information 13%   Disagree 2%

> "Most lower class Mexican-American families are reluctant to participate in counseling. Possible reasons are: (a) they feel uncomfortable and/or inadequate; (b) they may not be accustomed to participating in community activities; (c) they may feel they lack necessary information; (d) they may fear leaving the security of their house and immediate neighborhood; (e) if they are here illegally, they may be afraid they will be expelled; (f) they may believe in accepting either their situation or what authority figures have told them; (g) lack of babysitting services. The counselor needs to be aware of the possible existence of these barriers and more. He needs to visit the family in the home, take time to build trust and rapport so that that family will feel comfortable with him and able to ask questions, reveal information, fears, anxieties, etc. The key is to be sensitive, open, understanding, supportive and honest." (Hispanic)

When Hispanic parents resist such referrals, counselors should determine when the resistance is due to cultural rather than psychological causes and act appropriately.

Hispanics: Agree 94%   Insufficient Information 3%   Disagree 3%
Non-Hispanics: Agree 85%   Insufficient Information 13%   Disagree 2%

> "Mexican parents, as a rule, resist referrals. They come to my wife, who had a child in the first grade, for advice. My wife and I usually review the case and we advise the parents. In most instances, we advise the parents not to place their children in special classes." (Hispanic)

> "The effective counselor of Hispanics must be open to the fact that the lower socio-economic level Mexican-American can be expected to be more reticent, less verbal, less ready for counseling, and more resistant to change. Because of this the counselor will need to spend more time in working on small steps toward a goal which will include an explanation of the counseling process to the client, considerable time

devoted to establishing rapport and trust before beginning to work on resolution of problems. Families in most cases will not seek the counselor's services; in many cases they will not even know that such services exist. Counselors will need to use tact and compassion when they explain services to families to decrease the risk of misunderstanding. Families may feel that services are made available only when their children are 'in trouble.' They may be embarrassed or afraid to go to the school; they may feel that they have no place in determining what is best for their child. They may lack information regarding their rights and available services. They may have never participated in any 'public' activities before. Counselors need to begin by educating families as to the value of counseling services. They need to meet parents' needs by being flexible and sensitive. Creative counseling approaches should be experimented with. Home counseling and family group counseling may be effective. Counselors should above all keep individual differences uppermost in mind and strive to truly understand the individual, not a stereotypical notion based on national origin or socio-economic status." (Non-Hispanic)

Summary: Both groups of participants agreed that Hispanic parents who believe that handicapping conditions are caused by such things as alcohol abuse, witchcraft, punishments for leading a bad life, etc., may rely on curanderos and herbs to cure their children or hide their children from others in the community. Or believing that these handicaps are the will of God, they may be reluctant to attempt to change or improve their children's condition or believe that it would be futile to attempt to do so.

While the participants agreed that counselors should respect the beliefs of their counselees and not use the counseling process to change their cultural frames of reference, they also agreed that counselors should counsel them regarding the actual causes of their children's handicaps and the fact that their children may have much more potential than they appear to have. The participants also agreed tht counselors should attempt to persuade these parents to accept the services of educators, psychologists, doctors, etc., as well as herbalists, curanderos, and that counselors should coordinate their services with the parish priest when appropriate. To a lesser extent, they also agreed that counselors should work in conjunction with herbalists and curanderos when their counselees have strong confidence in these practitioners. Although a majority of the non-Hispanics agreed with all of the above statements, many of them reported that they lacked sufficient information or experience to have opinions.

While the Hispanic participants agreed that Hispanics are more likely than Anglos to believe that behavior is controlled by willpower rather than unconscious motivation, 50 percent of the non-Hispanic participants stated that they had insufficient information or experience to judge whether it was true. However, they agreed with the majority of the Hispanic participants, who felt that some Hispanic parents may believe that their children's misconduct or learning problems are caused by laziness or stubbornness rather than problems beyond their control. Both groups of participants also agreed that when counseling Hispanics with these beliefs, counselors should explain when children are unable rather than unwilling to do things expected of them and distinguish when parents are unable to believe this for cultural reasons and when they resist such interpretations.

The participants likewise agreed that, believing that behavior is subject to conscious control, some Hispanic parents tend to become defensive about their children's behavior and are more likely to use behavior modification and corporal punishment to correct their children. They agreed that when working with defensive parents or those who use these techniques, counselors should discuss their children's problems in ways which will not make them defensive and should avoid criticizing the disciplinary techniques they use. If these parents reject psychological counseling because they believe it is inappropriate or only for very disturbed people, counselors should understand the cultural reasons for this rejection and use techniques which avoid giving the parents the impression that they believe that they or their children are very disturbed or crazy.

Difference in Educational Experiences

Some Hispanic parents may come from countries where disabled children do not receive special education. Thus, they may not seek such services for their children. This may be especially true of early stimulation and intervention.

Hispanics: Agree 88%   Insufficient Information 6% Disagree 6%
Non-Hispanics: Agree 93%   Insufficient Information 6% Disagree 1%

Some Hispanic parents may come from countries where many of the disabled fulfill acceptable community roles without special education. This may be especially true of rural agricultural areas. As a result, some Hispanic parents may think that special services beyond medical treatment are unnecessary.

Hispanics: Agree 77%   Insufficient Information 10% Disagree 13%
Non-Hispanics: Agree 79%   Insufficient Information 19% Disagree 2%

Because of the limited training the disabled receive in these countries, some Hispanics may not be aware of the disabled's potential for learning with appropriate special education services.

Hispanics: Agree 90%   Insufficient Information 5% Disagree 5%
Non-Hispanics: Agree 94%   Insufficient Information 4% Disagree 2%

Because of their educational experiences in their native countries, some Hispanic parents are unaware of the existence of some of the learning handicaps which require special educational services in the United States. They may ask themselves, if the schools in their native countries never noticed such things, why is their child's school blaming their child's difficulty on something they have neither heard of before nor observed in their child at home? This may lead them to reject both the diagnosis and the services offered to their child.

Hispanics: Agree 76%   Insufficient Information 12% Disagree 13%
**Non-Hispanics: Agree 71%   Insufficient Information 23% Disagree 7%

Therefore, counselors should educate Hispanic parents about both their children's special needs and the ways special educational services can provide for these needs.

Hispanics: Agree 95%   Insufficient Information 2% Disagree 3%
Non-Hispanics: Agree 92%   Insufficient Information 6% Disagree 2%

Therefore, counselors should actively seek out or search for disabled children in need of services within the Hispanic community.

Hispanics: Agree 84%   Insufficient Information 5% Disagree 13%
Non-Hispanics: Agree 83%   Insufficient Information 11% Disagree 6%

"Until we present these students to the authorities in charge there will be little pressure on them to provide services." (Hispanic)

"Ha! I have a two-year waiting period before the students in my bilingual class are tested." (Non-Hispanic)

"You know someone with the time and inclination?" (Non-Hispanic)

Therefore, counselors should educate the Hispanic community regarding the needs and potential of disabled children and the importance of early intervention.

Hispanics: Agree 95%   Insufficient Information   2%   Disagree   3%
Non-Hispanics: Agree 91%   Insufficient Information   8%   Disagree   1%

Hispanics with limited education may have different concepts of what constitutes sufficient education.

Hispanics: Agree 88%   Insufficient Information   4%   Disagree   7%
Non-Hispanics: Agree 90%   Insufficient Information   9%   Disagree   2%

"Their concept of what constitutes a 'good' education may differ from ours. We need to learn what their concept is and inform them of what we can and cannot do in our programs. Value should be placed on their concept." (Hispanic)

"This applies to all people with limited education." (Non-Hispanic)

Therefore, counselors should ascertain the educational goals that these parents have for their children and what they think is a good education and inform them of what is possible and necessary nowadays in the schools their children attend.

Hispanics: Agree 95%   Insufficient Information   3%   Disagree   2%
Non-Hispanics: Agree 95%   Insufficient Information   4%   Disagree   1%

"What is possible, yes, tone down or tactfully introduce the necessary." (Hispanic)

Therefore, when working with these Hispanics, counselors should be prepared to spend a great deal of time providing information and answering questions about concepts and ideas which well-educated persons are familiar with.

Hispanics: Agree 89%   Insufficient Information   5%   Disagree   6%
Non-Hispanics: Agree 88%   Insufficient Information   7%   Disagree   5%

Counselors should be aware that although these parents may want to help their children, because of their own lack of experience and education they may be unable to provide the assistance that many other parents can provide—for example, helping their children with their homework.

Hispanics: Agree 94%   Insufficient Information   2%   Disagree   3%
Non-Hispanics: Agree 93%   Insufficient Information   3%   Disagree   4%

"Lower socio-economic Hispanic parents may have limited education in varying degrees which may be influential in the counseling process. The following descriptions of parents I have known may help to clarify the different needs that parents bring to the counseling situation. A mother who cannot sign her name or read in her native language; she is embarrassed to reveal this to the counselor. When she receives notices in Spanish from the school she cannot read them; she depends on her husband, who has only gone to the third grade in Mexico, to handle the families 'academic' needs. Another mother has attended school to the sixth grade in Mexico, she does seasonal cannery work. She can understand some English, but she does not speak or read it. She can help her children at home with their assignments in Spanish and can help them understand math problems, but when they bring English homework she cannot help them. One of her children has a learning disability, but she interprets this as stubbornness, laziness on her child's part. She constantly compares the learning disabled child to her siblings and criticizes her inabilities. Another young mother came to the U.S. with her family when she was in the third grade. She attended school in the U.S. until the eighth grade, at which time she dropped out because of pregnancy. She speaks and reads English and Spanish. She has trouble handling her children at home and is embarrassed when she is called to the school because of her childrens' school problems. A widowed Mexican-American man, who considers himself a Chicano, attends the university. He is having trouble with the demands of raising four motherless children, keeping up with his studying, and finding time to meet his personal needs. In working with the four individuals which I have described, the sensitive counselor would need to take the role of educator on a variety of different levels. With the illiterate parent, the counselor would be essential in helping the parent to understand documents to be signed, making home visits and phone conversations to see that information and advice was relayed directly to the parent, and using a form of Spanish that was understandable to the parent in discussing her child's needs. The second mother needs to learn the differences between American/Mexican educational approaches so that she can be more nurturing to her L.D. child. She needs information about her child's disability in Spanish. The third mother might benefit from information on child rearing and child development. She needs to be informed and encouraged to seek help through a parent center or other agency. The fourth parent will be able to converse on an intellectual level with the counselor, but he still may find it difficult to share his emotions regarding his difficulties with his family and personal needs. Despite the fact that he speaks good English, a bilingual/bicultural counselor could probably more easily empathize and meet his needs. In all these cases the counselor would need to reach out to these parents to maximize his effectiveness. Regardless of the families' educational levels, the counselor would serve as educator to some extent in all cases." (Non-Hispanic)

"Spanish-speaking parents believe in the educational system but do not know how to help their youngsters due to language barriers or low educational schooling themselves, i.e., Raza teenagers need extra tutoring in science courses, but how can a man with a second grade level of education help his son figure out an algebra equation scientifically?" (Hispanic)

"If parents can't read nor write, they can still help their children with their homework by sitting with them. Their interest and *presence* is really all that is required. A counselor can relate this to parents." (Non-Hispanic)

Summary: The participants agreed that some Hispanic parents who come from countries where children do not receive special education, lack information about special education, mental health, and counseling services in the United States, or have had little education themselves, may not have the same perspective about special education services as Anglo parents.

Participants also agreed that for these reasons it may be necessary to actively seek out Hispanic disabled children in need of these services and counsel their parents about their special needs and the ways in which special education services can fulfill these needs, especially if intervention occurs early enough. They also agreed that when working with such parents, counselors should ascertain their perceptions about what would be a good and sufficient education for their children, explain the true potential of their handicapped children nowadays with special education intervention, if necessary, and be prepared to spend time providing information and answering questions about ideas which well-educated persons are familiar with.

Prejudice

Because of previous misplacement of non-handicapped Hispanic children in special education programs, many parents are now suspicious of such placements for their children even when they are appropriate.

Hispanics: Agree 88%   Insufficient Information 7%   Disagree 5%
**Non-Hispanics: Agree 70%   Insufficient Information 26%   Disagree 5%

Thus, while in the past a simple statement of the problem in school would be enough to gain the support of many Hispanic parents, nowadays many Hispanic parents are justifiably suspicious of school personnel.

Hispanics: Agree 80%   Insufficient Information 12%   Disagree 8%
**Non-Hispanics: Agree 58%   Insufficient Information 28%   Disagree 14%

> "If it weren't this way, Hispanics would have to be slow learners." (Hispanic)

> "We have to keep this in mind in case it is applicable to a particular family we are working with." (Non-Hispanic)

> "Not many. Most would support the school personnel although some would fit the description." (Hispanic)

Therefore, counselors should be advocates for Hispanic exceptional students and their parents. They should:

- Inform school authorities and colleagues of discriminatory and prejudicial procedures, materials, etc., which are being utilized in the school and suggest specific ways of eliminating them;
- Inform others of the needs of Hispanic exceptional students and suggest specific educational, economic and social services and changes and modifications in school procedures, instructional methods, curriculum content and classroom management techniques which would help satisfy these needs;

- Interpret the results of assessment procedures in ways that would make the results culturally and linguistically relevant;
- Offer information regarding parental rights, create a format for parents to express their concerns on important issues relevant to their life-styles, and assist them in obtaining the knowledge and skills needed to impact on the system.

Hispanics: Agree 87%   Insufficient Information 5% Disagree 7%
Non-Hispanics: Agree 89%   Insufficient Information 9% Disagree 2%

"We have a moral obligation to our students whom we are paid to help. Not to be advocates, to take the easy way out, not rock the boat and stand by while Hispanic students continue to be treated in a discriminatory and prejudicial manner would be to abuse the trust we want to merit." (Non-Hispanic)

"Key element is whether administrators are or would be receptive to these suggestions. Until they have been made to see the light, little can be accomplished." (Hispanic)

Summary: Hispanic participants agreed that Hispanic parents may be suspicious of school personnel and about placing their children in special education programs because of previous mistakes. Non-Hispanic participants agreed with this but to a lesser degree. Both groups of participants also agreed that because of such mistakes, counselors should function as advocates for Hispanic exceptional students and their parents.

SUMMARY

The statements included in this chapter elicited less controversy among the participants than those in the previous chapters. The participants agreed with all of the following suggestions for counseling Hispanic parents. They agreed that counselors should:

1. actively encourage the participation of the Hispanic community in the planning and implementation of the counseling programs which serve them;
2. enlist the family's assistance when necessary and consider the inclusion of both the immediate and extended family in group counseling when appropriate;
3. maintain formal relationships with their counselees until they indicate otherwise;

4. allow more time than usual to accomplish their counseling goals;
5. encourage parents to play a more active and responsible role in the counseling process;
6. actively offer their services to parents who may be unaccustomed to professional counseling and assure them that they are entitled to the free services for which they are eligible;
7. spend the necessary time to develop rapport and trust with their counselees before actually attempting to counsel them;
8. turn to the father when they want parents to exert more authority over their children and to the mother if more nurturance and support is needed;
9. not encourage family members to change their behavior until the father of the family is ready to make the desired change;
10. not assume that parents of students who are fluent in English are also fluent themselves;
11. communicate with non-English-speaking parents in Spanish and avoid using educational jargon with parents who have learned English as a second language;
12. accommodate their counseling techniques to the way their counselees identify themselves culturally;
13. help parents with limited economic resources to participate in counseling by counseling them at home and assisting them to obtain the financial assistance, child care services, etc., they require in order to participate in counseling sessions;
14. encourage parents who allow their economic necessities to take precedence over their children's education to re-evaluate their values;
15. facilitate the attempts of parents whose problems are caused by social or economic injustice to correct these situations rather than counsel them to adjust to the situations;
16. overcome the mistrust many parents may feel toward school officials, counselors, etc., by building bridges to the Hispanic community before there are problems to be solved, empathizing with their feelings of mistrust, and advocating for them when they are discriminated against.
17. respect their counselee's incorrect beliefs about the causes of handicapping conditions while counseling them regarding the true causes and their children's true potential;
18. counsel parents who prefer to rely on curanderos, herbalists,

etc., to help their handicapped children to accept the services of educators, psychologists and doctors as well;

19. coordinate their efforts with those of parish priests, herbalists, curanderos, and others when this may facilitate the counseling process;

20. help parents to understand when their children's learning and behavior problems are caused by things which they are unable rather than unwilling to control and detect when their counselees are unable rather than unwilling to accept the interpretations and information offered them;

21. utilize non-threatening techniques when counseling defensive parents;

22. avoid giving parents who believe counseling is only for very disturbed or crazy people the impression that they believe these parents or their children require counseling for this reason;

23. actively search out disabled children whose parents may not perceive that their children require special education or related services.

Chapter 6

ASSESSMENT

INTRODUCTION

Assessors can choose among many types of procedures to evaluate Hispanic students. Some of the ways in which these procedures differ are noted below.

1. formal vs. informal procedures
2. criteria-referenced vs. norm-referenced tests
3. national vs. regional norms
4. universal vs. pluralistic norms
5. English vs. Spanish language tests
6. translations and adaptations from English language tests vs. tests originally prepared for use with Hispanic students; vs. culture fair tests
7. timed vs. untimed tests
8. procedures which permit feedback about how the student is doing vs. tests which do not permit such feedback
9. instruments which require guessing vs. those which do not.

This chapter includes the participants' opinions and comments regarding appropriate assessment procedures for Hispanic students. The first section deals with assessment in general, while the second section is concerned with the evaluation of Hispanic students for placement in special education programs.

174

GENERAL PRINCIPLES

Some Hispanics come from countries where students are seldom assessed individually as they are in the United States. The strangeness and unfamiliarity of this situation may make Hispanic students anxious to the point that their anxiety interferes with their ability to demonstrate their achievement and potential.

Hispanics: Agree 71% Insufficient Information 19% Disagree 19%
**Non-Hispanics: Agree 70% Insufficient Information 25% Disagree 5%

Therefore, assessors should make special efforts to set Hispanic students at ease prior to and during assessment. If, despite these attempts, Hispanic students demonstrate high levels of anxiety, the results of their assessments should be invalidated.

Hispanics: Agree 68% Insufficient Information 13% Disagree 20%
Non-Hispanics: Agree 78% Insufficient Information 10% Disagree 12%

> "No student should be evaluated when they are anxious because they cannot do their best." (Non-Hispanic)

> "The results should be reported, not discarded, but with qualifications which describe the students emotional state at the time." (Non-Hispanic)

> "It would be a good idea in theory to put them at ease, but you have to have some means to evaluate them." (Non-Hispanic)

The Hispanic culture fosters a close personal interdependence among family members and close friends. Children especially are encouraged to rely on the help, support and opinions of adults in the extended family.

Hispanics: Agree 93% Insufficient Information 2% Disagree 5%
Non-Hispanics: Agree 85% Insufficient Information 13% Disagree 2%

As a result, some Hispanic students perform better on tests when they receive immediate feedback about the results of their attempts and when they experience assessors as involved and supportive.

Hispanics: Agree 84% Insufficient Information 10% Disagree 6%
Non-Hispanics: Agree 78% Insufficient Information 17% Disagree 5%

> "This is true for all students." (Non-Hispanic)

> "If assessors want to be involved and supportive, they should not use standardized tests with Hispanics because such tests

were not developed for them. No matter how supportive the assessor acts, standardized tests provide negative feedback to the students who realize how they are doing and who wants negative feedback?" (Hispanic)

Therefore, when evaluating Hispanic students, assessors should maintain an involved and supportive posture rather than a detached or objective posture with them.

Hispanics: Agree 80% Insufficient Information 9% Disagree 11%
Non-Hispanics: Agree 78% Insufficient Information 16% Disagree 6%

"This is fine as long as it does not invalidate the results." (Hispanic)

Therefore, Hispanic students should not be assessed with standardized instruments which do not permit the assessor to provide encouragement and feedback to them.

Hispanics: Agree 42% Insufficient Information 17% Disagree 41%
**Non-Hispanics: Agree 27% Insufficient Information 27% Disagree 45%

"No one should be assessed this way." (Non-Hispanic)

"Only if there are other equally valid instruments." (Non-Hispanic)

"I think it's impossible to avoid these tests at times. However, notation should be made of any possible negative effects the child may seem to exhibit as a result of this." (Non-Hispanic)

"There are ways of getting around this problem. For example, building rapport before the testing is begun." (Non-Hispanic)

"The assessor can always be supportive and involved regardless of the instruments used for testing." (Hispanic)

Because Hispanics tend to feel that it reflects negatively on their self-worth to admit that they do not know something or cannot do something, Hispanic students who are less accustomed to asking questions and expressing doubts and confusions may not admit that they do not understand directions or items included in assessment procedures.

Hispanics: Agree 87% Insufficient Information 5% Disagree 8%
Non-Hispanics: Agree 75% Insufficient Information 16% Disagree 9%

Therefore, assessors should actively determine that Hispanic students understand the directions and the items utilized to assess them and encourage them to ask questions when they do not.

Hispanics: Agree 91%   Insufficient Information 4%   Disagree 5%
Non-Hispanics: Agree 89%   Insufficient Information 9%   Disagree 2%

The Hispanic culture discourages guessing (hablando sin saber). Thus, Hispanic students may be penalized on assessment procedures which require students to respond when they are uncertain of the corrrect answer.

*Hispanics: Agree 61%   Insufficient Information 18%   Disagree 21%
**Non-Hispanics: Agree 40%   Insufficient Information 50%   Disagree 10%

> "Have you ever asked directions in Mexico? They'll tell you how to get anywhere even if they've never heard of the place." (Hispanic)

> "Hispanic students in the United States know how to function in the two cultural styles." (Hispanic)

> "Are you kidding? My students guess all the time." (Hispanic)

Therefore, Hispanic students should not be assessed using instruments which require guessing..

Hispanics: Agree 35%   Insufficient Information 18%   Disagree 47%
**Non-Hispanics: Agree 23%   Insufficient Information 37%   Disagree 41%

> "They can be used as long as the students are told that guessing is acceptable." (Hispanic)

> "These tests should be used, however, in these types of assessment procedures, it should be emphasized to students that it's okay to guess and they should do so if they don't know an answer." (Non-Hispanic)

> "Depends on whether there are other instruments available." (Non-Hispanic)

> "There is a difference between pure guessing and using logic to figure out something you don't know or to at least eliminate obviously wrong choices. Hispanic students need to learn this skill as do many non-Hispanic students." (Hispanic)

The Hispanic culture does not expose Hispanic students to many of the items on standardized tests. Thus, many tests which claim to measure other things when used with Hispanic students measure the extent of their exposure to the dominant culture instead.

Hispanics: Agree 86%   Insufficient Information 9%   Disagree 6%
Non-Hispanics: Agree 84%   Insufficient Information 9%   Disagree 2%

> "This is one of the most important facts anyone who tests Hispanic students should know." (Hispanic)

Therefore, Hispanic students should not be assessed using standardized instruments which contain items to which they have not been exposed unless the purpose of the procedure is to measure their exposure to these items.

Hispanics: Agree 82%   Insufficient Information 7%   Disagree 11%
Non-Hispanics: Agree 81%   Insufficient Information 12%   Disagree 6%

> "Right on!" (Hispanic)

> "Disagree. These tests tell us what students know and do not know. Then we can teach to the test. That is, determine what needs to be taught and teach it." (Non-Hispanic)

Therefore, assessors should function as advocates for Hispanic students against the use of such tests. They should explain why standardized tests are biased against Hispanic students, encourage the development of local or regional norms (especially in regard to cultural, linguistic and socio-economic variables) and suggest the use of criterion-referenced tests and informal observation whenever possible.

Hispanics: Agree 86%   Insufficient Information 2%   Disagree 12%
Non-Hispanics: Agree 85%   Insufficient Information 8%   Disagree 7%

> "This is the only thing we should do about standardized tests and Hispanics. If we continue to permit Hispanic students to fail these tests, they will continue to believe that they are the failures when it is the tests and the biased tests that are failing to assess them accurately." (Hispanic)

Therefore, assessors should keep in mind that culturally determined test-taking styles, etc., of Hispanic students are not right or wrong, good or bad, acceptable or unacceptable when compared to those expected of students acculturated to the Anglo culture, but only the same or different. And they should avoid using these prejudicial concepts when interpreting the results of their assessment of Hispanic students.

Hispanics: Agree 90%   Insufficient Information 6%   Disagree 4%
Non-Hispanics: Agree 92%   Insufficient Information 5%   Disagree 2%

Summary: The participants agreed that Hispanics who came from countries where they aren't tested individually may become so anxious as to invalidate the results of the testing; that Hispanic students may perform better on tests when they receive immediate feedback and experience assessors as involved and supportive; and that Hispanic students may not admit that they do not understand directions or items on a test. Hispanic participants but not non-Hispanic participants also agreed that Hispanic students may be penalized on tests which require students to respond when they are uncertain of the correct answer.

The participants also agreed that assessors should attempt to make Hispanic students less anxious; that they should maintain an involved supportive posture with Hispanic students; and that they should make sure Hispanic students understand the directions and items on the tests. However, they did not agree that Hispanic students should not be assessed with instruments which do not permit assessors to provide them with the encouragement and feedback they need or with instruments which require guessing.

Finally, the participants not only agreed that Hispanic students should not be assessed with standardized instruments which contain items to which they have not been exposed, they also agreed that assessors should function as advocates against the use of such tests with Hispanic students.

Language

Because some Hispanic students may start school without the English language skills required for them to profit from instruction in English, assessors should determine whether Spanish-speaking students are fluent enough to be taught in English, English and Spanish, or Spanish only.

Hispanics:	Agree 94%	Insufficient Information 3%	Disagree 3%
Non-Hispanics:	Agree 95%	Insufficient Information 4%	Disagree 1%

Because Hispanic students who have been exposed to some oral English before starting school may be more fluent in oral English than written English, especially during their first few years in school, assessors should administer both oral and written forms of language tests, especially when they want to evaluate the English fluency of Hispanic students.

Hispanics:	Agree 95%	Insufficient Information 1%	Disagree 4%
Non-Hispanics:	Agree 95%	Insufficient Information 2%	Disagree 3%

Some Hispanic students may have developed two vocabularies. They may be dominant or proficient in English for information and experiences that pertain to school and education and dominant or proficient in Spanish for information which relates to home and community.

Hispanics: Agree 90%   Insufficient Information 2%   Disagree 3%
Non-Hispanics: Agree 86%   Insufficient Information 4%   Disagree 10%

Therefore, assessors may have to utilize both English and Spanish language procedures to determine the full extent of some Hispanic students' verbal ability.

Hispanics: Agree 95%   Insufficient Information 2%   Disagree 3%
Non-Hispanics: Agree 97%   Insufficient Information 2%   Disagree 2%

Hispanics speak many Spanish dialects because:

a. There are significant differences in Spanish spoken in the various Latin American countries;
b. Latin Americans from different countries tend to relocate within specific regions in the United States, i.e., Cubans in Florida, Puerto Ricans in the North East, Mexicans in the South West, etc.;
c. In some regions, i.e., Texas, Hispanics speak a dialect of Spanish which includes many English words (Tex-Mex).

Hispanics: Agree 91%   Insufficient Information 5%   Disagree 4%
**Non-Hispanics: Agree 71%   Insufficient Information 23%   Disagree 5%

Therefore, when assessing language dominance, assessors should select instruments which utilize the dialect spoken by the student and which provide appropriate regional norms.

Hispanics: Agree 86%   Insufficient Information 3%   Disagree 11%
Non-Hispanics: Agree 84%   Insufficient Information 8%   Disagree 8%

> "If possible, this would be the ideal. To have assessments in Spanish would be quite a feat." (Hispanic)

> "It's difficult enough to find valid assessments in Spanish, let alone appropriate regional assessments." (Hispanic)

> "I didn't realize tests in different dialects were available." (Non-Hispanic)

> "Americans from different sections of the country have the same problems. There is a *Standard for all language* that should be maintained." (Non-Hispanic)

Therefore, when assessing the knowledge, etc., of Spanish-speaking students with Spanish language instruments, assessors should determine which errors are due to dialect differences rather than lack of the knowledge, achievement, aptitude, etc., being tested.

Hispanics: Agree 91%   Insufficient Information   3%   Disagree   6%
Non-Hispanics: Agree 94%   Insufficient Information   3%   Disagree   3%

Hispanics may use words and expressions in ways which are different than the way they are used in the Anglo culture and vice versa. For example, Hispanics are accustomed to addressing people as doctor, ingeniero, and maestro as a sign of respect. However, when Hispanic students do the same thing in English and address their teachers as teacher, Anglo teachers may interpret it as disrespect. Likewise, Hispanics may address each other using such terms as gordo and flaco as signs of affection. However, when Anglos are addressed as fatty and skinny, they often interpret it as the opposite of affection.

Hispanics: Agree 95%   Insufficient Information   2%   Disagree   3%
Non-Hispanics: Agree 88%   Insufficient Information 11%   Disagree   1%

"I wish I had known this before because this has been bothering me for years." (Non-Hispanic)

Therefore, assessors should determine not only the extent of students' English vocabularies but the extent to which they are able to use their English words in culturally appropriate ways.

Hispanics: Agree 95%   Insufficient Information   1%   Disagree   4%
Non-Hispanics: Agree 94%   Insufficient Information   4%   Disagree   2%

"How does one go about assessing this?" (Non-Hispanic)

Hispanic non-verbal communication (body language) is different in very many ways from that used by Anglos. For example, when Hispanic students lower their eyes and bow their heads when being reprimanded, they are communicating respect for their elders. However, when Anglos assume the same posture, they may be communicating admission of guilt and willingness to accept their punishment.

Hispanics: Agree 90%   Insufficient Information   5%   Disagree   5%
Non-Hispanics: Agree 84%   Insufficient Information 15%   Disagree   2%

Therefore, assessors should determine whether Hispanic students are fluent in the use of appropriate English non-verbal communication.

Hispanics: Agree 84%   Insufficient Information   6%   Disagree   9%
Non-Hispanics: Agree 84%   Insufficient Information 15%   Disagree   2%

"Assessors should be fluent in the Hispanic system for non-verbal communication. Why must the Hispanic always conform?" (Hispanic)

"This seems like a good idea. However, I have not been taught how to do this, nor am I familiar with any test or procedure designed to do this, although I would like to learn more about it." (Non-Hispanic)

"Perhaps, 'and idiomatic expressions' should be added to this statement." (Unknown)

Because Spanish words and concepts do not translate into English and vice versa, assessors should avoid using items on literal translations of English language tests which lose their meaning in the translations.

Hispanics:	Agree	92%	Insufficient Information	2%	Disagree	2%
Non-Hispanics:	Agree	96%	Insufficient Information	2%	Disagree	2%

Summary: The participants agreed that assessors should determine whether Spanish-speaking Hispanic students are fluent enough to be taught in English or require Spanish instruction as well. They agreed that assessors should administer both oral and written language tests in both English and Spanish and, when possible, use Spanish language tests which include both the dialect spoken by the student and appropriate regional norms. They also agreed that assessors should avoid using literal translations of tests which lose their meaning in the translation. Finally, the participants agreed that assessors should determine whether students use their English vocabulary in culturally appropriate ways and are fluent in the use of English non-verbal communication when assessing their overall proficiency.

Achievement

The Hispanic community's priorities and goals for the education of their children are different from those of the Anglo community in many significant ways. Among other things, these differences affect the content of the academic curriculum, the values taught by the school and the pace at which students are expected to progress.

Hispanics:	Agree	76%	Insufficient Information	9%	Disagree	15%
**Non-Hispanics:	Agree	67%	Insufficient Information	21%	Disagree	12%

"This is very true. While like any other parents they want their children to do well in school, especially those of the lower socio-economic class are less into college degrees for their children and more into vocational learning. Also, some courses which we may consider enrichment, they may consider unnecessary." (Non-Hispanic)

"This depends on the community and the socio-economic level of the people who live within it." (Non-Hispanic)

"It seems to me that families which have settled here want their children to learn whatever is necessary to 'make it' here." (Non-Hispanic)

"The parents of my Hispanic students are eager for their children to learn English and do well. They are no different than any other group of parents." (Hispanic)

As a result, the contents of standardized achievement tests which are designed to reflect what is being taught in the average school at a particular grade level may not reflect what is being taught in schools and classes in which the curriculum is relevant to the needs and desires of Hispanic communities.

Hispanics: Agree 87%   Insufficient Information 7% Disagree 6%
Non-Hispanics: Agree 79%   Insufficient Information 15% Disagree 6%

"And they certainly do not reflect the achievement of a student who was born and partially educated elsewhere, Mexico, for example." (Non-Hispanic)

"I have the feeling the questions are trying to excuse the students from studying or working hard." (Non-Hispanic)

"The Hispanic community's priorities and goals may differ and these doubtlessly affect the success of the curriculum, the values taught and the pace. It may also be desirable that the community's priorities and goals determine the curriculum, the values taught and the pace. However, I believe that the over-application of this concept can readily result in school graduates who are unable to compete successfully in the world beyond the school. I also believe that application of this concept is at least partially responsible for the continuing clamor for proficiency testing and use of standardized instruments. While accommodations to individual and group needs is needed, careful guidelines are also needed to protect each student from self-fulfilling prophecies of slow progress to lowered expectancies." (Hispanic)

Therefore, assessors should utilize criterion-referenced tests which include items from curricula which are culturally relevant to Hispanic students to assess their achievement.

Hispanics: Agree 84%   Insufficient Information   7%   Disagree   8%
Non-Hispanics: Agree 85%   Insufficient Information   8%   Disagree   7%

"This is the best way to make the test fit the student and not vice versa." (Hispanic)

"Hispanic students living in the United States should be tested on the curriculum taught in the United States if that's where they're going to be living." (Non-Hispanic)

Since Hispanic students may be dominant or proficient in English for information related to school and in Spanish for information related to non-school areas, or they may utilize a combination of English and Spanish (Tex-Mex), a mono-lingual assessment may not reveal the complete extent of their knowledge.

Hispanics: Agree 90%   Insufficient Information   3%   Disagree   7%
Non-Hispanics: Agree 92%   Insufficient Information   5%   Disagree   3%

Therefore, assessors should assess the achievement of bilingual Hispanic students in both English and Spanish.

Hispanics: Agree 91%   Insufficient Information   2%   Disagree   7%
Non-Hispanics: Agree 94%   Insufficient Information   4%   Disagree   3%

"This is a must. Every school should have someone who can evaluate a student in Spanish. If they do not, they should go out and hire one or make sure that teachers teaching on waivers actually fulfill their obligation to become 'bilingual' teachers." (Hispanic)

"This would be a good idea if we had the money to do it. But for now, priorities require the insufficient funds for education to be spent for other things which benefit greater numbers of students." (Non-Hispanic)

"This is ideal. In reality we have neither the time or personnel to do this and never will." (Non-Hispanic)

Since Hispanic students may be more fluent in oral than written English and Spanish, written tests may not reveal the full extent of Hispanic students' knowledge, especially during the first few years of their exposure to school.

Hispanics: Agree 92%   Insufficient Information 2% Disagree 6%
Non-Hispanics: Agree 96%   Insufficient Information 2% Disagree 2%

Therefore, assessors should utilize both oral and written procedures when assessing the achievement of bilingual Hispanic students.

Hispanics: Agree 95%   Insufficient Information 1% Disagree 5%
Non-Hispanics: Agree 93%   Insufficient Information 5% Disagree 2%

Assessors' evaluation of bilingual Hispanic students' responses on achievement tests should never be influenced by the correctness of the grammar, spelling, etc., they use to express themselves unless the test is specifically designed to measure English language skills.

Hispanics: Agree 80%   Insufficient Information 6% Disagree 14%
Non-Hispanics: Agree 73%   Insufficient Information 13% Disagree 14%

Summary: The participants agreed that assessors should utilize criterion-referenced tests when the items on standardized achievement tests do not reflect what Hispanic students have been taught. They agreed that the achievement of bilingual students should be evaluated with oral and written tests in both English and Spanish and that errors in mechanical English such as spelling and grammar should not be considered unless the assessor is attempting to evaluate these students' English language skills.

IDENTIFICATION OF EXCEPTIONAL STUDENTS

Cognitive Learning Style

Hispanic students tend to have cognitive and learning styles which may be different from the teaching styles of their teachers. These differences, rather than supposed intellectual deficiencies, learning disabilities, etc., may account for the school-related problems of many Hispanic students.

Hispanics: Agree 84%   Insufficient Information 9% Disagree 7%
Non-Hispanics: Agree 79%   Insufficient Information 14% Disagree 8%

"It is no longer possible to deny that the cognitive styles of Mexican-Americans and Anglos are different. The research is conclusive. Therefore, as Ramirez and Castaneda have suggested, it is time that the school system, meaning teachers, become bicognitive and teach each child in the manner best suited to help him/her learn." (Hispanic)

"This is the real reason for the poor showing of many Mexican-Americans in our biased schools, not that they are lazy or stupid." (Hispanic)

"All teachers are different and have different styles of teaching. Students are not 'stereotyped' either. I taught elementary and high school in Mexico, also. I found students there are just like ones in the U.S. The problem lies more with the ones who are more illiterate, have lack of any formal education, and from more uneducated parents. There are the same problems among Americans (Black or White) as well as other cultures. Hispanics are not unique in this." (Non-Hispanic)

Therefore, Hispanic students should not be mislabeled learning disabled, etc., when the cause of their poor achievement is due to a mismatch between their cognitive learning styles and their teachers' teaching styles.

Hispanics:	Agree 89% Insufficient Information 6%	Disagree 5%
Non-Hispanics:	Agree 87% Insufficient Information 10%	Disagree 4%

"But often better to 'label' temporarily to help kids when no other services are available." (Non-Hispanic)

Therefore, an evaluation of the learning styles of Hispanic students should be included when such students are demonstrating academic or behavioral problems in school. This evaluation will enable the assessors to determine whether these teachers' teaching styles match their students' learning and cognitive styles.

Hispanics:	Agree 85% Insufficient Information 7%	Disagree 8%
Non-Hispanics:	Agree 84% Insufficient Information 11%	Disagree 5%

"This kind of evaluation should be done *BEFORE* students show academic or behavioral problems." (Hispanic)

"While I agree with the suggestion, I would like to know how to determine this." (Non-Hispanic)

"But students cannot always choose their teachers, and teachers certainly can't change their style to suit every student! Everyone is different, regardless of culture." (Unknown)

Learning Potential (Intelligence)

Hispanic students may not be able to demonstrate what they have learned or what they can do on tests which:
- are not in their native language;
- are timed;
- contain items to which they have not been exposed;
- are too thing rather than people oriented;
- do not allow for feedback from the assessor.

Hispanics:	Agree 92%	Insufficient Information 12%	Disagree 6%
Non-Hispanics:	Agree 85%	Insufficient Information 8%	Disagree 7%

"This is so obvious it doesn't need saying." (Hispanic)

"Hispanic kids like all kids can learn a lot of things including how to take tests." (Non-Hispanic)

Many tests attempt to determine learning potential (intelligence) by measuring achievement. The rationale of this approach is that differences in achievement on such tests reflect differences in potential. However, tests and other evaluative procedures which do not permit Hispanic students to demonstrate what they have achieved or can do for the reasons mentioned above provide a biased indication of their potential.

Hispanics:	Agree 89%	Insufficient Information 7%	Disagree 4%
Non-Hispanics:	Agree 87%	Insufficient Information 8%	Disagree 5%

"Worse than biased, inaccurate and misleading." (Non-Hispanic)

"I think trying to measure learning potential with a test is a waste of time and leads to an over identification of Hispanics, Blacks and poor students for classes for the retarded." (Non-Hispanic)

Therefore, the learning potential of Hispanic students should not be evaluated by these kinds of "intelligence tests."

Hispanics:	Agree 85%	Insufficient Information 7%	Disagree 8%
Non-Hispanics:	Agree 83%	Insufficient Information 12%	Disagree 5%

"Nor should the 'intelligence' or 'learning potential' of ANY student be solely assessed by such instruments." (Hispanic)

"The law requires assessors to evaluate students adaptive behavior as well." (Non-Hispanic)

"They can and should be used as part of a complete battery of tests." (Non-Hispanic)

Hispanic students who are not accustomed to taking individualized tests may become too anxious and insecure during the evaluation to demonstrate their knowledge and achievement. As a result, assessment procedures may not give a true indication of these Hispanic students' potential.

Hispanics: Agree 86%   Insufficient Information 6%   Disagree 8%
Non-Hispanics: Agree 76%   Insufficient Information 15%   Disagree 10%

Therefore, assessors should not use formal assessment procedures to evaluate the learning potential of Hispanic students who are unaccustomed to such procedures.

*Hispanics: Agree 61%   Insufficient Information 9%   Disagree 30%
**Non-Hispanics: Agree 41%   Insufficient Information 22%   Disagree 37%

"Formal tests should be used but only as part of a wide range of assessment techniques because they do provide useful information." (Non-Hispanic)

"But, it is possible to do many things to help them become accustomed to these procedures." (Non-Hispanic)

"If the instructor is sensitive, he can allow the student to retake the test until he can do it without becoming anxious." (Hispanic)

Therefore, assessors should use formal assessment procedures with such students but only as part of a complete and thorough battery of procedures.

Hispanics: Agree 83%   Insufficient Information 10%   Disagree 7%
Non-Hispanics: Agree 85%   Insufficient Information 11%   Disagree 4%

Emotional and Behavior Problems

The Hispanic culture requires good students to be passive learners—to sit quietly at their desks, pay attention, learn what they are taught and speak only when they are called upon. Anglo educational methods often require students to be active students —to show initiative and leadership, to volunteer questions and answers, and to question the opinion of others.

Hispanics: Agree 83%   Insufficient Information 3%   Disagree 14%
Non-Hispanics: Agree 79%   Insufficient Information 17%   Disagree 4%

"This only applies to students who have gone to school in other countries. However, many Hispanic students have only gone to school in the United States and they don't know what's required at school in their native country except of course what carries over from their home culture." (Non-Hispanic)

"I suppose . . . Little kids don't have this problem once they see how others do it." (Unknown)

"This is not commonly the case with Hispanics born in the United States." (Hispanic)

"Not in my room. Everyone is active and on task." (Non-Hispanic)

Hispanic students who cannot assume this more active role may be incorrectly perceived as insecure, shy, or excessively passive.

Hispanics: Agree 86%   Insufficient Information 4%   Disagree 11%
Non-Hispanics: Agree 85%   Insufficient Information 12%   Disagree 4%

Hispanic students who are trained to be dependent upon the opinions, values, and decisions of adults may seem to Anglo assessors to be overly dependent, immature, or even slow.

Hispanics: Agree 89%   Insufficient Information 3%   Disagree 8%
Non-Hispanics: Agree 83%   Insufficient Information 11%   Disagree 6%

Hispanic students who are brought up to be cooperative rather than competitive in their relationships with their peers may be seen by Anglo assessors as too passive and non-assertive.

Hispanics: Agree 90%   Insufficient Information 2%   Disagree 8%
Non-Hispanics: Agree 77%   Insufficient Information 14%   Disagree 10%

Hispanics who are not necessarily expected to admit responsibility or apologize when they have made a mistake or wronged another person may resist doing so, especially in front of their peers. Anglo teachers may misperceive their unwillingness as recalcitrance, stubbornness, or defiant behavior.

Hispanics: Agree 82%   Insufficient Information 8%   Disagree 10%
Non-Hispanics: Agree 78%   Insufficient Information 17%   Disagree 6%

"Especially true for students ten years old and up." (Non-Hispanic)

"I'm really in the dark about some of these things." (Non-Hispanic)

"I disagree that Hispanics aren't expected to admit responsibility or apologize. Of course they are. I expect my children to." (Hispanic)

Hispanic students are used to close personal relationships and physical contact with adults. When they seek this close physical contact in the primary grades, they may appear to be overly dependent on their Anglo teachers. When they exhibit the same behavior as teenagers, they may appear to be sexually aggressive.

Hispanics: Agree 67% Insufficient Information 14% Disagree 19%
**Non-Hispanics: Agree 63% Insufficient Information 25% Disagree 12%

"This is only true of some Hispanic students." (Hispanic)

"Again, I've read and heard this but I haven't seen it." (Non-Hispanic)

Hispanic students who help each other when they are called on, during examinations, or with their homework may be perceived to be cheating rather than cooperating by persons who are unfamiliar with the Hispanic culture.

Hispanics: Agree 82% Insufficient Information 9% Disagree 9%
Non-Hispanics: Agree 82% Insufficient Information 12% Disagree 6%

Cultural conflicts between Hispanic and Anglo expectations for children and adolescents may cause identity problems for Hispanic youth. Some Hispanic youth may resolve these identity crises by adopting exaggerated behavior patterns (such as those typical of Vatos Locos, Low Riders, etc.) which are designed to express their individuality. When students demonstrate these behavior patterns in school, they may threaten Anglo teachers and administrators, who may think that these Hispanic youth have emotional or behavioral problems.

Hispanics: Agree 87% Insufficient Information 6% Disagree 8%
Non-Hispanics: Agree 82% Insufficient Information 13% Disagree 5%

"This is just one of many important examples of the lack of communication between Hispanic students and Anglos." (Hispanic)

"I feel these are *perceived* as problems and then become such because these 'problems' are treated as problems and the cultural differences are misinterpreted and then also become problems. 'Cultural education' is needed by administrators also." (Non-Hispanic)

"These are not exaggerated behavior patterns, just unique and different ones." (Hispanic)

Therefore, assessors should distinguish between the previously mentioned culturally determined acceptable ways of behaving in schools and others which may indicate emotional or behavioral problems.

Hispanics: Agree 91%   Insufficient Information   4%   Disagree   5%
Non-Hispanics: Agree 91%   Insufficient Information   8%   Disagree   1%

"Assessors need to be educated about the Hispanic culture by Hispanic educators." (Hispanic)

Hispanic students who are experiencing failure or frustration in school because of mismatches between their cognitive and learning styles and the teaching styles of their teachers, lack of culturally relevant material in the curriculum, instruction in their non-dominant language, etc., may react to this frustration and failure by loss of interest, withdrawal, resignation, anxiety, rebelliousness, etc. These emotional and behavioral problems are the *result* of, not the *cause* of these students' difficulties in school.

Hispanics: Agree 94%   Insufficient Information   3%   Disagree   3%
Non-Hispanics: Agree 87%   Insufficient Information 10%   Disagree   3%

"I love the wording of this item—sums it all up beautifully!" (Hispanic)

Hispanic students who are required to compete against their will, criticized in front of their peers, denied the dependent relationship they are accustomed to have with adults, etc., may feel rejected, abused or picked upon by their teachers. They may become insecure and anxious. They may rebel against such treatment or withdraw from further attempts to succeed in school or relate to their teachers. In such cases, these emotional and behavioral problems are the *result* of, not the *cause* of, these students' difficulties in school.

Hispanics: Agree 91%   Insufficient Information   4%   Disagree   5%
Non-Hispanics: Agree 86%   Insufficient Information 11%   Disagree   4%

Therefore, assessors should distinguish between Hispanic students who have intrinsic emotional and behavioral problems which interfere with their adjustment to schools and those whose emotional and behavioral problems are caused by culturally and linguistically inappropriate school experiences.

Hispanics:　　　Agree 94%　Insufficient Information　2%　Disagree　4%
Non-Hispanics:　Agree 91%　Insufficient Information　6%　Disagree　2%

"This seems so logical to me. Yet, although I am a bilingual educator and have passed the language and culture tests, this is all new to me." (Non-Hispanic)

Summary: The participants agreed that when evaluating Hispanic students for possible placement in special education because they may have an intellectual deficit, a learning disability or a behavior disorder, assessors should determine whether these students' poor achievement or behavior problems are caused by a mismatch between their cognitive learning styles and their teachers' teaching styles rather than the supposed handicaps previously mentioned.

They agreed that the learning potential of Hispanic students should not be measured with tests which are not in their native language, are timed, contain items to which they have not been exposed, are too thing oriented rather than people oriented, or do not allow for feedback from the assessor, because these factors prevent them from demonstrating what they have learned or what they can do. By a small majority, Hispanic participants agreed that assessors should not use formal tests of learning potential with students who become too anxious to function adequately because they are unaccustomed to taking such tests. A much higher percent of the participants agreed that these tests should be used with such students but only as part of a complete and thorough battery.

The participants agreed that assessors should not attribute emotional problems or behavior problems to Hispanic students with the following cultural characteristics: do not play an active role in class; are dependent on the opinions, values, and decisions of adults; are cooperative rather than competitive; resist apologizing or admitting responsibility when they have made a mistake or wronged someone; seek close physical contact with adults; help each other when called on in class, during examinations, or with their homework; and resolve their identity problems by adopting exaggerated behavior patterns. They also agreed that assessors should determine whether Hispanic students' emotional and behavioral problems are intrinsic or caused by culturally and linguistically inappropriate school experiences.

SUMMARY

The participants agreed that when assessing Hispanic students, assessors should set them at ease, maintain an involved and supportive posture with them and actively determine that they understand the directions and items included in the procedures. They agreed that assessors should use both oral and written instruments and English and Spanish language instruments, and they should avoid using literal translations of tests which lose their meaning when evaluating bilingual students. When evaluating these students' fluency in English, assessors should also determine whether they use their English vocabulary in culturally appropriate ways and whether they are fluent in English non-verbal language.

The participants agreed that assessors should avoid certain errors. These included:

1. mislabeling students as having intellectual deficits, learning disabilities, or emotional and behavioral problems when their difficulties in school are caused by a mismatch between the students' cognitive learning styles and their teachers' teaching styles;
2. attributing emotional or behavioral problems to students whose behavior is culturally determined;
3. attributing intrinsic causes to the emotional and behavioral problems of students when their problems are caused by culturally and linguistically inappropriate educational experiences.

The participants agreed that assessors should not use procedures with Hispanic students which are not in their native language, are timed, contain items to which they have not been exposed, and are too thing rather than people oriented. However they disagreed that assessors should also not use instruments which do not allow for feedback or require guessing, nor did they agree that formal procedures should not be used with students who may become too anxious to function because they are unaccustomed to such procedures.

Chapter 7

CURRENT ISSUES

T his brief chapter includes the participants' responses to items designed to study their opinions regarding four questions.

Question 1: Do the participants believe it is practical to train non-Hispanic professionals to work with Hispanic students and their parents?

The participants' opinion regarding this question was studied by means of their responses to the following item.

Because of the significant differences between the Hispanic and Anglo cultures, it is extremely difficult to train Anglo professionals to work effectively with Hispanic students and their parents. Therefore, efforts to provide educational and counseling services to the Hispanic community should concentrate almost exclusively on the recruitment of Hispanics into the professions. Attempts to train Anglo professionals to work with the Hispanic community should be drastically curtailed.

Hispanics:	Agree 38% Insufficient Information 11%	Disagree 50%
Non-Hispanics:	Agree 11% Insufficient Information 10%	Disagree 79%

"Remove artificial barriers and hire Hispanic educators, especially in administrative positions that deal with the education of Hispanic students. This action would have a great impact in improving the quality of education for all students. Hispanics comprise over 20 percent of our human resources in California. Among this significant number of Hispanics, there is a sufficient number of educators with all the needed qualifications who have been denied access to positions where they would be effective in solving the problems facing Hispanic students." (Hispanic)

"In Mexico, most students are taught by authoritarian teachers who teach 60 kids in one room without ever cracking a smile. That's one reason why so many of them drop out of school in the fifth grade. Hispanic students need teachers who are loving, caring human beings. No importa que sea Hispano o no." (It does not matter if they are Hispanic or not.) (Hispanic)

"Is this question for real? I have known some Anglos who are just as sympathetic as Hispanics to the Hispanic cause. With the proper attitude, training, and heart, both Anglos and Hispanics can work together to better the system of education in the U.S." (Hispanic)

As can be seen from the data presented above, a majority of both the Hispanic and non-Hispanic participants disagreed that it would be a good idea to drastically curtail the attempt to train non-Hispanic professionals to work with Hispanics.

Question 2: Do the participants believe that it is realistic to expect that non-Hispanic professionals will adapt their techniques to the cultural needs of Hispanics?

This question was studied by means of the following item.

Despite what some people may prefer, the fact is that it is more realistic to encourage Hispanic students to adapt to the Anglo culture than to expect Anglos in general and Anglo professionals in particular to adapt their assessment, instructional, motivational, classroom management and counseling techniques to Hispanics.

Hispanics: Agree 33%   Insufficient Information 11%   Disagree 56%
Non-Hispanics: Agree 13%   Insufficient Information 16%   Disagree 71%

"The educator has the responsibility for learning to relate to Chicanos. The educator should live and work in Chicano barrios in order to approximate what it is like to be a Chicano in an alien society. Educators in training must experience at firsthand the agony and frustration of being a Chicano in a White society that has fractured the minds of people of Aztlan whose tyrannization began over 200 years ago. The training should include readings in the nature and need of the student; but what is more important, it should also include direct exposure to the environment of the student. This means that student teachers should live and learn on location in the barrios. In this manner, teachers will become exposed to the various life-styles that affect the behavior of the Chicano population. Hopefully, through this exposure, insight will be gained into the cultural aspects which affect the teaching situation and a better understanding will develop in the student teacher which will help him in establishing rapport with Chicano students." (Hispanic)

"What a loaded question! While it is more realistic, it is a cop out and does not solve the problem but again leaves the entire burden on the non-Anglo. I hope we never again settle for this approach in relation to solving the problems for *any* group in our society." (Unknown)

"You really cannot teach a non-minority how to be a minority or think like a minority because, as Piaget would say, the scheme or personal experience of one is different. However, a non-minority person can have empathy with a Third-World person and can be very much aware and sensitive to the perils of a minority member in our U.S. society so much so that he/she can 'relate' and be accepted by the subculture." (Hispanic)

The data presented above indicates that the participants disagreed that it was more realistic to expect Hispanic students to adapt to the non-Hispanic culture than to expect non-Hispanics to accommodate these techniques to Hispanics.

Thus, it appears from the participants' answers to these two questions that they agree that training non-Hispanic professionals to work with Hispanic students and their parents is a realistic goal.

Question 3: What do the participants think is more important in order to understand Hispanics who are living in the United States: to be aware of the specific differences between the Hispanic and Anglo cultures or to be aware of the implications of living in two cultures and the prejudice experienced as a result?

The following three items relate to this question.

It is more important for Anglo professionals who work with the Hispanic community to be aware of the implications of living in two different cultures than to be aware of the specific differences between the cultures.

*Hispanics: Agree 63%   Insufficient Information 9%   Disagree 28%
Non-Hispanics: Agree 47%   Insufficient Information 14%   Disagree 38%

It is more important for Anglo professionals who work with the Hispanic community to be aware of the implications of the prejudice Hispanics suffer than to be aware of the specific differences between the two cultures.

*Hispanics: Agree 61%   Insufficient Information 9%   Disagree 29%
Non-Hispanics: Agree 39%   Insufficient Information 17%   Disagree 45%

It is more important for Anglo professionals who work with the Hispanic community to be aware of the specific differences between the two cultures than to be aware of the implications of either living in two different cultures or the prejudice Hispanics suffer.

Hispanics: Agree 40%   Insufficient Information 9%   Disagree 51%
**Non-Hispanics: Agree 21%   Insufficient Information 20%   Disagree 59%

The participants' answers to the three items indicate that the Hispanic participants thought that an awareness of the implications of living in two cultures and the experience was more important than knowledge of the specific differences between the cultures. While the responses of the non-Hispanics are difficult to interpret, they did not appear to share the opinions of the Hispanic participants.

Question 4: Some theorists have suggested that there are three alternative ways for Hispanics to resolve their cultural conflicts: acculturation into the Anglo culture, maintenance of the Hispanic culture exclusively, or becoming bicultural. Which of these alternatives do the participants believe is the most desirable?

The participants' opinions about this question were elicited by the followng items:

The most desirable alternative is acculturation.

Hispanics: Agree 19%   Insufficient Information 11%   Disagree 71%
**Non-Hispanics: Agree 10%   Insufficient Information 22%   Disagree 68%

The most desirable alternative is traditional.

Hispanics: Agree 19%   Insufficient Information 11%   Disagree 69%
**Non-Hispanics: Agree 7%   Insufficient Information 23%   Disagree 70%

The most desirable alternative is dualistic.

Hispanics: Agree 68%   Insufficient Information 11%   Disagree 21%
Non-Hispanics: Agree 62%   Insufficient Information 16%   Disagree 22%

The most desirable alternative is the one that suits the individual.

Hispanics: Agree 87%   Insufficient Information   6%   Disagree   7%
Non-Hispanics: Agree 85%   Insufficient Information   7%   Disagree   8%

As can be seen from their answers to the items presented above, the participants favored a bicultural identification as opposed to acculturation or maintenance. However, what they favored most was the alternative which suits the individual.

Chapter 8.

GROUPS OF PARTICIPANTS COMPARED

T his chapter includes separate discussions of the responses of the Hispanic and non-Hispanic participants as well as comparisons between their responses.

HISPANIC PARTICIPANTS

Did the Hispanic participants agree among themselves about which cultural traits tend to characterize Hispanics living in the United States and their implications for instruction, classroom management and assessment of Hispanic students and counseling their parents?

As the data in Chapters 3 through 6 indicate, the Hispanics agreed that many but not all of the traits included in the study which have been attributed to the Hispanic culture actually do tend to characterize Hispanics (see Appendix 1). The Hispanics also agreed with all of the statements included in the study which described the effects of language differences, limited economic resources, limited education, prejudice and stereotyping on the lives of many Hispanics living in the United States (see Appendix 2). Finally, the Hispanic participants agreed with a number of specific suggestions for taking these cultural traits and factors into consideration when selecting instructional techniques, classroom management procedures, counseling techniques and assessment procedures. These suggestions are listed in Chapters 3 through 6.

Despite the facts that the Hispanic participants agreed among themselves in these ways, significant differences were observed among Hispanics who were born in different countries or whose ancestors were from different countries on a number of the items.[1] However, while these differences are statistically significant, they do not appear to be very important.

NON-HISPANIC PARTICIPANTS

Did the non-Hispanic participants agree among themselves about which traits are characteristic of Hispanics living in the United States and their implications for clasroom instruction, management, assessment and counseling?

The data in Chapters 3 through 6 and Appendices One and Two provide an affirmative answer to this question. However, the data also indicate that there were significant differences of opinion regarding the opinions expressed by non-Hispanics with varying amounts of experience working with Hispanic students and their parents.

Ideally, in order to analyze this factor, it would have been better to follow a group of non-Hispanics over a period of time and collect information about possible changes in their opinions regarding the items in the questionnaire as they gained more experience working with Hispanic students and their parents. This would have permitted the conclusion that any changes observed probably resulted from their increased experience. Comparing the opinions of participants with varying degrees of experience does not allow the same conclusions, since it could be that it was the very differences of opinion among the participants which led some of them to choose to work with Hispanics and others to choose not to do so. Keeping this limitation in mind, comparisons of the responses of three groups of non-Hispanic participants—those with less than one year of experience working with Hispanic students, those with at least one year but less than three years of experience and those with at least three years of experience—are presented next.

Table XV indicates the number of participants in each group.[2]

---

[1]Chi square analysis 0.05 level

[2]The responses of 23 non-Hispanics were added to the original pool of participants in order to increase the number of non-Hispanics with little or no experience.

TABLE XV

NUMBERS OF NON-HISPANIC PARTICIPANTS WITH
VARYING DEGREES OF EXPERIENCE

Years of Experience	Number of Non-Hispanic Participants
Less than 1	37
At least 1 but less than 3	21
More than 3	129
	Total 187

An analysis of the responses of these non-Hispanic participants regarding whether they agreed that the various cultural traits included in the study are characteristic of Hispanics living in the United States indicated statistically significant differences among the three groups on 124 traits and non-significant differences on 56 traits.[3] An analysis of their responses to the implications of these cultural traits—that is, how they should be taken into account by persons working with Hispanic students and their parents—revealed statistically significant differences among the three groups on 92 items and non-significant differences on 96 items.[3] Thus, it is clear that non-Hispanic participants with varying degrees of experience working with Hispanic students and their parents responded differently to the items in the questionnaire. Further analysis of the data indicated that they responded differently in two ways.

Firstly, as the data in Tables XVI and XVII indicate, the less experience the non-Hispanic participants had with Hispanic students, the more often they responded that they lacked sufficient experience or information to judge both the traits and implications included in the study.

TABLE XVI

NUMBERS OF TRAITS ABOUT WHICH PARTICIPANTS STATED
THEY LACKED SUFFICIENT EXPERIENCE OR INFORMATION

Percent of Participants Responding Insufficient Experience or Information	Years of Experience		
	Less Than 1 Year	More Than 1 Year But Less Than 3	At Least 3 Years
At least 40%	82	19	4
At least 50%	52	11	0
At least 60%	26	3	0
At least 70%	9	1	0

[3]Chi square analysis at 0.05 level of significance.

TABLE XVII

NUMBER OF IMPLICATIONS ABOUT WHICH PARTICIPANTS
STATED THEY LACKED SUFFICIENT EXPERIENCE OR INFORMATION

Percent of Partici-pants Responding In-sufficient Experience or Information	Years of Experience		
	Less Than 1 Year	More Than 1 Year But Less Than 3	At Least 3 Years
At least 40%	15	5	0
At least 50%	3	0	0
At least 60%	1	0	0
At least 70%	0	0	0

Secondly, differences were also observed among the three groups when the responses of only the participants who expressed an opinion were considered. That is, omitting the responses of those who stated that they lacked sufficient experience or information to judge, the three groups of participants differed regarding the opinions they expressed both about the cultural traits included in the study and their implications.

Cultural Traits. In general, the less experience non-Hispanics had working with Hispanic students and their parents, the less they agreed that the traits were more likely to be characteristic of Hispanics living in the United States than of Anglos. Specifically, on forty-five of the fifty-five traits about which the three groups differed, the less experience the non-Hispanics had, the less they agreed that the traits are more characteristic of Hispanics than of Anglos.

Implications. There were four different types of implications included in the study.

1. Implications which require a change in techniques or methodology by professionals in order to accommodate to the cultural characteristics of Hispanics, i.e., "Therefore, educators should not lower course grades or punish Hispanic students in other ways when family responsibilities prevent them from completing assignments, arriving on time or attending class."

2. Implications which require that Hispanic students or their parents adapt to the prevailing culture of the school system with help from the professionals, i.e., "Therefore, educators should help Hispanic students to accept necessary public criticism."

3. Implications which require that professionals should accommodate to Hispanic students or their parents while helping

them to adapt to the prevailing culture, i.e., "Therefore, educators should provide the approval and feedback these students require but only temporarily while they are encouraging the students to function more independently."

4. Implications which require that Hispanic students or their parents both adapt to the prevailing culture of the school system and maintain their traditional cultural characteristics, i.e., "Educators should encourage these students to be both able to function independently when necessary and to also rely on the encouragement and feedback of adults when necessary."

One hundred and one of the implication items were of the first type. That is, they required professionals to accommodate their techniques to the culture of the Hispanic students and parents with whom they worked. In general, the more experience non-Hispanics had working with Hispanic students, the more they agreed that professionals should accommodate to Hispanic students and their parents. Specifically, on thirty-eight of these items, the more experience non-Hispanics had, the more they agreed that professionals should accommodate their methodology to the Hispanic culture; on four items, the more experience non-Hispanics had, the more they disagreed that professionals should accommodate their methodology to the Hispanic culture; and on fifty-nine items there were no differences among the groups (see Appendix 3).

The non-Hispanic participants with varying degrees of experience working with Hispanic students also differed in regard to a few of the implications in the three other categories mentioned above. However, these differences did not appear to follow any pattern.

Current Issues. The three groups of non-Hispanics also differed on two of the current issues discussed in Chapter 7. The more experience the non-Hispanics had working with Hispanic students and their parents, the more they disagreed that attempts to train non-Hispanics to work with Hispanics should be drastically cut and the less they agreed that it is unrealistic to expect non-Hispanic professionals to accommodate their techniques to Hispanics. Thus, it appears that the more experience the non-Hispanics had working with Hispanics, the more they agreed that training non-Hispanics to work with Hispanic students and their parents is a realistic goal.

HISPANIC AND NON-HISPANIC PARTICIPANTS COMPARED

Were there differences of opinion between the Hispanics and non-Hispanic participants?

The data presented in Chapters 3 through 6 clearly indicate that the non-Hispanic participants responded more often than the Hispanic participants that they lacked sufficient experience or information to judge. The data in these chapters also indicate the specific instances in which they did not agree with the Hispanic participants either that certain cultural traits are more characteristic of Hispanics living in the United States than Anglos or with the implications of these cultural differences.

The Hispanic and non-Hispanic participants also differed on a number of the current issues included in Chapter 7. The non-Hispanic participants disagreed more than did the Hispanic participants with statements to the effect that attempts to train non-Hispanic professionals to work with Hispanics should be curtailed and that it is unrealistic to expect non-Hispanic professionals to accommodate their techniques to Hispanics. In addition the non-Hispanics did not agree with the Hispanics that an awareness of the implications of living in two cultures and of the prejudice Hispanics experience in the United States is more important than the knowledge of the specific differences between the Hispanic and Anglo cultures.

PART III

CONCLUSIONS AND RECOMMENDATIONS

Chapter 9.

CONCLUSIONS AND RECOMMENDATIONS

LIMITATIONS

In general, conclusions are only as good as the data on which they are based. The conclusions derived from this study are no exception to this rule. Therefore, a brief discussion of the limitations of the data included in this study is warranted. On the one hand, it might seem that a sample which consisted of almost five hundred individuals (469 in the original sample plus the additional 23 non-Hispanics) which included both Hispanic and non-Hispanic regular educators, bilingual/cross-cultural educators, special educators, counselors and psychologists would provide a worthwhile basis for drawing inferences about the opinions of the large population they represent. On the other hand, the extent to which the sample actually represents this larger population is unknown, since the responses of only those persons who learned about the study and volunteered to participate in it are represented in the sample.

This factor places definite limits on the validity of any conclusions based on the data. However, the large number of participants, the obvious seriousness of their responses, their widespread geographical distribution and the fact that they represent the major professions engaged in assessing and instructing Hispanic students and counseling their parents justify the drawing of at least tentative conclusions from the data included in the study. These conclusions are presented next.

CONCLUSIONS

1. Although Hispanics living in the United States trace their roots back to many different Latin American countries, there is still a common denominator of Hispanic culture in the United States, especially for Hispanics in the same socio-economic class.

This conclusion is based on two facts. Both Hispanic and non-Hispanic participants agreed with this statement. On most items, Hispanics living in different parts of the country and with roots in different Latin American countries reached a high percentage of agreement among themselves about whether or not the specific cultural traits included in the study are characteristic of Hispanics living in the United States.

2. Hispanics not only believe that there is a Hispanic culture in the United States, they also agree about many specific ways in which professionals can take these cultural factors into consideration when they work with Hispanic students and their parents.

This conclusion is derived from the fact that a large percentage of the Hispanic participants agreed among themselves regarding the appropriateness of many suggestions about ways in which professionals should modify their techniques when working with Hispanics with specific cultural traits.

3. In general, there is more agreement among Hispanics about which cultural traits tend to characterize Hispanics living in the United States than there is about how these traits should be taken into account when working with Hispanic students and their parents.

This conclusion is based on the fact that in many instances the percentage of Hispanics who agreed that a particular trait tends to characterize Hispanics was higher than the percentage of Hispanics who agreed about the specific way in which professionals should modify their techniques when working with Hispanics with that cultural trait.

4. Hispanics know more about their culture than do non-Hispanics.

This conclusion is based on the fact that non-Hispanics, especially those with less experience with Hispanics, were more likely to respond insufficient experience or information to judge whether cultural traits attributed to the Hispanic culture actually tend to characterize Hispanics living in the United States.

5. When working with Hispanic students and their parents, professionals should take into consideration the effects of living in two different cultures and any prejudice they may experience as members of an ethnic minority group. They should also be aware of the effects of socio-economic class differences and differences in educational levels when they work with lower socio-economic class Hispanic students and their parents.

This conclusion is based on two facts. The Hispanic participants agreed that when professionals work with Hispanics, it is more important for them to be aware of the implications of living in two different cultures and the prejudice Hispanics suffer than to be aware of the specific differences between the Anglo and Hispanic cultures. Both the Hispanics and non-Hispanic participants agreed with all of the statements which described the effects of socio-economic and educational differences on the lives of low socio-economic class Hispanic students and their parents.

6. Hispanic professionals are more aware of the effects of living in two cultures and prejudice on the lives of Hispanics than are non-Hispanics.

This conclusion is based on the fact that the non-Hispanic participants did not agree with the Hispanic participants that it is more important for professionals to be aware of the implications of living in two different cultures and the prejudice Hispanics suffer than to be aware of the specific differences between the Anglo and Hispanic cultures.

7. The more experience non-Hispanics have working with Hispanic students and their parents, the more knowledge they have about the Hispanic culture and the more they believe that professionals should accommodate their techniques to the cultural realities of the Hispanics they work with.

This conclusion is derived form the facts that less experienced non-Hispanic participants were more likely to state that they lacked sufficient experience or information to judge whether the cultural traits included in the study were characteristic of Hispanics living in the United States and less likely to agree that professionals should accommodate their techniques to the cultural characteristics of the Hispanics who they work with.

8. The more experience non-Hispanics have working with Hispanics, the more their opinions about the cultural implications for instruction, classroom management, assessment and counseling agree with those of Hispanics.

This conclusion is based on two facts. The more experience the non-Hispanic participants had, the more they agreed with Hispanics that certain traits are characteristic of Hispanics living in the United States and that the best way for professionals to take many of these traits into consideration when working with Hispanics is to accommodate their techniques to the cultural realities of the Hispanics who they work with.

9. Professionals such as counselors, educators and psychologists who work with Hispanic students and their parents should be trained to take their cultural characteristics into consideraton when they instruct, assess or manage the classroom behavior of these students or counsel their parents.

This conclusion is based on three facts. Both groups of participants agreed that information about the Hispanic culture, if presented in an appropriate manner stressing the dangers of over-generalizations and the individual differences in acculturation, socio-economic level, etc., among Hispanics, could be very useful in preparing professionals to work with Hispanic students and their parents. Both groups of participants disagreed that it would be unrealistic to expect non-Hispanic professionals to accommodate their assessment, instructional, classroom management and counseling techniques to Hispanics. Both groups of participants disagreed that attempts to train non-Hispanic professionals to work with Hispanics should be drastically curtailed.

RECOMMENDATIONS

1. Taken together, these conclusions lead to the proposition that counselors, educators, psychologists and others who work with Hispanic students and their parents should be knowledgeable about the Hispanic culture, the prejudice Hispanics may suffer, the implications of living in two cultures and the ramifications of socio-economic class differences when they are relevant. These professionals should determine which of these traits and life experiences actually characterize the Hispanic individuals they work with, and they should take these individual differences into consideration when selecting appropriate instructional, classroom management, counseling and assessment techniques.

Professionals who are not able to do this should be helped to do so. Hopefully, the specific information presented in this book will be useful in this endeavor.

2. When preparing professionals to take cultural factors into consideration when they work with Hispanics, special care should be taken to insure that they are aware of:

- cultural traits which Hispanics believe characterize Hispanics but which non-Hispanics either disagree that they characterize Hispanics or report that they lack sufficient experience or information to judge;
- modifications in techniques which Hispanics believe should be made when working with Hispanics but which non-Hispanics, especially those with little experience working with Hispanics, either disagree with or state that they lack sufficient experience or information to judge.

3. Instruments for evaluating an individual's knowledge of the Hispanic culture and its implication for educating Hispanic students should be available. These instruments should be used to:

- provide feedback to persons working with or preparing to work with Hispanic students and their parents regarding their knowledge about the Hispanic culture;
- individualize instruction in personnel preparation programs;
- evaluate the cultural competency of individuals seeking employment and/or certification as professionals competent to instruct, assess or counsel Hispanic students or their parents.

Hopefully, the information included in this study could prove helpful in the development of such instruments.

APPENDICES

HISPANIC PARTICIPANTS' OPINIONS REGARDING WHETHER TRAITS ATTRIBUTED TO HISPANICS LIVING IN THE UNITED STATES ACTUALLY CHARACTERIZE THEM

In this appendix, traits which have been attributed to the Hispanic culture are grouped together in terms of the extent to which the Hispanic participants agreed that they actually tend to characterize Hispanics living in the United States. Group One consists of those traits which the participants agree, with very little controversy, are characteristic of Hispanics (between 80% and 98% of the participants agreed). There was also considerable agreement among the participants (between 70% and 79%) that the traits in Group Two also tend to characterize Hispanics living in the United States. While a majority of the participants agreed that the traits listed in Group Three are characteristic of Hispano-Americans, a great many participants disagreed with the majority opinion. Group Four consists of those traits about which there was no agreement that they tended to characterize Hispanics living in the United States.

GROUP I

HIGH AGREEMENT

Importance of the Family and Group

Hispanics tend to experience the family as a fountain of emotional and economic security and support. The family is the most valued institution in the Hispanic culture. The individual owes his primary loyalty to the family. Hispanics have a strong identification with and loyalty to their family and community. They are brought up to believe that contributing to and sacrificing for the benefit of the group is more important than personal aggrandizement. As a result, they may be highly motivated to do things that have significance for their families, friends and community. They may prefer to work in groups.

Relationships

Relationships with Friends

In the Hispanic culture, friends are people who have proven over time to be dependable, trustworthy and worthy of respect. They are not acquaintances. Friendship is not a here today, gone tomorrow relationship. Once a friendship has been established, friends will share and make sacrifices for each other much the same as they would for their extended families. They would not do the same for casual acquaintances who in the Anglo culture may be considered friends.

Hispanics are generous with their belongings with friends and family. They practice the dictum "it is better to give than to receive." Hispanic children are also taught to share their belongings with others.

Formal Relationships

One of the ways in which Hispanics demonstrate their respect for each other is through the maintenance of certain formal conventions like the use of the formal "usted" rather than the informal "tu" in conversation. Hispanics may mistake an Anglo's less formal approach to interpersonal relationships as a sign of disrespect. This applies both to adults and children who have formal relationships with adults with whom they tend to use the formal "usted" form.

Smooth Interpersonal Relationships

One area in which Anglos and Hispanics are likely to be markedly disparate is the area of manners, courtesy, and interpersonal relations. Anglos are taught to value openness, frankness, and directness. They are much more likely to express themselves simply, briefly, and frequently bluntly. The traditional Hispanic approach requires the use of much diplomacy and tactfulness when communicating with another individual. Hispanics often find themselves in difficulty if they disagree with an Anglo's point of view. To them, direct argument or contradiction appears rude and disrespectful. On the surface they may seem agreeable, manners dictating that they not reveal their genuine opinion openly unless they can take time to tactfully differ. Thus, they are less likely to express their disagreement with others or their unwillingness to do what others ask or expect from them. This is especially true of children who are taught to respect their elders.

Physicalness

Hispanics are more physical than Anglos in their relationships. Hispanics stand closer together when talking or relating. They tend to show affection and acceptance through touching. Friends are likely to kiss when they meet. Males are likely to hug each other or pat each other on the back as well as shake hands. And it is not unusual for people to hold others by the arm or place their hands on their shoulders when conversing.

Hispanics also tend to utilize physical punishment rather than deprivation of love and affection when disciplining their children. Moreover, once they have punished their children, they tend to forgive them rather than to remain angry, resentful or to hold a grudge. When they are told that the school is having difficulty with their children, some Hispanic parents will respond that they will hit them or advise school personnel to hit them.

Attitude Towards Authority

Many Hispanics come from cultures which emphasize respect for authority. This is especially true of those whose families have not been a part of the power structure. They are generally used to being told what is right by government officials, priests, educators, etc., and to obey.

In the counseling situation, where counselees are supposed to assume responsibility for the outcomes or decisions, this attitude will make the process more difficult. Out of respect for teachers and school authorities, parents may accept imposed decisions rather than exercise their rights or act out their disagreement.

Because of their respect for authority and their previous educational experiences, some Hispanics may express agreement with the decisions made about their children during counseling sessions, individualized education planning meetings, etc., when they do not understand the decisions or disagree with them.

Coming from countries where citizens are expected not to question the law but to trust in the authorities, they may have difficulty participating in the educational decision-making process as described by PL 94-142. Unaccustomed to the concept of parents' rights in general and unaware of their specific rights under the law, it may be difficult to fulfill the role ascribed to them by PL 94-142, especially when it is in their children's best interest that they demand that school systems respect their rights or those of their children.

Some Hispanic parents come from cultures where they are taught to be wary of signing documents. When they are asked to sign forms necessary for the evaluation of their children or the provision of special education services, they may be reluctant to do so.

Role of Children

Hispanic children are brought up to look up to their elders, especially their parents, and respect their wishes, opinions, attitudes and advice and to model themselves after adults whom they like. As a result, they may function better when adults are involved and supportive and provide encouragement and feedback about how they are doing both when they are working in the classroom and when they are being assessed.

They are brought up to obey rather than to question why or disagree, to be quiet around their elders and to listen and learn rather than to speak and participate.

They often have an active role to play in the family. They may be responsible for helping to care for the younger children, have many chores at home and serve as translators when their parents do not speak English. When these responsibilities interfere with their attendance at school, homework and study time, Hispanics tend to view the student's responsibilities to the family as more important than their responsibility to school.

Sex Roles

In traditional Hispanic families, the father tends to function as the authority and decision maker while the mother is the nurturer and comforter.

Modesty

Because Hispanics, especially females, tend to be modest about exposing their bodies, some students may feel very uncomfortable about wearing shorts to physical education classes, showering in the presence of others and being examined by doctors and nurses.

Learning Styles

The Hispanic culture emphasizes learning by doing. As a result, some Hispanic students learn more by touching, seeing, manipulating and experiencing concrete objects than by discussing or reading about ideas. When there is a difference between their cognitive styles and their teachers' teaching styles, these differences rather than supposed intellectual deficits, learning disabilities, etc., may account for their school-related problems.

Attitude Toward Religion and the Supernatural

Some Hispanic students may believe in the supernatural, ghosts, magic, religion, saints, etc., more than their Anglo peers do.

Attitude Towards Emotional and Behavioral Problems

In comparison to Anglos, Hispanics are more likely to believe that behavior is controlled on a conscious level through will-power rather than unconscious intra-psychic motivation.*

As a result, some Hispanic parents may believe that their children's misconduct or learning problems are caused by laziness and stubbornness rather than emotional, psychological or neurological problems beyond their control.

Believing that behavior is subject to conscious control, Hispanic parents are more likely to utilize behavior modification techniques in order to control their children's behavior than techniques which are designed to change their children's dynamics or resolve their problems. Because of their belief, they also tend to view their children's behavior as a reflection of the family and their ability as parents. They may become defensive when their children's misbehavior is brought to their attention.

Attitudes Toward Counseling

Hispanics who are accustomed to seeking the help of family members with their personal problems may not feel the need to discuss things with strangers, regardless of their professional qualifications. They may even experience the counseling process as an invasion of their privacy by a stranger.

Hispanics who believe that behavior is controlled on a conscious level may not have a great deal of faith in psychological counseling as a problem-solving approach and are more likely than Anglos to resist the use of these approaches with their children or themselves.

They may believe that psychological counseling is only suitable for the very disturbed or crazy.

Hispanics are proud and self-reliant. When they need assistance, they tend to go to their families rather than public agencies for support. Many of them come from countries where public welfare type programs are virtually non-existent. Because of their pride and previous experience, they may be reluctant to accept free services for themselves or their children from public agencies.

---

*Twenty-four percent of the Hispanic participants reported that they lacked sufficient information and experience regarding this item.

GROUP II

SOMEWHAT MORE CONTROVERSIAL

Pace of Life

Hispanics tend to be more concerned with doing a job well regardless of the amount of time required than they are in finishing rapidly so they will have more time for the next task.

Hispanics tend to prefer to work at a relaxed pace, even if it means taking longer to finish something.

Among Hispanics conducting business or meetings in general is somewhat of a social affair. Digressions from the topic at hand make for a more personal, relaxed atmosphere. Counselors who have an Anglo "let's-get-down-to-business" or "let's-stick-to-the-point" approach may misperceive these digressions as avoidance or resistance.

Personal vs. Impersonal

Hispanics tend to judge people in terms of their personal qualities—who they are, rather than in terms of their accomplishments—what they are. Success, honor and prestige are attributed to good people rather than to people who have achieved a considerable amount in a material sense. As a result, some Hispanic students may not be as motivated by the work ethic to accomplish, achieve, and succeed according to the criteria utilized in the schools.

In comparison to the Anglo culture, the Hispanic culture emphasizes people over ideas.

As a result, some Hispanic students may relate better to a person-centered rather than thing- or idea-centered curriculum.

What motivate Hispanics to be punctual are not impersonal reasons such as it is efficient for everyone to arrive at the same time and begin at the same time. Hispanics may feel that the meeting or work could have started without them if necessary. On the other hand, personal relationships do concern them. For example, they may be very concerned that their lack of punctuality not be interpreted as a sign of disrespect or a lack of courtesy toward others and arive on time to make sure they do not seem disrespectful.

Sex Roles

Hispanic families often have different expectations for their sons and daughters. Despite women's liberation and the non-sexist attitudes currently prevailing in the United States, many Hispanic parents have different expectations for their sons and daughters. They still protect girls and expect them to be mothers' helpers and to eventually marry, have children and focus their energies in the home. On the other hand, boys are expected to grow up to be more independent, to be more involved in activities outside the home and to be breadwinners. Thus, some Hispanic girls may not be highly motivated to succeed academically, to go to college or to complete vocational training programs.

Because the Hispanic culture tends to be patriarchal, some Hispanic male students, especially adolescents, may have difficulty complying with female authority figures.

Unwillingness to Admit Inability

Hispanics, especially males, tend not to admit to not knowing something or being unable to do something. Hispanics are expected to be sensitive to the needs, feelings and desires of others so that it is unnecessary for others to be embarrassed by asking for help or understanding or to be left alone. Males especially may rely on the sensitivity of others and express their needs in indirect or subtle ways.

Formal Relationships

Although there was little disagreement that Hispanic children are brought up to have more formal relationships with adults, there was slightly less agreement that as a result these students may be uncomfortable with the less formal relationships usually observed between Anglo teachers and Anglo students.

Role of Children

While there was little controversy that Hispanic children are brought up to be dependent on and to look up to their elders, there was slightly less agreement regarding how this upbringing affects their school functioning as reflected in the following statements.

Some Hispanic students may have difficulty when educators want them to form their own opinions and' make their own decisions independently of their teachers.

Hispanics tend to be more interested in and dependent on the approval of others than Anglos who are more likely to be receptive to more impersonal and materialistic forms of recognition.

Physicalness

Finally, while there was a great deal of agreement among Hispanic participants that Hispanic parents tend to use physical punishment rather than deprivation of attention and affection when disciplining their children, a smaller percentage of them agreed that when educators deprive Hispanic students of attention and affection in order to discipline them, these students may feel that they have been rejected rather than justly punished.

GROUP III

AGREEMENT WITH A GREAT DEAL OF CONTROVERSY

Interpersonal Relationships

Non-Competitive Behavior

Hispanics tend to believe that it is bad manners to try to excel over others in the group or to attempt to be recognized for their individual achievement. To be called *sofisticado*—acting as if you are better than others—is an insult. As a result, many Hispanic students will avoid competing with their peers for fear of being criticized or rejected by them.

Hispanic children are discouraged from attempting to excel at the expense of others. Overt competition between individuals is discouraged. As a result, Hispanic students may be reluctant to volunteer answers when they know them or to compete in academic games such as spelling bees and arithmetic baseball.

They may also pretend not to know the correct answer when called on.

Hispanic students may allow other students to copy their homework or their answers on examinations in order to show their helpfulness, brotherhood and generosity. They may not consider this to be bad behavior.

Group Processes

In the Hispanic culture, it is not impolite for more than one person to speak at a time during group discussions. Multiple conversations may be carried out simultaneously without anyone being considered rude or discourteous.

When a group of Hispanics disagree, they may resolve the issue by continuing to discuss it until it becomes apparent that a concensus has been reached without polling the group or calling for a vote.

Disciplinary Methods

Hispanic parents tend to speak more politely and indirectly when they criticize or discipline their children. In the United States, educators are much more gruff and direct with students. Some Hispanic students, especially males, may interpret the gruff or more direct manner of Anglos as an indication that educators do not consider them worthy or deserving of a proper relationship. When educators speak to them in a matter-of-fact or authoritarian manner, they may feel insulted, angry or resentful and lose respect for these educators and the desire to cooperate or conform.

Friends

Hispanic students who are asked to work in groups to which they have been assigned may be reluctant to cooperate fully if the group members are acquaintances rather than friends in the Hispanic sense of the word.

Concept of Time

Punctuality

The Hispanic concept of punctuality is different than the Anglo concept. If a meeting is called for two o'clock, people are expected to arrive some time after that. If a party or dance is set for nine o'clock, people may be expected to arrive at eleven or even later. An agreement to repair a TV for Wednesday means that it will probably be ready some time after Wednesday.

When Hispanic students arrive a little late or complete a project some time after it is due, they may assume that they have been punctual and Hispanic parents may not arrive "on time" for meetings and counseling sessions when "on time" is defined in Anglo terms.

Present vs. Future Time Oriented

Hispanics tend to be more present time oriented. Finishing a conversation now may be more important than keeping an appointment later. Living to the fullest now and enjoying what the present has to offer may be more important than saving, planning and striving for future satisfactions and security.

The anticipation of a large reward or satisfaction in the future may be much less motivating than a smaller satisfaction in the here and now.

Pace of Life

At home, Hispanic children are permitted to do things at their own pace without adhering to strict time schedules.

As a result, Hispanic students may not complete classroom work as fast as their Anglo peers.

When required to rush or stop working before they have finished in order to begin the next task with their peers, they may become anxious, nervous, rebellious, etc.

Spontaneity and Impulsiveness

Hispanics tend to be more spontaneous in their actions. They are not as concerned about hiding their feelings or acting on them. They are less likely to reflect first or ask themselves, "how will it look, or will it turn out alright?" before acting on an impulse. They have what some call a "Latin temperament."

Hispanics tend to react spontaneously and impulsively to life. When faced with problems, they tend to look for immediate solutions without reflecting on their implications for the future. Thus, some Hispanic students may be more impulsive and less reflective than their Anglo peers when asked to solve problems or answer questions in school.

Sex Roles

Hispanic boys are taught to be protective of their sisters and other girls, escorting them to and from school, protecting them from other boys, handling their money, etc., in general performing a macho role; Hispanic girls are encouraged to assume a submissive role toward brothers and other boys. As a result, both sexes may feel uncomfortable when they are required to work and play together as equals.

Hispanic students prefer to work in school in groups of their own sex. They may feel uncomfortable when well-meaning egalitarian non-sexist Anglo educators require that the sexes work or engage in athletic activities together.

Unwillingness to Acknowledge Responsibility

Hispanics are less likely to verbally acknowledge responsibility for mistakes and errors or to apologize when they have wronged someone.

Instead of blaming themselves for errors, they frequently attribute it to adverse circumstances. They didn't miss the bus because they arrived too late. Instead, they blame the bus for leaving before they arrived. They did not get drunk because they chose to drink too much. They got drunk because too much liquor was served at the fiesta.

Fatalism

"Haga uno lo que haga todo es lo que Dios quiere" (do what we will, everything is in the hands of God) is a saying that sums up the fatalistic philosophy of many Hispanics. Believing that God rather than man controls the events of their lives, many Hispanics try to accept and appreciate what Anglos try to control and overcome. This may make it difficult for some Hispanics to believe that their handicapped children can be helped.

Some Hispanics believe that their misfortunes are inflicted on them by God as punishments for their sins. They may believe that their handicapped children are the crosses God has given them to bear. As a result, they *may be* reluctant to attempt to thwart God's will by trying to change the condition of their children.

Superstition

Some Hispanics believe that drinking too much, looking at the moon at the wrong time, leading a bad life, etc., may cause the birth of handicapped children. Holding themselves personally responsible for their children's disabilities, they may feel so guilty and ashamed that they may attempt to hide their children from others in the community.

Some Hispanics believe that mental retardation, blindness, emotional problems, etc., can be caused by mal de ojo, brujeria, alcohol abuse, looking at the moon at the wrong time, etc. As a result, they may prefer to rely on prayer, curanderismo, herbs, brujas and other methods as ways of alleviating their children's difficulties rather than the services offered by the schools and other agencies.*

---

*Somewhat less controversial than the previous statement.

GROUP IV

LACK OF AGREEMENT

Interpersonal Relationships

Group Processes

Anglos expect that people who are working together will all share the load equally and think that a group member who is not a loafer, an idler, or a person who is taking unfair advantage of the efforts of others. However, Hispanics tend not to be upset by a group member who does not do his or her share of the work because he or she is less qualified, less motivated, or less interested.

Non-Competitive

Because of their belief that it is bad manners to try to excel over others, Hispanic students may resist being singled out in front of peers for praise and reward.

Quality of Work

In comparison to Anglos, quality of work is not a high priority for Hispanics. The quality of the product or the result of their effort may be less important than accomplishing and finishing the task.*

---

*A majority disagreed that this trait was characteristic of Hispanics living in the United States.

HISPANIC PARTICIPANTS' OPINIONS REGARDING STATEMENTS ABOUT HISPANICS LIVING IN THE UNITED STATES

This appendix contains a list of statements about the conditions under which many Hispanics live in the United States which a high percentage of Hispanic participants agree with. Unless otherwise indicated, at least 80 percent of the participants agreed with each of the statements.

Different Socio-Economic Levels

Hispanic students who are raised by parents with little formal education and scant financial resources may not be exposed to the materials and experiences many middle class, educated parents provide their children. As a result, they may lack some of the readiness skills expected of students in the lower grades.

These students may suffer cultural shock in school because of the differences between what is available to them at home, where they may have to wear out, make do, or do without, and what is provided by the school system. These differences may do harm to these students' self-concepts and make it difficult for these students to adjust to school.*

---

*Only 73 percent of the Hispanic participants agreed with this statement.

Some teenage Hispanic students whose families have serious economic problems may believe it is more important for them to earn money to help their families than to graduate from high school or to go on to college.

Many of the academically oriented courses offered in the middle and secondary schools may seem irrrelevant to the vocational needs of these students.

Hispanic families with limited economic resources in need of counseling are often in a double bind if counselors cannot be flexible in scheduling appointments and availability of services. Typically, jobs which lower-economic people have are not flexible regarding work hours, absenteeism, etc. Parents often cannot leave work to attend daytime appointments. If counseling facilities are far from neighborhoods, parents often find it a hardship to arrange transportation, provide for babysitters, etc. Special treatments, counseling fees for private therapy, etc., are often impossible to include in the family budget. Time to attend regular counseling sessions, even if they are scheduled during non-working hours, is often not possible due to family obligations of housework, meal preparation, child care. Family priorities must often take precedence over attendance at school functions, meetings, etc. Among poor families, the necessities of day-to-day existence, such as trips to the grocery store or laundromat, emergency health needs, car trouble, etc., are of primary importance.

Hispanics who have serious economic problems often justifiably perceive the causes of their frustrations, anger, etc., on the social and economic situation around them.

Different Educational Experiences

Hispanics with limited education may have different concepts of what constitutes sufficient education.

Hispanics who have had little education may lack information about special education, mental health and counseling services.

Some Hispanic parents may come from countries where disabled children do not receive special education. Thus, they may not seek such services for their children. This may be especially true of early stimulation and intervention.

Some Hispanic parents believe that special education services are a waste of time because they recall their own educational experiences in their native countries where only regular educational services were offered.

Some Hispanic parents may come from countries where many of the disabled fulfill acceptable community roles without special education. This may be especially true of rural agricultural areas. As a result, some Hispanic parents may think that special services beyond medical treatment are unnecessary.*

Because of the limited training the disabled receive in these countries, some Hispanics may not be aware of the disabled's potential for learning with appropriate special education services.

Because of their educational experiences in their native countries, some Hispanic parents are unaware of the existence of some of the learning handicaps which require special educational services in the United States. They may ask themselves, if the schools in their native countries never noticed such things, why is their child's school blaming their child's difficulty on something they have neither heard of before nor observed in their child at home? This may lead them to reject both the diagnosis and the services offered to their child.*

Although these parents may want to help their children, because of their own lack of experience and education they may be unable to provide the assistance that many other parents can provide—for example, helping their children with their homework.

They may prefer concrete action on the part of counselors as opposed to talking in the resolution of their problems and concerns. They want action-oriented counselors who can be change agents, who will do their best to change the situation which is causing the problem, rather than counselors who think they should adjust to or adapt to these conditions.

Language Differences

Some Hispanic parents are not fluent enough in English to participate in counseling sessions and school meetings held in English or to understand communications in English sent home

---

*Only 73 percent of the Hispanic participants agreed.

from school. Because they do not speak English to their children, some Hispanic students are not fluent enough in English when they start school to profit from instruction in arithmetic, science, etc., when the language of instruction is English. Immersing them in a completely English program may cause them to fall behind in these subjects.

Even after these children have been exposed to English at school, they may be Spanish dominant for words and concepts related to home and community. Teachers who are unaware of these students' incomplete mastery of English may create learning problems for them by assuming that they understand everything taught to them in English.

Prejudice and Stereotyping

History, geography, social roles, etc., are often studied exclusively in terms of the Anglo point of view. Too often, students are taught that Columbus rather than the Native Americans discovered America, that Ponce de Leon was a fool who was looking for a fountain of youth and that Latin Americans are lazy procrastinators who live in small underdeveloped pueblos.

When their foods are not mentioned during discussions of what are good foods to eat in order to have a balanced diet, their music is not played during assemblies and music appreciation classes, etc., Hispanic students may feel that they and their culture are inferior, at least in the eyes of their teachers.

Since Hispanic students are used to foods, music, holidays, language and customs which are very different from what Anglos are accustomed to, Hispanic students may have difficulty relating to the Anglo-oriented classroom.*

Some Hispanics have lost their trust and respect for Anglo institutions because of the prejudicial treatment they have received from employers, landlords, real estate agents, neighbors, welfare case workers, indifferent school officials, etc. This lack of trust may extend to counselors even when counselors do not merit such mistrust.

---

*Only 67 percent of the Hispanic participants agreed with this statement.

These Hispanic parents may also assume that counselors share the prevalent stereotype of Hispanics, such as they are disinterested in their children's school performance, lazy, stupid, dishonest, procrastinators, etc.

Those dependent on social welfare programs and undocumented aliens may be unwilling to confide in counselors for fear that the information might be used against them.

Because of previous misplacement of non-handicapped Hispanic children in special education programs, many parents are now suspicious of such placements for their children even when they are appropriate.

Thus, while in the past a simple statement of the problem in school would be enough to gain the support of many Hispanic parents, nowadays many Hispanic parents are justifiably suspicious of school personnel.

Identity Conflicts

Like many other people with roots in more than one country or culture, Hispanics have many alternative ways of viewing who they are. They may identify with the country and culture in which they or their families originated and conceive of themselves as Spaniards, Mexicans, Puerto Ricans, Cubans, Chileans, etc. They may identify with both their original and current cultures and think of themselves as Cuban-Americans, Puerto Rican-Americans, Mexican-Americans, Chicanos, Spanish-Americans, etc., or they may identify themselves solely in terms of their current residence and consider themselves to be Americans.

Many Hispanic youth are faced with the necessity of surviving in two cultures—the Latino culture at home and in the community and the Anglo culture at school. When they find that they can neither be "All American" or "Todo Latino," they may identify with a youth culture like the Low Riders, Vatos Locos, or Guardian Angels. This may lead them to dress, speak and walk differently than the other students in school.

IMPLICATIONS ABOUT WHICH NON-HISPANIC PARTICIPANTS WITH VARYING DEGREES OF EXPERIENCE EXPRESSED DIFFERENT OPINIONS

This section contains the forty-two implications about which non-Hispanics with varying degrees of experience expressed different opinions.

Group One contains the thirty-eight items about which the more experienced non-Hispanics had working with Hispanics the more they agreed.

Group Two contains the four items about which the more experience the non-Hispanics had, the less they agreed. The asterisks indicate the amount of difference between the three groups.

The greatest differences were observed in relation to items with three asterisks and the least difference, although still a considerable difference, was observed in relation to items with only one asterisk.

GROUP ONE

* Therefore, educators should include community-oriented projects in the curriculum.
** Therefore, educators should use family pride to motivate Hispanic students by saying such things as "your family will be proud of you."

** Therefore, educators should de-emphasize competition and stress cooperation when attempting to motivate some Hispanic students.

* Therefore, educators should encourage students to ask each other for help and arrange for peer tutoring.

** Therefore, educators should develop the close personal relationships with their Hispanic students which will motivate their students to seek their teachers' approval and to model themselves after them.

*** Therefore, educators should use praise, hugs, pats on the back and other personal rewards with Hispanic students more than checks, gold stars and materialistic forms of reinforcement such as sweets and toys.

*** Therefore, educators should adjust the contents of the curriculum to the needs of these Hispanic students. This may include offering more vocationally oriented courses and arranging for cooperative work study programs.

* Therefore, such limited English proficient students should receive a bilingual education. They should be taught such subjects as math, science, etc., in Spanish while they are being helped to become proficient enough in English to profit from English language instruction in these subject areas.

** Even after they are proficient in English they should be provided with enough Spanish language instruction to maintain their Spanish proficiency if they wish to do so.

* Therefore, educators should adapt their curriculum and instruction techniques to the knowledge and experiences Hispanic students bring to school. This will prevent them from being educationally behind as soon as they enter the school system.

* Therefore, educators should provide these students with the guidance and approval they need in order to make decisions in the classroom.

* Therefore, educators should provide these students with encouragement and feedback about how they are doing that they require in order to work effectively.

*** Therefore, educators should not over-emphasize the expression of opinions with such students until they demonstrate that they are comfortable with this role in school.

** Therefore, educators should personalize the curriculum. This can be done by having students solve math problems about people, shopping in stores rather than just numerical computational problems, teaching about human geography, how people live in different regions, rather than physical geography, etc.

*** Therefore, educators should include these interests (the supernatural, ghosts, magic, religion, saints, etc.) when teaching reading, writing and oral communication skills.

* Therefore, educators should de-emphasize the lecture approach and emphasize direct experience with these Hispanic students.

* Therefore, educators should provide Hispanic students with short-term assignments. Daily or weekly assignments would be preferable to term projects. When term projects are necessary, they should be broken down into short-term objectives leading toward long-term goals.

*** Therefore, educators should not assume that when Hispanic students express their joy or anger in class it will lead to even more acting-out behavior and they should not feel obliged to "nip such problems in the bud" or to stop them before they occur.

*** Therefore, educators should allow Hispanics to work on their homework together.

*** Therefore, educators should allow Hispanic students to help each other when they are called on to answer in class.

* Therefore, educators should not insist that all Hispanic group members share equally in the work if the group members themselves do not mind if some do not.

** Therefore, when Hispanic students miss school or come unprepared, educators should determine when conflicting family responsibilities are the cause and accommodate their expectations and teaching methods to the students' and parents' realities.

*** Therefore, educators should not lower course grades or punish Hispanic students in other ways when family responsibilities prevent them from completing assignments, arriving on time, or attending class.

** Therefore, when educators find it necessary to reprimand Hispanic students for tardiness or to encourage them to be punctual, they should focus more on the interpersonal than impersonal results of their lateness. Such statements as "if you respect your classmates you will get here when we need you" may have more effect than statements such as "we could not finish on time" or "we waited fifteen minutes because we had to wait for you."

*** Therefore, when it is necessary to discipline such students, it may be more effective for the discipline to be administered by a male even when the classroom teacher is a female.

* Therefore, educators should respect the wishes of Hispanic students by not requiring that the sexes work and play together if specific individuals are not inclined to do so.

** Therefore, educators should not use deprivation of affection to manage Hispanic students.

*** Therefore, educators should be indirect rather than direct and frank, and respectful rather than disrespectful, when reprimanding or disciplining Hispanic students.

*** Therefore, they should strive to become their students' friends by sharing their feelings, attitudes, opinions and personal lives with them.

* Therefore, educators should try to not back away from Hispanic students when they stand too close for comfort.

* Therefore, educators should not shame Hispanic students by requiring them to make verbal acknowledgements of their mistakes and wrongdoings in ways which are culturally unacceptable to them.

*** Therefore, educators should welcome the development of such group loyalty and they should use it when they manage their classes.

*** Therefore, Hispanic students should not be assessed with standardized instruments which do not permit the assessor to provide encouragement and feedback to them.

*** Therefore, Hispanic students should be encouraged to guess while being assessed with such instruments.

* Therefore, when counselors believe that it is necessary to put such parents at ease, to relax them, make the situation seem less formidable, etc., they should not use informality in their relationships as a technique. Such an unfamiliar unexpected relationship may make Hispanic parents even more uncomfortable and uneasy in the situation.

* Therefore, counselors who are not accustomed to being in such close proximity to others when they speak may be tempted to increase the distance between themselves and the Hispanic parents they are counseling by sitting behind a desk, etc. However, counselors should allow their Hispanic counselees to determine the distance between them in order to make their counselees more comfortable in the counseling session.

*** Therefore, when counseling Hispanic parents, counselors should plan for sufficient time to accomplish their goals even if it takes more time or many more sessions.

*** Therefore, counselors who disagree with the use of corporal punishment should not criticize Hispanic parents who use it, nor perceive them to be ineffective or abusive parents because they hit their children.

*** Therefore, counselors should not utilize the counseling relationship as a vehicle to encourage Hispanic parents to change from their own cultural frame of reference to the reference of the majority or dominant culture at the expense of their own desires and identity, even if counselors believe that it would be to the advantage of the parents or their children to do so.

GROUP TWO

* Therefore, educators should be sensitive to the needs for anonymity of some of their Hispanic students and avoid using the question-and-answer technique with them.

* Therefore, educators should not insist that when Hispanic students express themselves they use an Anglo style rather than the more poetic Hispanic style.

* Because these students do not function independently, educators should de-emphasize the use of trial-and-error learning, the inquiry method and other forms of independent study.

* Therefore, when counseling parents who believe fervently in these methods, counselors should consider working in conjunction with people in the community such as priest, curanderos, herbalista, who provide these kinds of treatments.

BIBLIOGRAPHY

Acevedo, Romero: *An Approach for Counseling Mexican-American Parents of Mentally Retarded Children.* ERIC ED 055 385.

Acuna, Rodolfo: *Occupied America: The Chicano's Struggle Toward Liberation.* San Francisco, Canfield Press, 1972.

Adkins, Patricia G. and Young, R.G.: Cultural perceptions in the treatment of handicapped school children of Mexican-American parentage. *Journal of Research and Development in Education,* 9:83-90, 1976.

Aguilar, Jaquacio: Initial contact with Mexican-American families. *Social Work,* 17(3):66-70, 1972.

Almanza, Helen P. and Mosley, William J.: Curriculum adaptations and modifications for culturally diverse handicapped children. *Exceptional Children,* 46(8):608-615, 1980.

Alzaga, Florinda: The three roots of Cuban heritage. *Agenda: A journal on Hispanic issues.* Jan./Feb. 1980. Disseminated by: National Origin Desegregation Component Office of Equal Educational Opportunity New Jersey State Department of Education.

Ambert, Alba N.: The identification of LEP children with special needs. *Bilingual Journal,* Fall, 17-22, 1982.

Ambert, Alba and Dew, Nancy: *Special Education for Exceptional Bilingual Students: A Handbook for Educators.* Milwaukee, Midwest National Origin Desegregation Assistance Center, University of Wisconsin, Milwaukee, 1982.

Aragon, John and Marquez, L.: *Spanish Americans: Language and Culture.* Reston, Council for Exceptional Children, 1973.

Aragon, John A. and Ulibarri, Sabine R.: Learn, amigo, learn. *Personnel and Guidance Journal,* 50(2):86-95, 1971.

Aramoni, Aniceto: Machismo. *Psychology Today,* 69-72, 1972.

Arnold, Richard D. and Wist, Anne H.: Auditory discrimination abilities of disadvantaged Anglo and Mexican-American children. *Elementary School Journal,* 70(6):295-299, 1970.

Baca, Leonard: *A Survey of Testing, and Placement Procedures to Assign Mexican-American Students into Classes for Educable Mentally Retarded in the Southwest.* University of Northern Colorado, 36:01-A, 214, 1974.

Baca, Leonard and Bransford, Jim: Meeting the needs of the bilingual handicapped child. *Momentum*, 12(2):49-51, 1981.

Baca, Leonard M. and Bransford, Jim: *An Appropriate Education for Handicapped Children of Limited English Proficiency*. Special Education in America—its Legal and Governmental Foundations Series. Reston, The Council for Exceptional Children, 1982.

Baca, Leonard M. and Cervantes, Hermes T.: *The Bilingual Special Education Interface*. University of Colorado, Denver, Times Mirror/Mosby, 1984.

Baca, Leonard and Lane, Karen: A dialogue on cultural implications for learning. *Exceptional Children*, 40:8, 1974.

Baecher, Richard E.: *The Instruction of Hispanic American Students: Exploring their Cognitive Styles*. Jamaica, Bilingual Press/Editorial Bilingue, Department of Foreign Languages, City University of New York.

Banks, James: *Multiethnic Education: Practices and Promises*. Bloomington, Phi Delta Kappa Educational Foundation, 1977.

Bender, Paula S. and Ruiz, Rene A.: Race and class as differential determinants of underachievement and underaspiration among Mexicans and Anglos. *Journal of Educational Research*, 68:51-5, 1974.

Benitez, Mario A. and Villareal, Lupita G.: *The Education of the Mexican American: A selected bibliography*. Rosslyn, National Clearinghouse for Bilingual Education, 1979.

Benson, Douglas K.: *A Select Bibliography of Sources on the Teaching of Hispanic Culture*. ERIC ED 192 558.

Bergin, Victoria: *Special Education Needs in Bilingual Programs*. Rosslyn, National Clearinghouse for Bilingual Education, 1980.

Bilingual Special Education Packet. Rosslyn, National Clearinghouse for Bilingual Education.

Bilingual Special Education Personnel Preparation. National task-oriented seminar, Washington, D.C., Access Inc., 1981.

A Bilingual Special Education Task Oriented Workshop Materials. Washington, D.C., Access Inc., 1980.

Bransford, Louis A. et al. (Eds): *Cultural Diversity and the Exceptional Child*. Reston, Council for Exceptional Children, 1973.

Brown, George H., Rosen, Nan L., Hill, Susan T., and Olivas, Michael A.: *The Condition of Education for Hispanic Americans*. Washington, D.C., U.S. Government Printing Office, 1980.

Bryant, Brenda and Meadow, Arnold: School-related problems of Mexican-American adolescents. *Journal of School Psychology*, 14(2):139-150, 1976.

Building Bridges of Understanding with the People of Latin America. Provo, Brigham Young University, 1979.

Burke, Fred G.: *Beyond Multicultural Education: The Case for Ethnic Literacy*. Trenton, New Jersey State Department of Education, National Origin Desegration, 1980.

California State Department of Education. Spanish-speaking pupils classified as EMR. *Integrated Education*, 7:28-33, 1969.

Carrasquillo, Angela: *New Directions for Special Education Through a Bilingual Bicultural Approach*. Paper presented at the annual international convention. The Council for Exceptional Children. April 1977, 13p. ERIC ED 139 173.

Carrillo, Frederico M.: *The Development of a Rationale and Model Program To Prepare Teachers For The Bilingual-Bicultural Secondary School Programs.* San Francisco, R & E Research Associates, 1977.

Caskey, Owen L. (Ed.): *Guidance Needs of Mexican-American Youth.* ERIC ED 036 347.

Caskey, Owen L.: *Community Responsibilities and School Guidance Programs for Mexican-American Youth.* ERIC ED 041 646.

Cervantes, Robert A.: *Hispanic Underachievers: The Neglected Minority.* Paper presented at the Hispanic English Dominant Student Conference; San Diego State University Lau Center, 1982.

Chinn, Philip C.: The exceptional minority child: issues and some answers. *Exceptional Children,* 45(7):532-536, 1979.

Chinn, Philip C.: Curriculum development for culturally different exceptional children. *Teacher Education and Special Education,* 2(4):49-58, 1979.

Cohen, Bernard H.: *Multiculturalism and Bilingual Education In Our Schools: The American Way.* Nyack, Bernard Cohen Research and Development Incorporated.

Cohen, R.E.: Principles of preventive mental health programs for ethnic minority populations: the acculturation of Puerto Ricans to the United States. *American Journal of Psychiatry,* 128(12):1529-1533, 1972.

Collier, Catherine (Ed.): *Bueno-Musep. bilingual special education. Annotated bibliography,* 1-4, Multicultural Special Education Project, Boulder, University of Colorado, 1982.

Collier, Catherine and Martinez, Leona: *Summary proceedings of a working institute on bilingual special education.* Boulder, Bueno Center for Multicultural Education, Oct. 30-31, 1982.

Communicating and Working with Parents in the Multicultural Classroom. 1-93, 1977. ERIC ED 177 046.

Condon, Elaine C., Peters, Janice Y. and Sueiro-Ross, Carmen: *Special Education and The Hispanic Child: Cultural Perspectives.* Philadelphia, Teacher Corps. Mid-Atlantic Network Temple University, 1979.

Conference Proceedings, R & D speaks: Bilingual/Multicultural Education, November 12-13, 1979. Austin, Southwest Educational Development Laboratory, 1980.

Contreras, Maximiliano: *Crossing: A Comparative Analysis of the Mexicano, Mexican-American and Chicano.* San Pedro, Travel/Study, Inc., 1983.

Cross, William C. and Maldanado, Bonnie: The counselor, the Mexican-American and the stereotype. *Elementary School Guidance and Counseling,* 6:1, 27-31, 1971.

Currier, Richard L.: The hot-cold syndrome and symbolic balance in Mexican and Spanish-American folk medicine. *Ethnology,* 5(3):251-263, 1966.

Darcy, Natalie: Bilingualism and the measurement of intelligence: Review of a decade of research. *Journal of Genetic Psychology,* 103:259-282, 1963.

Dean, Raymond S.: Analysis of the PIAT with Anglo and Mexican-American children. *Journal of School Psychology,* 15:4, 1977.

Dean, Raymond S.: Predictive validity of the WISC-R with Mexican-American children. *Journal of School Psychology,* 17:1, 1979.

De Blaisse, Richard R.: *Counseling with Mexican-American Youth.* Austin, Learning Concepts, 1976.

De Blassie, Richard R.: *Testing Mexican-American Youth*. Hingham, Teaching Resources, 1980.

de la Rocha, Petris (Proj. Coord.): *Chimextla Project, A Summary Report on Educational Needs of Latinos*. County of San Mateo, Office of Educational Services (San Mateo), San Mateo County Community College District, 1980.

Demos, George D.: Attitudes of Mexican-American and Anglo-American groups toward education. *Journal of Social Psychology*, 67:249-256, 1962.

A dialogue on cultural implications for learning. *Exceptional Children*, 40(8):552-563, 1974.

Diaz-Guerrero, Rogelio: Neurosis and the Mexican family structure. *American Journal of Psychiatry*, 112:411-417, 1955.

Diggs, Ruth W.: Education across cultures. *Exceptional Children*, 40(8):578-503, 1974.

Dillard, John M.: Multicultural approaches to mainstreaming: A challenge to counselors, teachers, psychologists and administrators. *Peabody Journal of Education*, 57(4):276-290, 1980.

Earle, Jane: The story of the Chicano education project. *Today's Education*, 66(4):76-77, 1977.

Edgerton, Robert B. and Karno, Marvin: Mexican-American bilingualism and the perception of mental illness. *Archives of Genetic Psychiatry*, 24:286-290, 1971.

The Education of the Mexican-American: A Selected Bibliography. Rosslyn, National Clearinghouse for Bilingual Education, 1979.

Escobedo, Arturo E.: *Chicano Counselor*. Lubbock, Trucha Publications, 1974.

Fabrega, Horacio and Wallace, Carole Ann: Value identification and psychiatric disability: An analysis involving American of Mexican descent. *Behavioral Science*, 13:362-371, 1968.

Felder, Dell: The education of Mexican-Americans: Fallacies of the monoculture approach. *Social Education*, 34(6):639-647, 1970.

Figueroa, Richard A.: The system of multicultural pluralistic assessment. *School Psychology Digest*, 8(1):28-36, 1979.

Flores, Juan M.: *Chicano Education: Clearer Objectives and Better Results*. ERIC ED 198 968.

Fuchigami, Robert Y.: Teacher education for culturally diverse exceptional children. *Exceptional Children*, 46(8):634-641, 1980.

Furlong, Michael J. et al.: Effects of counselor ethnicity and attitudinal similarity on Chicano students' perceptions of counselor credibility and attractiveness. *Hispanic Journal of Behavioral Sciences*, 1(1):41-53, 1979.

Gallegos, Robert L. et al.: *Bilingual/Bicultural Education—Special Education: An Interface*. ERIC ED 187 081.

Garcia, Angela B. and Zimmerman, Barry J.: The effect of examiner ethnicity and language on the performance of bilingual Mexican-American first graders. *The Journal of Social Psychology*, 87:3-11, 1972.

Garcia, Ricardo L.: Mexican-Americans learn through language experience. *Reading Teacher*, 28:301-305, 1974.

Garcia, Ricardo L.: *Fostering a Pluralistic Society Through Multi-Ethnic Education*. Bloomington, Phi Delta Kappa Educational Foundation, 1978.

Garcia, Ricardo L.: *Education for Cultural Pluralism: Global Roots Stew.* Bloomington, Phi Delta Kappa Educational Foundation, 1981.

Garcia-Moya, Rodolfo and Starks, Joann: *Bueno, Summary Proceedings of a Working Institute on Bilingual Special Education.* Boulder, Bueno Center for Multicultural Education, January 5-8, 1982.

Gavillan-Torres, Eva M.: Interdisciplinary approach to the education of Hispanic handicapped children. *Education Journal Limited,* 2(4):24-26, 1980.

Goldman, Roy D. and Hartig, Linda K.: The WISC may not be a valid predictor of school performance for primary grade minority children. *American Journal of Mental Deficiency,* 80:583-587, 1976.

Gollnick, Donna M. and Chinn, Phillip C.: *Multicultural Education in a Pluralistic Society.* St. Louis, C.V. Mosby, 1983.

Gonzales, Eloy and Ortiz, Leroy: Social policy and education related in linguistically and culturally different groups. *Journal of Learning Disabilities,* 10(6):332-338, 1977.

Gonzalez, Carlos: *An Overview of the Mestizo Heritage: Implications For Teachers of Mexican-American Children.* San Francisco, R & E Research Associates, Inc., 1976.

Gonzalez, Gustavo: Language, culture, and exceptional children. *Exceptional Children,* 40(8):565-570, 1974.

Goodale, Ronda and Soden, Marcia: *Disproportionate Placement of Black and Hispanic Students in Special Education Programs.* New Orleans, Paper presented at the Council for Exceptional Children Conference on the Exceptional Bilingual Child, February, 1981.

Grossman, Herbert: *What Counselors Educators and Psychologists Should Know About the Hispanic Culture in Order to Work More Effectively with Hispanic Exceptional Students and their Parents.* Sacramento, California State Department of Education, 1983.

Guerra, Manuel H. et al.: *The Retention of Mexican-American Students in Higher Education with Special Reference to Bicultural and Bilingual Problems.* ERIC ED 031 324.

Gutkin, Terry: Bannatyme patterns of Caucasian and Mexican-American learning disabled children. *Psychology in the Schools,* 16:178-183, 1979.

Haro, Carlos, M.: Truant and low-achieving Chicano student perceptions in the high school social system. *Aztlan,* 8:99-131.

Henkin, Carole S. and Henkin, Alan B.: Culture, poverty and educational problems of Mexican-Americans. *The Clearinghouse,* 50:316-319, 1977.

Hepner, Ethel M.: Self-concepts, values and needs of Mexican-American under-achievers or must the Mexican-American child adapt a self-concept that fits the American school? ERIC ED 048 954.

Hernandez, Alicia: Enriching self-concept through bicultural approaches: Group counseling for Chicanas. Project Mexico, ERIC ED 134 294.

Hernandez, Luis: The culturally disadvantaged Mexican-American student. Part I, *Journal of Secondary Education,* 42(2):59-65, 1967.

Hernandez, Luis: The culturally disadvantaged Mexican-American student. Part II, *Journal of Secondary Education,* 42(3):123-128, 1967.

Hilliard, Asa G.: Cultural diversity and special education. *Exceptional Children,* 46(8):584-588, 1980.

Holtzman, Elsa H., Goldsmith, Ross P. and Barrera, Carmen: *Field Dependence Field Independence.* Austin, Dissemination and Assessment Center for Bilingual Education, 1979.

Hoopes, David S.: *Intercultural Education.* Bloomington, Phi Delta Kappa Educational Foundation, 1980.

Hosford, Ray E. and Bowles, Stephen A.: Determining culturally appropriate reinforcers for Anglo and Chicano students. *Elementary School Guidance and Counseling,* 8(4):290-300, 1974.

Howard, Douglas P.: *Pitfalls In The Multicultural Diagnostic/Remedial Process: A Central American Experience.* University of Costa Rica, Paper presented at the Conference of the Council for Exceptional Children, 1980-1981.

Hurtado, Juan and Ochoa, Alberto: *Special Education and the Bilingual Child.* San Diego, National Origin Desegregation Lau Center, San Diego State University, 1982.

Issues in Bilingual, Bicultural Special Education Personnel Preparation. Washington, D.C., Access, Inc., 1980.

Investigation of Mental Retardation and Pseudo Mental Retardation in Relation to Bilingual and Sub-Cultural Factors. ERIC ED 002 810.

Jaramillo, Mari-Luci: *Cautions When Working With The Culturally Different Child.* ERIC ED 115 622.

Jaramillo, Mari-Luci: Cultural conflict curriculum and the exceptional child. *Exceptional Children,* 40(8):585-587, 1974.

Jones, Reginald (Ed.): *Mainstreaming and the Minority Child,* Reston, Council for Exceptional Children, 1976.

Jorstad, Dorothy: Psycholinguistic learning disabilities in 20 Mexican-American students. *Journal of Learning Disabilities,* 4(3):143-149, 1971.

Justin, Neal: Mexican-American reading habits and their cultural basis. *Journal of Reading,* 16:467-473, 1972-1973.

Kagan, Spencer and Madsen, Millard C.: Rivalry in Anglo-American and Mexican children of two ages. *Journal of Personality and Social Psychology,* 24:214-220, 1972.

Kagan, Spencer and Madsen, Millard C.: Cooperation and competition of Mexican, Mexican-American and Anglo-American children of two ages under four instructional sets. *Developmental Psychology,* 5(1):32-39, 1971.

Kagan, Spencer and Zahn, Lawrence C.: Field dependence and the school achievement gap between Anglo-American and Mexican-American children. *Journal of Educational Psychology,* 67(5):643-650, 1975.

Kamp, Susan and Chinn, Philip C.: *A Multiethnic Curriculum for Special Education Students.* Reston, Council for Exceptional Children, 1982.

Karno, Marvin and Edgerton, Robert B.: Perception of mental illness in a Mexican-American community. *Archives of General Psychiatry,* 20:233-238, 1969.

Karno, Marvin and Morales, Armando: A community mental health service for Mexican-Americans in a metropolis. *Comprehensive Psychiatry,* 2:116-121, 1971.

Keller, Gary D.: *The Systematic Exclusion of the Language and Culture of Boricuas, Chicanos and Other U.S. Hispanos in Elementary Spanish Grammar Textbooks Published in the United States.* Ypsilanti, Bilingual Press/Editorial Bilingue, Department of Foreign Languages and Bilingual Studies, Eastern Michigan University, 1974.

Keston, Morton J. and Jimenez, Carmina: A study of the performance on English and Spanish editions of the Stanford-Binet intelligence test by Spanish-American children. *Journal of Genetic Psychology,* 85:263-269, 1954.

Kiev, Asi: *Curanderismo: Mexican-American Folk Psychiatry.* New York, Free Press, 1968.

Killian, L.R.: Wisconsin, Illinois Test of Psycholinguistic Abilities and Bender Visual-Motor Gestalt Test performance of Spanish-American kindergarten and first-grade school children. *Journal of Consulting and Clinical Psychology,* 3(7,1):38-43, 1971.

Killian, L.R.: Cognitive test performance of Spanish-American primary school children—a longitudinal study. Final report. ERIC ED 060 156.

Kirk, Samuel A.: Ethnic differences in psycholinguistic abilities. *Exceptional Children,* 39:112-118, 1972.

Kirk, Samuel and Elkins, John: *Ethnic Differences and Learning Disabilities in Head Start Children.* Leadership Training Institute in Learning Disabilities, Washington, D.C., Department of Health, Education and Welfare, June, 1974.

Knapp, Robert R.: The effects of time limits on the intelligence of test performance of Mexican and American subjects. *Journal of Educational Psychology,* 51(1):14-19, 1960.

Kuvlesky, William P.: *Minority Group Orientations: Are Rural Mexican-American Youth Assimilation Prone or Pluralistic?* ERIC ED 192 959.

La Belle, Thomas J.: Differential perceptions of elementary school children representing distinct socio-cultural backgrounds. *Journal of Cross-Cultural Psychology,* 2(2):145-156, 1971.

Lambert, Nadine M.: Contributions of school classification, sex and ethnic status to adaptive behavior assessment. *Journal of School Psychology,* 17:1, 1979.

Landurand, Patricia et al.: *Bridging the Gap Between Bilingual Education and Special Education.* ERIC ED 191 253.

Leary, Mary Ellen: Children who are tested in an alien language: Mentally retarded? *New Republic,* 162(22):17-18, 1970.

Leutke, Barbara: Questionnaire results from Mexican-American parents of hearing impaired children in the U.S. *American Annals of the Deaf,* 121:565-568, 1976.

Levandowski, Barbara: The difference in intelligence test scores of bilingual students on an English version of the intelligence test as compared to a Spanish version of the test. *Illinois School Research,* 11(3):47-51, 1975.

LeVine, Elaine S. and Bartz, Karen W.: Comparative child-rearing attitudes among Chicano, Anglo and Black parents. *Hispanic Journal of Behavioral Sciences,* 1(2):165-178, 1979.

LeVine, Elaine S. and Padilla, Armando: *Crossing Cultures in Therapy:*

Pluralistic Counseling for the Hispanic. Monterey, Brooks/Cole, 1980.

Longsheet, Wilma S.: *Aspects of Ethnicity.* New York, Teachers College Press, 1978.

Madsen, Millard C.: Developmental and cross-cultural differences in the cooperative and competitive behavior of young children. *Journal of Cross-Cultural Psychology,* 2(4):365-371, 1971.

Madsen, Millard C. and Shapira, Ariella: Cooperative and competitive behavior of urban Afro-American, Anglo-American, Mexican-American and Mexican village children. *Developmental Psychology,* 3(1):16-20, 1970.

Maes, Wayne R. and Rinaldi, John R.: Counseling the Chicano child. *Elementary School Guidance and Counseling,* 8(4):279-284, 1979.

Marion, Robert L.: Minority parent involvement in the IEP process: A systematic model approach. *Focus on Exceptional Children,* 10:8, 1979.

Marion, Robert L.: Communicating with parents of culturally diverse exceptional children. *Exceptional Children,* 46(8):616-623, 1980.

Martinez, Cervando: Community mental health and the Chicano movement. *American Journal of Orthopsychiatry,* 43(4):595-601, 1973.

Martinez, Joe L. (Ed.): *Chicano Psychology.* New York, Academic Press, 1977.

Martinez, Samuel C.: *Hijos del Sol: An Approach to Raza Community Mental Health.* Monograph I, Oakland, La Familia Counseling Service, 1981.

Mason, Evelyn P.: Comparison of personality characteristics of junior high students from American Indian, Mexican and Caucasian ethnic backgrounds. *The Journal of Social Psychology,* 73:145-155, 1967.

Mason, Evelyn P.: Cross-validation study of personality characteristics of junior high students from American Indian, Mexican and Caucasian ethnic backgrounds. *Journal of Social Psychology,* 77:15-24, 1969.

Mendiville, Miguel: A Hispanic perspective on curriculum reform and design. *Social Education,* 108-110, February, 1979.

Mercer, Jane R.: Sociocultural factors in labeling mental retardates. *Peabody Journal of Education,* 48:188-203, 1971.

Mercer, Jane R.: Crosscultural evaluation of exceptionality. Focus on *Exceptional Children,* 5:8-15, 1973.

Mercer, Jane R.: Sociocultural factors in educational labeling. Prepared for the NICHD Conference held in Niles, Michigan. *Current Issues in Mental Retardation,* April 18-20, 1974.

Mercer, Jane R.: *Identifying the Gifted Child.* First Symposium on Chicano Psychology, Irvine University of California, 1976.

Mercer, Jane R.: In defense of racially and culturally non-discriminatory assessment. *School Psychology Digest,* 8(1):98-115, 1979.

Mexican-American Cultural Differences. A Brief Survey to Enhance Teacher Pupil Understanding. ERIC ED 041 665.

Mexican-Americans: The Rising Voice. A reprint from the San Jose Mercury News, San Jose, 1981.

Miranda, Manuel R. (Ed.): *Psychotherapy with the Spanish Speaking: Issues in Research and Service Delivery. Monograph 3,* Los Angeles, Spanish Speaking Mental Health Research Center, University of California, 1976.

Moreno, Steve: Problems related to present testing instruments. *El Grito,* 25-28, Spring 1970.

Mowder, Barbara A.: Assessing the bilingual handicapped student. *Psychology in the Schools*, 16(1):43-50, 1979.

Mowder, Barbara A.: A strategy for the assessment of bilingual handicapped children. *Psychology in the Schools*, 17(1):7-11, 1980.

Nall, Frank C.: Role expectations: A cross-cultural study. *Rural Sociology*, 21(1):28-41, 1962.

Nicholl, Worth L.: *The Rhetoric of Culture Pluralism Vs. The Drive Toward Total Assimilation: The Mexican-American Cultural Component of Federally Funded Bilingual Projects.* San Francisco, R & E Research Associates, Inc., 1978.

Non-discriminatory Testing. A Selective Bibliography. Reston, Council for Exceptional Children, 1976.

Oakland, Thomas (Ed.): *Psychological and Educational Assessment of Minority Children.* New York, Brunner/Mazel, 1977.

Ochoa, Alberto M. and Hurtado, Juan: *Special Education and the Bilingual Child.* San Diego, National Desegregation Lau Center, San Diego State University, 1982.

Omark, Donald R. and Erickson, Joan G. (Eds.): *The Bilingual Exceptional Child.* San Diego, College-Hill Press, 1983.

Padilla, Amado M., Ruiz, Rene A. and Alvarez, Rodolfo: Community mental health services for the Spanish speaking/surnamed population. *American Psychologist*, 892-905, 1975.

Padilla, Elena: *Up from Puerto Rico.* New York, Columbia University Press, 1958.

Palomares, Uvaldo and Negron, Frank (An Interview): Aspira today, accountability tomorrow. *Personnel and Guidance Journal*, 50(2):109-116, 1971.

Palomares, Uvaldo H.: Viva la Raza. *Personnel and Guidance Journal*, 50(2):118-121, 1971.

Palomares, Uvaldo and Haro, Juan (an interview): An interview with Juan Haro. *Personnel and Guidance Journal*, 50(2):121-129, 1971.

Palomares, Uvaldo and Welch, Janet: Portrait of a counselor. *Personnel and Guidance Journal*, 50(2):131-135, 1971.

Palomares, Uvaldo H.: Nuestros sentimientos son iguales, la diferencia es en la experiencia. *Personnel and Guidance Journal*, 50(2):137-144, 1971.

Penalosa, Fernando: The changing Mexican-American in southern California. *Sociology and Social Research*, 51(4):405, 1967.

Penalosa, Fernando and McDonagh, Edward C.: Education, economic status and social-class awareness of Mexican-Americans. *Phylon*, 29(2):119-126, 1978.

Personke, Carl R. and Davis, O.L.: Predictive validity of English and Spanish versions of a readiness test. *Elementary School Journal*, 70:2, 79-85, 1969.

Philippus, M.J.: Successful and unsuccessful approaches to mental health services for an urban Hispano-American population. *American Journal of Public Health*, 61(4):820-830, 1971.

Phillips, Beeman N. (Ed.): *Assessing Minority Group Children.* New York, Behavioral Publications, Inc., 1973.

Prago, Albert: *Strangers in Their Own Land: A History of Mexican-Americans.* New York, Four Winds, 1973.

Price-Williams, D.R. and Ramirez, Manuel: Ethnic differences in delay of gratification. *Journal of Social Psychology*, 93:23-30, 1974.

Ramirez, Manuel: Identification with Mexican family values and authoritarianism in Mexican-Americans. *Journal of Social Psychology*, 73:3-11, 1967.

Ramirez, Manuel: Cognitive styles and cultural democracy in education. *Social Science Quarterly*, 53(4):895-904, 1973.

Ramirez, Manuel: The relationship of acculturation to cognitive style among Mexican-Americans. *Journal of Cross-Cultural Psychology*, 5(4):424-432, 1974.

Ramirez, Manuel and Castaneda, Alfredo: *Cultural Democracy, Bicognitive Development and Education*. New York, Academic Press, 1974.

Ramirez, Manuel, Taylor, Clark and Peterson, Barbara: Mexican-American cultural membership and adjustment to school. *Developmental Psychology*, 4(2):141-148, 1971.

Reilly, Robert P.: *A Selected And Annotated Bibliography of Bicultural Classroom Materials For Mexican-American Studies*. San Francisco, R & E Research Associates, Inc., 1977.

Reschly, Daniel J. and Reschly, Jane E.: Brief reports on the WISC-RI. Validity of WISC-R factor scores in predicting achievement and attention for four sociocultural groups. *Journal of School Psychology*, 17(4):355-361, 1979.

Roberts, Alan H. and Greene, Joel E.: Cross-cultural study of relationships among four dimensions of time perspective. *Perceptual and Motor Skills*, 33:163-173, 1971.

Roca, Pablo: Problems of adapting intelligence scales from one culture to another. *The High School Journal*, 124-131, 1955.

Rodriguez, Fred: *Mainstreaming: A Multicultural Concept Into Teacher Education-Guidelines for Teacher Trainers*. Saratoga, R & G Publishers, 1983.

Rodriguez, Jose: An inservice rationale for educators working with Mexican-American students. In Gonzales, Tobias and Gonzales, Sandra (Eds.). *Perspectives on Chicano Education*. Stanford, Chicano Fellows, Stanford University.

Rodriguez, Richard F. et al.: *Issues in Bilingual/Multicultural Special Education*. ERIC ER 205 366.

Rodriguez, Richard F.: *The Mexican-American Child in Special Education*. Las Cruces, ERIC, CRESS, New Mexico State University, 1982.

Rodriguez, Roy C. et al.: Bilingualism and biculturalism for the special education classroom. *Teacher Education and Special Education*, 2(4):69-74, 1979.

Roos, Peter D.: Analysis of four issues pertaining to the right of limited English-speaking students to a linguistically appropriate education. San Francisco, Mexican-American Legal Defense and Educational Fund, 1978.

Rubel, Arthur J.: Concepts of disease in Mexican-American culture. *American Anthropologist*, 62(5):795-814, 1960.

Rueda, Robert S. and Prieto, Alfonso G.: Cultural pluralism: Implications for teacher education. *Teacher Education and Special Education*, 2(4):4-10, 1979.

Rueda, Robert S., Rodriguez, Richard F. and Prieto, Alfonso G.: Teachers' perceptions of competencies for instructing bilingual/multicultural exceptional children. *Exceptional Children*, 48(3):268-269, 1981.

Ruiz, Rene A. and Padilla, Armando M.: Counseling Latinas. *Personnel and Guidance Journal*, 55(7):401-408, 1977.

Sabatino, David A. et al.: Perceptual, language and academic achievement of English, Spanish and Navajo-speaking children referred for special classes. *Journal of School Psychology*, 62:451-458, 1972.

Sabatino, David A. et al.: Special education and the culturally different child: Implications for assessment and intervention. *Exceptional Children*, 563-567, 1973.

Samuda, Ronald J: *Psychological Testing of American Minorities*. New York, Harper and Row, 1975.

Santos, Maria and Montez, Toby: *A Bibliography for Counselors Working with Chicano Students*. Oakland, National Hispanic University, 1981.

Sato, Irvings: The culturally different gifted child—the dawning of his day? *Exceptional Children*, 40(8):572-576, 1974.

Saville-Troike, Muriel: *A Guide to Culture in the Classroom*. Rosslyn, National Clearinghouse for Bilingual Education, 1978.

Schmidt, Linda and Gallessich, June: Adjustment of Anglo-American and Mexican-American pupils in self-contained and team-teaching classrooms. *Journal of Educational Psychology*, 62(4):328-332, 1971.

Sena, Esteban: The organization and administration of guidance and counseling services for Chicano students. *Journal of Non-White Concerns in Personnel and Guidance*, 7(3):138-143, 1979.

Shaftel, George: The needs and anxieties of the Spanish-speaking students. *California Journal of Secondary Education*, 28(3):168-170, 1953.

Smith, George W. and Caskey, Owen L. (Eds.): *Promising School Practices for Mexican-Americans*. ERIC ED 064 003.

Southern California's Latino Community. A series of articles reprinted from *The Los Angeles Times*, Los Angeles, 1983.

Spalding, Norma: Learning problems of Mexican-Americans. *Reading Improvement*, 7(2):33-36, 1970.

Stewart, Ida S.: Cultural differences between Anglos and Chicanos. *Education Digest*, 41:29-31, 1976.

Sullivan, Allen R.: *Issues in Assessing Multicultured Youths—Its Implications for Teachers*. ERIC ED 115 621.

Swanson, Elinor N. and Deblassie, Richard R.: Interpreter and Spanish administration effects on the WISC performance of Mexican-American children. *Journal of School Psychology*, 17(3):331-335, 1979.

Ten Houten, Warren D.; Lei, Tzuen-Jen; Kendall, Francoise; and Gordon, C. Wayne: School ethnic composition, social contexts and educational plans for Mexican-Americans and Anglo high school students. *American Journal of Sociology*, 77(1):89-107, 1971.

Thomas, Donald: *Pluralism Gone Mad*. Bloomington, Phi Delta Kappa Educational Foundation, 1981.

Thomas, Paulette J.: Administration of a dialectical Spanish version and standard English version of The Peabody Picture Vocabulary Test.

Psychological Reports, 40:747-750, 1977.

Torrance, Paul E.: Readiness of teachers of gifted to learn from culturally different gifted children. *Gifted Child Quarterly,* 137, 145, Autumn 1974.

Vasquez, James A. and Gold, Clotilde: *Counseling and Minorities: A Bibliography.* Rosslyn, National Clearinghouse for Bilingual Education, 1980.

Vasquez, James A.: *Factors That Affect Learning Among Minority Youth: A Partial Bibliography.* Los Angeles, Evaluation, Dissemination and Assessment Center, California State University, 1981.

Vasquez, James A., Gonzales, Susan E. and Pearson, Mary E.: *Testing and Ethnic Minority Students: An Annotated Bibliography.* Rosslyn, National Clearinghouse for Bilingual Education, 1980.

Veir, Carole: *A Comprehensive Bibliography of Readings in Bilingual Special Education.* Tempe, Arizona State University, Department of Special Education.

Vigil, Diego: Adaptation strategies and cultural life styles of Mexican-American adolescents. *Hispanic Journal of Behavioral Sciences,* 1(4):375-392.

Vivo, Paquita: The Puerto Ricans—two communities, one culture. *Agenda: A Journal of Hispanic Issues,* 28-29, 1980.

Wagner, Helman: A comparison of selected differences in adolescence in Mexico and the United States. *Adolescence,* 12(47):381-384, 1977.

Warren Ross, Helen: Wepman Test of Auditory Discrimination: What does it discriminate? *Journal of School Psychology,* 17(1):47-54, 1979.

Watson, Bill and Van Etten, Carlene: Bilingualism and special education. *Journal of Learning Disabilities,* 10(6):331-338, 1977.

Williams, Jane Case: *Improving Educational Opportunities for Mexican American Handicapped Children.* ERIC ED 018 326 *Working With the Bilingual Community,* Rosslyn, National Clearinghouse for Bilingual Education, 1979.

Zirkel, Perry A.: Spanish-speaking students and standardized tests. *Urban Review,* 5(6):32-34, 1972.